Conflict, Education and Peace in Nepal

Also Available from Bloomsbury

Peace Education, edited by Monisha Bajaj and Maria Hantzopoulos
Education and International Development, edited by Tristan McCowan and Elaine Unterhalter
Education and Reconciliation, edited by Julia Paulson
Educational Transitions in Post-Revolutionary Spaces, Tavis D. Jules and Teresa Barton
Teaching for Peace and Social Justice in Myanmar, edited by Mary Shepard Wong
Educating for Peace and Human Rights, Maria Hantzopoulos and Monisha Bajaj
Education for Social Change, Douglas Bourn
Borderless Higher Education for Refugees, edited by Wenona Giles and Lorrie Miller
Education in Radical Uncertainty, Stephen Carney and Ulla Ambrosius Madsen

Conflict, Education and Peace in Nepal

Rebuilding Education for Peace and Development

Tejendra Pherali

BLOOMSBURY ACADEMIC
LONDON • NEW YORK • OXFORD • NEW DELHI • SYDNEY

BLOOMSBURY ACADEMIC
Bloomsbury Publishing Plc
50 Bedford Square, London, WC1B 3DP, UK
1385 Broadway, New York, NY 10018, USA
29 Earlsfort Terrace, Dublin 2, Ireland

BLOOMSBURY, BLOOMSBURY ACADEMIC and the Diana logo are
trademarks of Bloomsbury Publishing Plc

First published in Great Britain 2022
Paperback edition published 2024

Copyright © Tejendra Pherali, 2022

Tejendra Pherali has asserted his right under the Copyright, Designs and
Patents Act, 1988, to be identified as Author of this work.

For legal purposes the Acknowledgements on pp. viii–ix constitute an
extension of this copyright page.

Cover image © hadynyah/Getty Images

All rights reserved. No part of this publication may be reproduced or transmitted in
any form or by any means, electronic or mechanical, including photocopying,
recording, or any information storage or retrieval system, without prior
permission in writing from the publishers.

Bloomsbury Publishing Plc does not have any control over, or responsibility for, any
third-party websites referred to or in this book. All internet addresses given in this
book were correct at the time of going to press. The author and publisher regret any
inconvenience caused if addresses have changed or sites have ceased to exist, but
can accept no responsibility for any such changes.

A catalogue record for this book is available from the British Library.

A catalog record for this book is available from the Library of Congress.

ISBN: HB: 978-1-3500-2875-3
PB: 978-1-4729-8806-5
ePDF: 978-1-3500-2876-0
eBook: 978-1-3500-2877-7

Typeset by Newgen KnowledgeWorks Pvt. Ltd., Chennai, India

To find out more about our authors and books visit www.bloomsbury.com
and sign up for our newsletters.

Contents

List of Figures	vi
List of Tables	vii
Acknowledgements	viii
List of Abbreviations	x

1	Introduction: Education, Conflict and Peace	1
2	Armed Conflicts, Education and Peacebuilding	23
3	Educational Development and Conflict in Nepal	45
4	Impact of the 'People's War' on Educational Professionals	67
5	Young People as Victims of Conflict and Political Actors	95
6	Education, National Identity and Post-Conflict Reforms	123
7	Education for Peace and Development	145
8	Conclusion: Rethinking Education for Peace with Social Justice	173

References	195
Index	223

Figures

1.1	Country map indicating research districts	18
4.1	Liwang town, Rolpa	94
5.1	Balkalyan HS School, Rolpa	96
5.2	Children on the way to school – Sharada HS School, Doti	116
6.1	A primary school in Sankhuwasabha	139
7.1	The extended concepts of violence and peace	148
7.2	Mahendra HS School, Sankhuwasabha	160
7.3	The complementary roles of empowerment and social inclusion	165
8.1	The VPLP Framework: Multi-directional interactions between education and conflict	181

Tables

3.1	The Structure of the School System in Nepal	53
5.1	Forced Disappearances during the People's War	104
6.1	Percentage of Caste/Ethnicity Group Representation in Special and Gazette Class	140
8.1	The VPLP Framework to Analyse Multiple Roles of Education in Conflict	182
8.2	Conflict Analysis Framework in Education	186

Acknowledgements

In February 2006, few months before the historic Comprehensive Peace Accord (CPA) was signed between the Communist Party of Nepal-Maoist (CPN-M) and Government of Nepal (GoN), I was offered a position to work with a brilliant team in the newly established country office of Search for Common Ground (SFCG) in Kathmandu. I led a baseline study to investigate the role of youth in peacebuilding and community decision-making at a crucial time when the Maoists and parliamentary parties had forged an agreement to jointly oppose the monarchy, and thousands of Maoist cadres had entered the Kathmandu valley to stage mass demonstration. After the CPA, I travelled across the country to interview Maoist youths who had begun to engage openly in political organizing. Conversations with these 'comrades' were fascinating. Their oratory skills, which they had developed as part of their political socialization within the Maoist ranks, and their ability to critique Nepal's political history, socio-economic conditions and the existing political system from a Marxist perspective were incredibly impressive. My early curiosity about interactions between conflict and education in Nepal's Maoist rebellion began from this research experience and while working with SFCG colleagues, Serena Rix Tripathee, Michael Shipler and Rajendra Mulmi and youths who had joined later as part of the community peacebuilding initiatives led by this International Non-Governmental Organisation (INGO). So, I am most grateful to the SFCG colleagues for helping me to find my academic interest in the field of education and conflict.

I am also deeply indebted to the head teachers, teachers, parents and students of six schools, most of whom had endured the effects of Maoist insurgency, and some had been part of the Maoist rebellion. This book would not have been possible without their contributions. For confidentiality reasons, I am refraining from mentioning their names in this note, but I have deep respect for them and would like to express my humble gratitude.

I am also grateful to Professor Alan Smith, Professor Mario Novelli, Tony Vaux, Professor Dean Garratt, Professor David Huddart, Professor Mark Brundrett, Derek Kassem, Dr Pramod Bhatta, Professor Robin Shields, Professor Stephen Carney, Dr Julia Paulson, Professor Lynne Davies, Dr Sara Parker,

Professor Elaine Unterhalter and Professor Brad Blitz, who have either inspired me with their research in the field of education and conflict or supported me directly to build my academic career over the past one decade. I have also learnt enormously from discussions with over four hundred MA students who have studied my module Education, Conflict and Peace at UCL Institute of Education and numerous attendees of Education in Conflict and Emergencies Seminar Series which has been running for over eight years. I am also grateful to Professor Keiichi Ogawa from Kobe University, Japan, and colleagues in the Multicultural and Social Innovation Center at Chulalongkorn University, Thailand, who have welcomed me to their institutions as a visiting scholar over the past few years and provided me with several platforms to present my research.

I would also like to thank Taylor and Francis for their permission to reproduce ideas in Chapter 4, which initially appeared in *Comparative Education*, 52(4), (2016): 473-91 and Elsevier for their permission to reuse some sections in Chapter 6, which were published earlier in the *International Journal of Educational Development*, 34, (2014): 42-50.

Finally, it would not have been possible to complete this book without the selfless support of my family who have endured my absence during many weekends and on many special occasions especially during the summer of 2021 when I spent eight weeks to complete this book. Asha, Akash and Abhay have always been a massive support throughout this process. I am most grateful to them.

I am personally responsible for all weaknesses in the book.

Abbreviations

ANTO	All Nepal Teachers Organization
CDC	Curriculum Development Centre, Government of Nepal
CPA	Comprehensive Peace Accord
CPN-M	Communist Party of Nepal-Maoist
DFID	Department for International Development
DOE	Department of Education
GCPEA	Global Coalition to Protect Education from Attack
GoN	Government of Nepal
HDI	Human Development Index
INEE	Inter-Agency Network for Education in Emergencies
INGO	International Non-Governmental Organization
INSEC	Informal Sector Service Centre
ICRC	International Committee of the Red Cross
ICJ	International Commission of Jurists
MoE	Ministry of Education
NA	Nepal Army
NHRC	National Human Rights Commission
NEPC	National Education Planning Commission
NESP	New Education System Plan
NCS	National Civil Service
NC	Nepali Congress
NGO	Non-Governmental Organization
PLA	People's Liberation Army
PTA	Parent-Teacher Association
SDGs	Sustainable Development Goals
SEE	Secondary Education Examination
SFCG	Search for Common Ground
SLC	School Leaving Certificate
SMC	School Management Committee
SSRP	School Sector Reform Plan
UK	United Kingdom
UMN	United Mission to Nepal

UN	United Nations
UCPN-M	United Communist Party of Nepal-Maoist
UNESCO	United Nations Educational, Scientific and Cultural Organization
UNICEF	United Nations Children's Fund

1

Introduction: Education, Conflict and Peace

When a 'middle school' was established in March 1973 at the top of the Palpa district's Gokhunga mountain, it was expected that people in the surrounding villages of Bhuwan Pokhari would naturally seize the opportunity to send their children to school. But it soon became apparent that Dalits[1] and Janajatis[2] were less enthusiastic about the prospects of schooling. Due to their poor economic conditions, they were unable to afford the materials and indirect costs of education; also, the benefits of education were not obvious to them, because given the social conditions and caste-based domination that they faced, they could not easily discern how education could change their life. Investment in girls' education was also seen as irrational and culturally undesirable, because the girls would be married off to another family which meant that there was no direct return on investment in education for the parental family (Stash and Hannum, 2001). The result was that the majority of students in the school represented upper castes, especially the Brahman, Chhetri and Newar[3] families.

What also came with the 'middle school' was 'modern education' that labelled traditional Nepali society as backward and needing to catch up with the ideals and development of Western societies such as Europe, North America, Australasia and Japan. The Western concept of development (e.g. technological advancement, modern infrastructure such as roads, bridges, electricity, telecommunication, improved health, eradication of deadly diseases, industrialization and mass production) accompanied by a focus on teaching relevant subjects in schools

---

[1] Dalits are considered one of the most marginalized caste groups in South Asia and they have been historically treated as 'untouchables' and continue to experience social exclusion in Nepal (Bishwakarma, 2019; Poudel, 2007; Pyakurel, 2021).
[2] Janajatis are indigenous peoples of Nepal. The Nepal Federation of Indigenous Nationalities specifies fifty-nine indigenous groups based on their distinct languages, cultures and beliefs. Janajatis constitute more than one-third of Nepal's population and, except for the Newars, all of them have been discriminated against, subjugated, dominated and exploited in terms of land, territories, resources, language, culture and political and economic opportunities (Jha, 2019; Subba et al., 2014).
[3] While the Newars are classified as Janajati, historically they have enjoyed the same economic and social privileges as the hill-high caste groups.

left no space for traditional Nepali notions of learning and becoming learned. This whole new shift was felt necessary to catch the speed of *bikas* (development) and prosperity. Pigg (1992: 499) vividly describes:

> In daily life, bikas becomes the idiom through which the relationship between local communities and other places is expressed. There are places of much bikas (*dherai bikas*), little bikas (*thorai bikas*) and no bikas (*bikas chhaina*). Bikas is quantifiable in this way because in common usage it connotes things: new breeds of goats and chickens, water pipes, electricity, videos, schools, commercial fertilizer, roads, airplanes, health posts and medicines. Bikas comes to local areas from elsewhere; it is not produced locally. Most material aspects of bikas – and these material benefits matter most to the majority of Nepalese citizens – are manufactured, often from unusual materials such as plastics. Other items, such as roads and hydro-electric plants, rest on technical knowledge obtained in places of greater bikas than villages. Moreover, much bikas is administered from Kathmandu and staffed at the higher levels by people posted to local projects from other places. From these associations grows the popular notion that bikas is concentrated, to varying degrees, in other places and that villages are places of relatively little bikas.

The idea of modernity spread rapidly deep into our minds that this was the only ideal model of development, and our social structures, economic policies and education system must be geared towards achieving this development goal. Science education, mathematics, English language and, few years later, computer education, were seen as a cure for the disease of ignorance (that we did not know what Western Europe and North America had achieved!) that was supposedly preventing us from living like the Westerners – 'modern' and developed. Formal education made little connection with our local traditional knowledge, conventional livelihood skills, our relationship with nature and cultural practices that were deeply rooted in the local environment: forests, rivers and mountains. These traditional practices, which were the foundations of our civilization, became symbols of backwardness, which would gradually fade away. English language was an important element of educational success. Anyone who did well at school was expected to leave the village for higher education in a town and then to the capital city and then to the Western world if they were capable of securing an opportunity for further education. Education in the 'middle school' did not prepare us for a better life in the village; rather it taught us to look down on the village, dismiss the local knowledge and identify with the life and culture 'outside' of the village. It was to do with 'development' and 'modernization', which was offered in the urban culture (Pigg, 1992).

This outward facing idea of development also introduced some transformative visions in modern education: that access to education would liberate people from oppressive social structures and enable them to create better ones; and 'educated persons' (Skinner and Holland, 1996) would participate in 'state-building, national integration and unity' and 'question and challenge the legitimacy of caste and gender-based discrimination' (Carney and Rappleye, 2011: 6).

Those who were able to fulfil the societal expectations framed by the development discourse gradually escaped from the village in search of 'more' development, first to the closest urban centre and then to the capital city, and some to the 'ideal' Western world. This process only extracted the best brains from the village, who rarely returned to their roots. I often find myself in such a situation and even though I tackle my guilt of abandonment, like many others of similar backgrounds, by occasional charitable gestures back to the village and support to the 'middle school' which I attended, modern education has completely uprooted us from the origin with only nostalgia in residue. Development in the real sense was too slow to arrive. The modernization project has for decades ridiculed the indigenous cultures and stolen local people's self-confidence, throwing them into the trap of external dependency.

My Roots and Reflections

On Social Inequalities

Born in a socially privileged Brahman[4] family, my childhood experiences represented the social, cultural and political environment of the 1980s in a typical village in the western mountains of Nepal. Casteism is a strong social marker in South Asia that is characterized by rituals, social hierarchies, discrimination and exploitative power relationships. It is no longer a 'rigid ritual stratum' but has lately become a collective political identity that is used to negotiate power and resources (Subedi, 2016). Brahmans in my village enjoyed the highest social status and generally better economic and political privileges. The prerogatives of being a Brahman also included the 'cultural capital' (Bourdieu, 1986) that often manifested in influential social action, high educational aspirations and access to social networks that were connected to political authority. We lived

---

[4] In the caste system, Brahman is the priestly caste whose responsibility was to engage in teaching, learning and production of knowledge. In Nepal, elite Brahmans have always been close to the monarchy and enjoyed social, economic and political privileges.

in a village that was dominated by the community of indigenous ethnic groups (predominantly, Magars) and Dalits who often helped us in our farms, but we never went to work in theirs. Socially, we had harmonious relationships with all but there was a clear set of rules with regard to social, cultural and personal proximities. For example, I could sometimes go and play with friends from indigenous castes but was not allowed by my parents to eat anything cooked in their homes. I could not invite them into my house, nor could I join in the local ethnic events, such as folk music and dance performances, which would take place during festive periods. I was expected to maintain a distance to preserve my caste identity as a Brahman, aspiring to become someone in a position of power and influence. There was a sense that my socializing with Magar children would jeopardize our family's status as Brahmans. The society treated me as someone who was part of a closed cultural group with high ambitions for success that was to be accomplished above and beyond my village, and most unequivocally above my fellow Magar friends in the neighbourhood. My elder brothers completed their school education and secured professional jobs in the public sector but their childhood friends from lower castes either never went to school or if they did, started late and dropped out early. Even during my time, all my Magar friends dropped out before reaching the secondary level, either to work in the farm or to be employed in factories or as domestic helpers in neighbouring India.

Our tailor, an elderly man who stitched my clothes, would stay outside the four walls of our house. As a Dalit, he was treated as impure and untouchable. During festive times, father used to buy clothes for everyone in the family and our tailor would set out his sewing machine outside in the front yard to stitch our new clothes. My mother would purify us with a sprinkle of gold-dipped water every time the tailor touched us to take measurements for clothes. In the school, Dalit children never touched the container of drinking water. If they felt thirsty, children from high castes would have to pour water into their cupped hands under their mouth. At school, it was rare for any student from a Dalit or indigenous background to perform academically at the same level as high-caste children, and low achievement of low-caste children was a norm which was completely unsurprising to both teachers and those children's parents. This meant that teachers also held low educational expectations for children from the Dalit and indigenous backgrounds (Pherali, 2011). While my teachers, all Brahman males, were well acquainted with my father and always set high learning targets for me (and children from high castes) and expected us to secure top grades in every exam, the children from lower ethnic and caste groups were left to their own destiny. There were hardly any girls in the class, and when I reached the final year of my primary school only one girl out of fifteen of us was studying and she sat alone on the front bench while rest of us sat in the rows behind. At the lower secondary level, a few fellow students including a few girls joined from feeder primary schools in the region but most of the girls dropped out after completing the seventh grade. All these educational and social experiences were part of my upbringing, and no social or educational space was available to question and debate these inequalities. The processes of 'social reproduction' (Bourdieu, 1984) were normalized though subtle discourses and structural inequalities permeated the social and education system. On reflection, the education system was complicit in systematically marginalizing girls and children from *Dalit* and indigenous communities such as Tharu, Magar, Rai, Limbu, Sherpa, Gurung and others by failing to retain them in the system (Lawoti, 2005).

On Childhood Stories

Childhood stories can have enormous impact on individuals' social attitudes and perspectives about life. I was fortunate to have a father who was a great storyteller. Stories were part of everyday conversations, during household chores and during long journeys we used to make together to visit our relatives. The stories always carried powerful moral lessons reflecting the importance of righteous upbringing, religious values and honourable cultural behaviour. My father's stories ranged from narration of his own life experiences to exciting events from Hindu epics such as the *Ramayana*, *Mahabharata* and *Vedic Puranas*. As a Brahman and scholar of Sanskrit literature, he not only preached moral, ethical values from the Vedas but also practised these in his everyday life. Then, he would talk about his struggle to bring about social change in the community and involvement in politics, as well as the challenges he faced in securing a decent livelihood for us as a family. I relished listening to his personal adventures with leopards when he was a goat herder at a young age. Then he would get emotional every time he recalled his memories with his parents and the loss he suffered when they passed away. Every moral lesson that emerged from the story had relevance to our contemporary social environment. These were more interesting lessons than those at school, where education was dominated by rote learning and the content was mostly decontextualized, disconnected from our life and generally monotonous. These childhood stories not only taught me compassion, cultural values and ethics but also shaped my attitudes and personality in life. One of his stories goes as follows:

> In the early 1940s, we used to have bonded labourers in our house who would work in our farm, rear our cattle and fetch water from the stream. My mother used to give some grain as wages at the end of the day which the workers would take home to feed their families. I was unhappy about this exploitation but could not challenge the practice as that was the standard practice in the village so, as a young person, I could not challenge the wage system. I desperately wanted to help the farm workers so, started giving them more grain without my mother's knowledge. As a result, they preferred working for us to other landowners. This created a tension, and we were blamed for spoiling the wage system. My mother eventually discovered it and told me off. But later, when I grew older and started managing our family affairs, I freed some labourers who were bonded to other landowners in the village by paying off their debts. Even though they did not have to come and work for us, they had nowhere else to go, so they continued working for us with much better wages, some respect and dignity.

I simply enjoyed listening to these narratives when I was young but now reflect on them critically using my rational thinking as an adult, wider social awareness and political economy perspectives. These stories signify intimacy and affection in my father's relationship with his parents, strong family traditions of devotion and responsibility as well as practical actions to resist injustices in the feudalistic social system. The inability of my mother to tell similar stories (not because she could not but because it was culturally not her place to prepare me for a future!) and my father's occasional patronizing remarks about her as a 'naïve woman' denoted her disempowered status in the family and society in general. She represented women's social status not only within Nepali society generally during those times but also interestingly in a family that was socially privileged as compared to many others. My mother was married at the age of eleven, gave birth to eleven of us and raised us while performing all household chores including working in the farm. My father epitomized a personality of contrasts: someone who believed in the glory of family traditions but also deeply cared about ethics, compassion and kindness to those who struggled. He was concurrently a loving husband and a male chauvinist; privileged Brahman, not wealthy but a generous master; a dignified social worker and progressive politician; inspirational father; devoted Hindu and a secularist. He embodied multiple identities, some of which were shaped by the conditions of his epoch and the rest were his deliberate and conscious choices based on his principles and beliefs. These descriptions paint a picture of the social and cultural life in which I grew up and were the values that influenced my upbringing and still, critically and reflexively, continue to inform my positionalities in research and writing.

Development of Education in Nepal: A Historical Account

Until 1950, educational access was limited to only a few children from the ruling class and the authoritarian Rana oligarchy categorically denied the public access to schools. The regime was alarmed by the role of education in engendering political consciousness, leading to possible dissent and demands for civil liberty and democratic rights. Establishing a school for the purpose of providing education to the general public was a punishable act. The Rana rulers believed that educating the public would be to risk their control over state power and economic resources.

The monarchs were reduced to figureheads and confined within their palace under the strict control of the Rana rulers, who precluded them from interacting with ordinary citizens. This Rana oligarchy, which had lasted for over a century, was overthrown in 1951 by an alliance between the Nepali Congress party, a major political force struggling for democracy, and the subdued monarch Tribhuvan, who was desperate to regain power. The overthrow of the regressive autocratic regime and the advent of democracy ended the dark anti-education era that had kept ordinary Nepali citizens away from the light of education.

Heavily influenced by traditional rote-learning Sanskrit-based education, the Nepalese education system inherited the disposition of British colonial education imported from the Indian subcontinent during and after the British Raj in India. The first school in Nepal, Durbar High School, was established in 1853 with the main purpose of educating children from the ruling families and their courtiers. Apart from Durbar High School, there were only thirteen high schools in the country that provided very limited access to the children mostly from the highly privileged socio-economic class. There were also some Sanskrit and monastic schools offering religious education to selected Buddhist and Hindu children from superior castes. The Rana oligarchy systematically pursued 'a programme of Hinduization' that legitimized the ethnolinguistic hierarchy of castes and ethnic groups headed by the hill high castes (e.g. Brahmans, Chhetris and Newars) (Hutt, 2004: 2). The state-imposed hierarchy was likewise seen in the education sector in which access to education was exclusive to children from socially and economically privileged backgrounds.

The state-imposed monopoly of the Nepali language across all sectors, including in education, led to gradual deterioration of the languages and cultures of indigenous communities. In addition, a few people from affluent backgrounds were able to gain higher education in India. The collapse of the

Rana oligarchy in February 1951 provided the state and communities a historic opportunity for mass education. The task of educational development was enormous as almost 97 per cent of the population was unable to read and write at that time (World Bank, 2001). Communities began to utilize the democratic freedom that followed the demise of the oppressive Rana rule to establish literacy centres across the country, many of which were established by Gurkha soldiers who had returned home after serving in British forces in the Second World War. Nevertheless, schools were established by community leaders representing hill high castes predominantly in their own neighbourhoods to allow their children an easy access to school. The low castes and ethnic minorities faced sociocultural barriers and lacked cultural capital (Bourdieu, 1986), preventing them from participating in the process of educational development. As a result, schools were often too distant for Dalits, indigenous groups and ethnic minorities, and despite the government's effort to improve literacy and school enrolment, many Dalit children and those from ethnic minorities and indigenous populations still remained out of school.

Nine years after the overthrow of the Rana regime and the political turmoil that followed, the first parliamentary elections were held in 1959, providing the first democratically elected government. During this period, the first higher education institution of Nepal, Tribhuvan University, was established as a vehicle for Nepal's journey to modernity and development. However, the political tensions between the monarchy and parliamentary parties led to the dismissal of the elected government and dissolution of the parliament in 1961 by then king Mahendra, who introduced a unitary Panchayat system, banning parliamentary democracy and placing the monarchy above the constitution. The political regression had no adverse effects on expansion of school education in the subsequent decades. The number of schools continued to grow throughout the country despite the unfavourable political climate for supporters of multiparty democracy (World Bank, 2001). With the authoritative monarchy at the centre of Nepal's sociopolitical transformation, the educational reforms also revolved around the national project of producing a citizenry that was loyal to the monarchy, which was an integral part of Nepali nationalism (Onta, 1996). In 1971, the Panchayati government introduced a comprehensive National Education System Plan to nationalize schools and take absolute control of teacher recruitment, curricular provision, assessment and accreditation, and monitoring and supervision of educational processes across the country (GoN, 1971). All community schools were brought under the management of the Ministry of Education through its regional offices, and the education system began to concentrate on creating national identity through one religion (Hinduism), one language (the Nepali language) and one national symbol of unity (the monarchy) (Shah, 1993). This was a state-sponsored project of national homogenization, which denied diversity of languages and cultures in Nepali society, to promote national unity under common political and cultural values and principles. These values and principles were those of the ruling class of hill high-caste Hindus and were enshrined in the constitution to provide a blueprint for the process of nation-building. At the core of educational development was the national political agenda which aimed at producing patriotic citizens loyal to the monarchy, Panchayat system and the nation.

While the state monopolized formal education for its political purpose of producing citizens loyal to the system, many teachers across the country were clandestinely involved in political activism against the regime. They played a vital role in raising political awareness and mobilizing masses in the communities against the repressive Panchayat system. After the restoration of multiparty democracy in 1990, teachers' involvement in party politics became more visible through their affiliate unions. Unsurprisingly, the senior leadership of most political parties still consists of many former teachers who had predominantly worked in the rural areas of the country during the Panchayat period.

After the political change of 1990, like many other developing countries, Nepal also became a playground of neoliberal policies (Regmi, 2021), embarking upon a rapid process of privatization of the public sectors, including education. The 1990s saw a momentous growth of private schools and colleges in urban settings (Bhatta and Pherali, 2017). These educational institutions operate as private companies without financial support from the government; charge fees from parents; provide an English medium education and primarily target urban, financially able parents who can afford to pay for their children's education. The government has repeatedly made attempts to regulate the private education sector but with little success (Poudyal, 2017). Research shows that the private/public divide in education worsens socio-economic divisions as the increased levels of spending on private education are associated with wage dispersion and the education premium (Huber, Gunderson and Stephens, 2020). The direct impact of privatization of education in Nepal is that public schools have become concentrations of children with disadvantaged backgrounds, as school choice depends on the parental ability to pay (Joshi, 2020). For the very reason that private schools were operating as commercial enterprises and reproducing social inequalities, these schools were particularly targeted for violent attacks by the Maoists (Caddell, 2006). During the Maoist 'People's War' (1996–2006), many private schools were forced to close, causing an influx of students into already struggling public schools.

Education and Conflict: An Interdisciplinary Field of Research, Policy and Practice

In the last two decades, the field of education and conflict has received significant attention in academic research, policy debates and in the work of humanitarian and development practitioners (Davies, 2004; INEE, 2010; Novelli and Cardozo, 2008; Pherali, 2019; Smith and Vaux, 2003; UNESCO, 2011). This is due to increased recognition of education as a human right – that all children irrespective of their religion, ethnicity and socio-economic backgrounds have the right to education; and due to persistent violations of this right in contexts of political tension, state fragility and civil wars. The long-standing development paradigm that draws on human capital formation and poverty alleviation through investment in education and economic growth (Barro, 2013; Becker, 1975; Schultz, 1961) has also been challenged due to its insensitivity towards the production of inequalities and lack of attention to non-economic factors, such as institutional stratification, social and cultural capital, identities, cultural values and struggle for civil liberties (Bourdieu, 1984; Hoxby and Avery, 2013; Marginson, 2019). Hence, there is a consensus among development agencies and international organizations that educational reforms must support the agenda of equity, inclusion and conflict-sensitivity and serve a wider goal of social transformation (INEE, 2013; Novelli, Lopes Cardozo and Smith, 2019; UNESCO, 2018). Furthermore, the dominant assumption – that poverty causes conflict – has led to increased donor interest in conflict-affected countries with increased funding in the education sector (Novelli, 2010). The strategic goal and underlying motivation of educational donors seems to be around maintaining stability by keeping youth in education and training; increasing their employability to provide a sustainable livelihood and promoting non-violence and social cohesion through peace education programmes.

The debates about education and armed conflict can be loosely presented under three key themes. Firstly, there is a theoretical analysis of multidimensional interactions between education and conflict. Education is portrayed as a victim of conflict – that teachers, pupils and educational infrastructures are targeted for violent attacks to undermine the political authorities (GCPEA, 2020; UNESCO, 2011). This has particularly increased as the nature of modern warfare has changed since the fall of the Soviet Union and end of the Cold War. Unlike most interstate conflicts in the history of humanity, new wars are largely fought within nation states and tend not to occur within demarcated zones. This has resulted in growing civilian casualties that largely include vulnerable populations including children, the elderly and people with disabilities. Worldwide, it is estimated that over two million children were killed in conflicts between 1998 and 2008, while another six million were disabled and over 300,000 were recruited as child soldiers (UNICEF, 2010a cited in Mundy and Dryden-Peterson, 2011). In educational terms, children living in conflict-affected countries are the worst affected. In 2011, out of 57 million children out of school globally, almost 28.5 million primary and secondary school-aged children in conflict-affected countries were being denied access to school (Save the Children, 2013). Growing violence in different parts of the world, including Afghanistan, Myanmar, Syria and Iraq, has driven around 28 million children away from their home (UNICEF, 2017).

Education can not only be a contributor to peace, stability and positive social change but also be complicit in an ideological process of social control and manipulation (Bush and Saltarelli, 2000; Davies, 2005; Pherali, 2016b). The changing nature of violent conflicts, especially since 9/11, has redefined the relationship between education and conflict, both in terms of suspicion of education as a tool for radicalization as well as the potential role it could play in mitigating the causes of violent extremism. In practical terms, schools can serve as recruitment sites or indoctrination camps for rebels (GCPEA, 2020; Watchlist, 2005), while education is also a critical space for implementing the state's counter-insurgency policies (Novelli, 2017). More importantly, formal education is manipulated by the state to promote a particular version of national identity and political ideology, which may not necessarily represent the cultural and social diversity within the national boundaries. In those contexts, cultural minority groups refuse to participate in the formal education system (Lall, 2020; Pherali, 2021) and in some instances where armed groups are active, educational institutions, teachers and students may be targeted for violent attacks. These tensions may be further complicated by global policy frameworks that tend to universalize educational approaches without necessarily appreciating the local needs, histories, power relationships between different social groups and conflict dynamics.

Bush and Saltarelli (2000) draw upon a wide range of examples from around the world to demonstrate that education has both 'negative' and 'positive' faces. They argue that education is used as a tool to perpetrate structural violence.

For example, formal education which is distributed unevenly across different social, cultural and regional groups reproduces horizontal inequalities which could fuel violent conflicts (Langer and Kuppens, 2019). Imposition of a non-native language as a medium of instruction represents cultural violence against minorities, reducing their chance of social development. Denial of education to certain ethnic, caste, racial or religious groups could limit their opportunities to participate equitably in the political and economic affairs of their society, leading to social divisions between those who have been privileged to benefit from educational opportunities and those deprived of them. Other areas of contestation in education include manipulation of history to serve the interests of political elites; misrepresentation of the 'other' in textbooks and disparities of educational outcomes across different economic, ethnic and regional groups (Bush and Saltarelli, 2000). On the other hand, a good quality inclusive education has the potential to promote an ethnically tolerant environment; desegregate the mind to bring people together from across dividing lines; appreciate linguistic and cultural diversities and promote peace and social cohesion through inclusive educational policies. Most importantly, education when practised as a process of 'conscientization' helps unleash human potential, creativity, innovations – that we advance as a just society (Freire, 1974). It also has the power to emancipate human beings from ignorance, provide critical consciousness and empower people against oppression (Freire, 1974; Pherali, 2016b).

Secondly, education is disrupted during armed conflicts, and children and families are uprooted from their homes (UNICEF, 2017). The Stockholm International Peace Research Institute (SIPRI) reported that the number of armed conflicts rose from forty-one in 2014 to fifty in 2015, due to rapid expansion of the Islamic State (IS) into twelve additional countries mainly in the Middle East (SIPRI, 2016). Except for the conflict between India and Pakistan, these conflicts are all intrastate civil wars, with foreign military forces present in some cases. Children's right to protection, well-being and education is seriously jeopardized and these countries are falling behind in meeting the education milestones of the Sustainable Development Goals (SDGs, 2015). Violent conflicts and protracted crises severely disrupt children's daily routine including their access to education, and young people who lack access to quality learning are also vulnerable to ideological indoctrination and manipulation by extremist or violent political groups. The rationale for upholding children's right to education in times of emergencies draws on the principle that education is a basic human right and it cannot wait until the crisis ends. More importantly, maintaining education during conflict and crisis can help to protect children from being recruited into the conflict. It can provide a sense of normality and hope for a better future by creating opportunities for spatial and social mobility. However, the very reason that schools provide a sense of normality, representing a functioning state, make them 'tactical targets' of the opposing armed groups (van Wessel and van Hirtum, 2013). Education also provides an enabling platform for other humanitarian services in emergencies: access to shelter, basic health services, nutritious food, clean water and sanitation could be provided through schools as well as knowledge about disaster risk reduction, critical thinking and peacebuilding skills. In other words, educational interventions in crisis situations can save lives by providing child-friendly spaces; sustaining communities by providing a sense of normality; providing knowledge to cope and deal with adversities and making people more resilient. In this regard, the Inter-Agency Network for Education in Emergencies (INEE) has developed a set of minimum standards for education in humanitarian situations which serve as guiding principles for the education community who support education in conflict and protracted crises (INEE, 2010).

Thirdly, there is also recognition that education has an important role in peacebuilding and state-building. DFID (2010) emphasizes the four elements of building peaceful states and societies:

1. Address causes and effects of conflict and fragility (e.g. addressing social exclusion and discrimination);
2. Support inclusive political settlements and processes;
3. Develop core state functions (e.g. security, law and justice and financial and macroeconomic management); and
4. Respond to public expectations (e.g. basic public services such as health, education, water, energy, fairness, free elections, free media and protection of human rights).

Education is not only a part of basic service delivery but it also has the potential to address the effects and causes of conflict. Most importantly, education can provide fundamental skills for conflict resolution, such as dialogue, mediation, negotiation and discussion, which are useful to 'transform the way the world deals with conflict, away from adversarial approaches toward cooperative solutions' (SFCG, 2020: n.p.). Education is an integral part of the process that enables conflict-affected generations to find new ways to deal with the legacies of violence and develop capacities to deal with differences. An educated population is more likely to engage in democratic processes and contribute to the establishment of effective state institutions, such as the judiciary, security institutions and representative democracy, which maintain the rule of law and stability. More importantly, investment in higher education would enable a post-conflict society to produce a skilled workforce who could contribute to economic regeneration (Milton and Barakat, 2016; Pherali and Lewis, 2019). It has also been argued that education should be recognized as a central player in peace processes (Novelli and Smith, 2011) so that educational inequalities that lead to conflict could be corrected in the process of post-war peacebuilding (UNICEF, 2016a). Conflict-sensitive educational reforms can contribute to broader goals of peacebuilding by redressing systemic fault lines around educational exclusion of minorities and disadvantaged social groups, recognizing minority voices in the curriculum and promoting peace, resilience and mutual understanding.

The 'People's War' and Education in Nepal

On 13 February 1996, a splinter faction of the large, diverse Communist Party of Nepal was inspired by Mao's peasant-led revolution in China to announce a 'People's War' in Nepal. This faction became known as the United Communist Party of Nepal, Maoist (UCPN-M). It began by carrying out attacks on police posts in three districts: Rolpa and Rukum in the mid-west and Sindhuli in the east, instigating 'planned assaults' on two factories in Gorkha and Kathmandu and raiding the house of a civilian in the eastern district of Kavre (*The Worker*, 1996). The communist rebellion in Nepal was completely at odds with Fukuyama's (1992) proclamation that the fall of the Soviet Union and collapse of the communist ideology had paved the way for Western liberal democracy to become an irreversible, universal political doctrine. It was also unexpected from the perspective of the national political situation, as the country had recently seen a mass movement successfully overthrow the authoritarian Panchayat regime, and the multiparty democracy which had been set up was beginning to show slow but consistent progress in the Human Development Index (HDI) (Lawoti and Pahari, 2010).

The 'People's War' was initiated with the aim of overthrowing the monarchy that had ruled over Nepal for the past two and half centuries and establishing 'a new socio-economic structure and state' (Bhattarai, 2003; Maoist Statements and Documents, 2003). The root causes were the long-standing grievances of the disenfranchised peoples and the pervasive social, economic and political disparities across castes, gender, religions, geographies and ethnicities. Social inequality was deeply entrenched in the hierarchical caste system in which hill high-caste groups such as Brahman, Chhetri/Thakuris and Newars enjoyed the economic and social privileges of society while Dalits, Madhesi and indigenous groups were largely marginalized (Murshed and Gates, 2005).[5] Secondly, the advent of liberal democracy in 1990 not only curtailed the monarchy's absolute power but also raised people's expectations for good governance, economic opportunities and better life conditions. Disappointingly, the governments during this period were unstable; political leaders were involved in self-serving power politics and there were regular strikes and demonstrations, hurting people's everyday business. It was also a period that saw rapid global connectivity and sweeping neoliberal reforms, triggering labour movements and expansion of the private sector in key domains such as education, health and finance. The political optimism among the people gradually turned into widespread frustration as the living conditions of most rural populations did not improve and the long-standing structural inequalities remained unchanged. Thapa and Sijapati (2004) have argued that the political failure or ineptitude of the post-1990 governments paved the way for the declaration and rapid expansion of the 'People's War'. However, there were deeply rooted socio-economic structures that perpetuated poverty, inequalities and discrimination against people based on their caste, gender and ethnic identities which provided political justification for an armed rebellion (Bhattarai, 2003; Deraniyagala, 2005; Do and Iyer, 2007). Over seventeen thousand people lost their lives during the conflict, not to mention the social and economic damage. The Comprehensive Peace Accord (CPA) was signed eventually between the Government of Nepal and the CPN-M on 21 November 2006.

There is a plethora of literature that examines the Maoist movement in Nepal from political, economic and sociological perspectives (e.g. Do and Iyer, 2007; Hutt, 2004; Karki and Seddon, 2003; Kumar, 2005; Lawoti, 2005; Lawoti and Pahari, 2010; Thapa and Sijapati, 2004). Education is often omitted in these analyses and even in the few exceptions (Rai, 2018; Standing and Parker, 2011; Valente, 2014), only certain aspects of education are analysed, pointing to the need for a comprehensive analysis of education and armed conflict in Nepal. Hence, this book attempts to fill this gap by presenting a detailed analysis of interactions between education, conflict and peace, particularly from the

---

[5] Geographically, Nepal is divided into a northern, more hilly or mountainous region, and a southern lowland region. People from the northern region are known as 'Pahadi' (northerners). The southern region is known as the Tarai or Madhes, and many of the inhabitants describe themselves as 'Madhesi' though others reject that label. While there are high-caste and low-caste people in both regions, the high-caste people in the north have historically had access to power while the southern region has been exploited and disadvantaged.

position of teachers and students who experienced the conflict. It builds upon conceptual and theoretical ideas that deal with multidirectional links between these concepts to examine the role of education in the emergence, growth and transformation of the 'People's War'. One of the key arguments of the book is that education in Nepal played a complicit role in conflict, primarily benefitting the traditionally privileged social groups in Nepali society and hence perpetuating the existing structural inequalities which were the major cause of the rebellion. During the conflict, schools were caught in the middle and teachers and students were abducted and maimed by both the Maoists and the security forces. Schools also became a domain of financial and human resource extraction, sanctuaries for warring forces as well as political spaces that were used to promote critical education, providing intellectual strengths to the violent rebellion. Many teachers and students throughout the country were part of the Maoist movement which viewed the rebellion as a political struggle aiming to address the historical grievances of ethnic minorities, Dalits and indigenous populations. In the post-conflict era, teachers have been demoralized due to the experience of violence, fear and uncertainties in the past, and have lost faith in the system for ensuring their professional well-being. This has resulted in growing corruption and rent-seeking in the school system, with teachers relying on their affiliated political party for support rather than the state authority.

Researching the Impact of Conflict on Education

Civil wars have long-term effects on human lives. These are not only limited to economic loss but also involve the destruction of war-torn societies' social and cultural assets (Ghobarah, Huth and Russett, 2003). Particularly, forced displacement of families, professionals, teachers and artists strip the community of its cultural capital, identity and wealth, which is difficult to replenish at the end of war. The cessation of violence may provide an opportunity for reconstruction (Buckland, 2005) but the multidimensional impacts of the violent conflict require long-term programmes of healing and rebuilding. It is therefore crucial to study indirect and enduring impacts of violence, trauma and loss of livelihoods on populations so that effective programmes are put in place to restore confidence, dignity and hope for future.

Education is an integral part of a nation's economic and social development through which foundations for sustainable peace are built. Post-war educational reconstruction must therefore involve not only the reinstatement of educational infrastructure and resumption of teaching and learning, but also reconfiguration of the system, policies and educational approaches to address the educational causes of conflict. These causes may include grievances around exclusionary educational policies, such as imposition of a non-native language as a medium of instruction, non-recognition of learners' cultural identity in the curriculum, discriminatory pedagogical practices and lack of educational opportunities. Hence, from a conflict perspective, educational problems need to be examined within the broader context of social structures and distribution of power between different cultural groups in the society. This book attempts to serve that very purpose by comprehensively examining the impact of the armed conflict on school education in Nepal. In this process, the chapters in the book will serve four broad aims: a critical analysis of the historical context of education and its relevance to the armed conflict in Nepal; a narrative analysis of the experiential dimensions of the violent conflict by drawing upon effects on teachers, parents, education officers and children, describing a range of their responses to the conflict; developing a holistic understanding of the impact of the armed conflict on school education by integrating the range of responses from the schools; and finally, developing an understanding of, and explaining the implications for, educational reforms in a new post-conflict political context.

Methodology

This book primarily draws on an extensive qualitative study in eight different secondary schools selected across six districts of the five geopolitical regions of Nepal (see Figure 1.1). These districts included Doti (far eastern region where a school was attacked by security forces), Rolpa (mid-western region where the 'People's War' originated), Kapilvastu (a district in the south western plains bordering India where the Maoist conflict was followed by ethnic/religious violence in 2007), Kathmandu (the capital in the central Region), Udaypur (south eastern region connecting the mountains and southern plains) and Sankhuwasabha (a mountainous district in the north eastern region which borders Tibet). Three of the total eight schools were private/institutional that served children from economically better off families, and the representation of girls and children from low-caste groups, particularly Dalits, was very low in these schools. The five public schools included in the study generally had a higher number of boys attending the school when the study was conducted, and

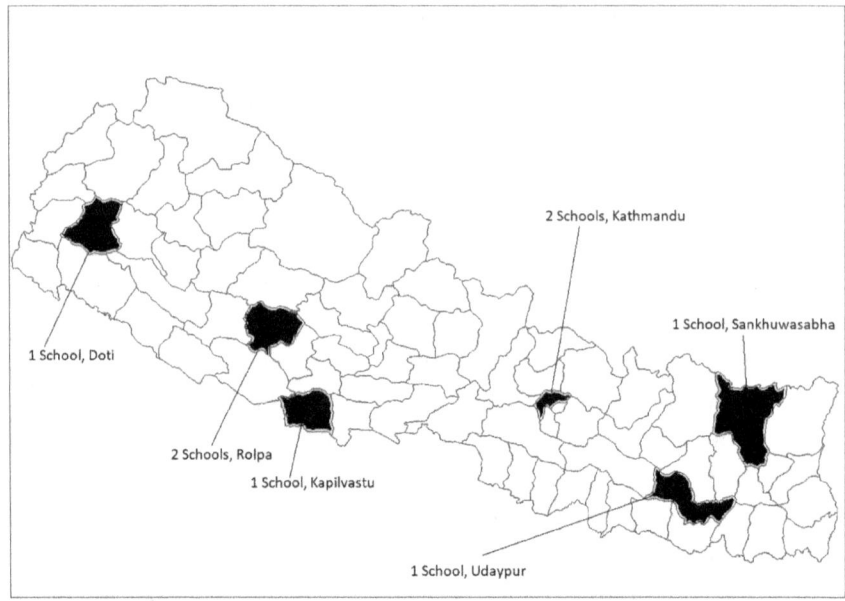

Figure 1.1 Country map indicating research districts.

the students generally represented diverse caste, ethnicity and gender. Figure 1.1 indicates the geographical regions of the fieldwork.

The study was undertaken using a narrative inquiry, a research strategy within the domain of qualitative research, to analyse violent experiences of educational stakeholders (Clandinin and Connelly, 2000; Connolly, 2007). In the first comprehensive study, three main research methods were employed to gather the primary data: individual interviews, focus group discussions and narrative writing. During the fieldwork, eight head teachers, eight teachers and seven education officers representing the six research districts and the Department of Education were interviewed, whereas eighty-eight teachers (eight groups) and seventy-six parents (eight groups) participated in the focus group discussions. The study was carried out from June to October 2008. On an average, I spent one week with research participants chatting, dining and walking together prior to interviewing them formally. During my stay in the field, I was also able to meet with local people in teahouses, local shops and community places, which provided deep insights into the research setting (schools and surrounding communities) and the sociopolitical character of the community.

Additionally, 240 students aged between fifteen and twenty-two completed a narrative writing task titled 'The Armed Conflict and My Experiences', in which they wrote about their experiences of the 'People's War' and the subsequent ethnic violence in some southern districts of the country. More details about this innovative research method and reflections on narrative inquiry with young people will be presented in Chapter 5.

The discussion presented in this book is also informed by some of my subsequent research work in Nepal – a study into the role of education in post-conflict peacebuilding (2010–13); a political economy analysis of education in 2011 (Pherali, Smith and Vaux, 2011) and an examination of new patterns of privatization in Nepal (Bhatta and Pherali, 2017).

Methodological Assumptions

Polkinghorne (2007: 471) notes that narrative research is the 'study of stories' and 'narrative researchers study stories they solicit from others: oral stories obtained through interviews and written stories through requests'. This makes narrative research 'both phenomena under study and method of study' (Clandinin and Connelly, 2000: 4). As a method of research, it utilizes a range of 'field texts' including life experience, autobiography, journals, field notes taken during the research, letters, conversations, interviews with participants, family stories, photos and other related artifacts (Clandinin and Connelly, 2000: 98–115). As Hendry (2007: 495) also notes, 'through telling our lives, we engage in the act of meaning making'. She further argues that 'we are our narratives. They [narratives] are not something that can be outside ourselves because they are what give shape to us, what gives meaning' (Hendry, 2007: 495). This leads to a need for negotiation between the researcher's inherent narrative and those of the participants in the study, which mutually enhance the 'act of meaning making' (Hendry, 2007).

I provide a historical analysis of Nepalese society and the education system and locate the interconnection between education and conflict within the broader spectrum of social and political development in Nepal. In this process, my own conscious 'self', derived from my social and cultural background, engages with the stories to situate them in a particular context so that the meanings are socially constructed and 'co-constructed' as the human beings 'engage with the world they are interpreting' (Crotty, 1998: 43). But these stories cannot be analysed fully unless they are placed within the broader sociopolitical context of contemporary Nepali society and negotiated with the interpreter's preconditions and prejudices. Here, prejudices are not necessarily a negative condition. Annells (1996: 707) argues that it is impossible to 'eliminate one's own concepts in interpretation' rather 'it is actually an advantage not to be freed from prejudice in a hermeneutical situation' where prejudice is a prerequisite for a meaningful engagement with the research data. As outlined earlier in this chapter, I have witnessed discriminatory practices and educational exclusion against women and subordinate castes such as Dalits and indigenous peoples which now make me feel uncomfortable. The pervasiveness of this social injustice, which has become one of the problematic characteristics of the Nepali social system, represents what Bourdieu (1984) calls 'symbolic violence'. Hence, the analysis is located within the historical backdrop of Nepal's socio-economic realities in which the education system largely failed to address these social divisions. As argued elsewhere, the emergence of the armed rebellion was a response to some of these unjust social and political conditions in which education became both an aid to as well as victim of the conflict (Pherali, 2011).

My exposure to the world of narratives and critical engagement with the unjust social and cultural realities of Nepali society have led me to adopt narrative inquiry as a research strategy for giving 'voice to those traditionally marginalized, and providing a less exploitative research method than other modes' (Hendry, 2007: 489). This allows for the stories not simply to be seen in isolation, but in the context where they have been conceived and narrated, as an effective way to understand the lived experiences of the research participants. More importantly, the researcher's own disposition and sociocultural background play an important role in the process of narrative interpretation. Hendry (2007: 489) also mentions that 'by acknowledging the social construction of knowledge, narrative has provided a methodology that has taken into account the situated, partial, contextual, and contradictory nature of telling stories'.

Organization of the Book: The Big Picture and Contextualization

In Chapter 2, I provide an overview of the field of education and conflict, reviewing the theoretical and empirical debates, attacks on education and the impact of armed conflicts on the provision of education and its stakeholders, including teachers, students and education officers globally. Chapter 3 mainly focuses on the historical context of the 'People's War' and education in Nepal with a particular focus on the social, political and economic dimensions of Nepali society in which the armed rebellion emerged and expanded with significant effects on all domains of life. In this chapter, the genesis of the armed conflict is located in the processes of educational development to provide insights into interactions between education and violent conflict. In Chapter 4, I present an analysis of the school-based response to conflict in Nepal and discuss the multitude of ways the Maoist rebellion and state oppression affected teachers and other educational professionals during the conflict. Particularly, this chapter explores teachers' perspectives about interconnections between education and the Maoist rebellion, and reports on experiential dimensions of violence in schools and communities. Chapter 5 focuses on children's experiences of war as well as the role young people played during conflict. The analysis will be situated in the UN Convention on the Rights of the Child and draw upon debates about children's right to political participation. I show that young people in rural Nepal were often exposed to political discourses that challenged exploitation of the poor, ethnic and caste-based discrimination, unequal land distribution and injustices affecting marginalized populations. This kind of political socialization instilled a feeling of resistance among young people who were not just victims of Nepal's Maoist rebellion but also active participants in the movement. Chapter 6 highlights the pertinent issue of national identity, which has become a controversial political agenda amid attempts for sustainable peace. Specifically, I present a critical analysis of the role of education in the creation of national identity and argue that historically disadvantaged communities in Nepal are increasingly reclaiming their ethnic and indigenous identities, which is paving the way for multiple national identities within one sovereign nation. Chapter 7 highlights avenues for post-conflict educational reforms and the role of education in promoting social justice, inclusive democracy and development. Finally, Chapter 8 concludes with some reflections on how education can strengthen its positive role for national reconciliation, good governance and inclusive development at all levels.

2

Armed Conflicts, Education and Peacebuilding

Violent Conflicts and Education: A Global Context

Since the end of the Second World War, the nature of major armed conflicts in the world has shifted from interstate wars to predominantly intrastate civil wars. In 2006, all the thirty-two active armed conflicts reported in twenty-three locations in the world were intrastate civil wars (Harbom and Wallensteen, 2007), the majority of which were occurring in the poorest countries of the world. In recent years, the world has seen a steady increase in the number of armed conflicts. For example, thirty active conflicts were recorded globally in 2010 (Themnér and Wallensteen, 2011). The rise of violence in the Middle East and the expansion of the Islamic State (IS) since 2010 increased the number of armed conflicts to forty-one in 2014 before reaching fifty-four in the year 2019 (Strand et al., 2020). In 2020, active armed conflicts were taking place in at least thirty-nine states, out of which twenty were being fought in sub-Saharan Africa and only two armed conflicts occurred between states – the ongoing clashes between India and Pakistan in Kashmir and the high-intensity border conflict between Armenia and Azerbaijan (SIPRI, 2021). Even though the conflict fatalities seem to have decreased to 120,000 in 2020, a 30 per cent reduction since 2018, the severity of the accompanying humanitarian crisis including forced displacement of the civilian population, food insecurity, violation of human rights and lack of basic services such as health and education has increased significantly (SIPRI, 2021).

The most serious victims of these wars are the innocent civilians who are killed, abducted or forced to flee their homes to live a harsh life as refugees when the wars are in progress (Ahlstram, 1991; SIPRI, 2005). The effects of armed conflicts always exceed the usually noticeable loss of human lives and destruction of infrastructure; cause long-term effects on civilian health (Ghobarah, Huth and Russett, 2003) and on the economic well-being of the countries suffering from wars (Kang and Meernik, 2005) and prevent these countries from being able to achieve the development goals including the ones on education (Stewart, 2003; UNESCO, 2011). World Bank (2011: 49) in their *2011 World Development Report* noted:

> More than 1.5 billion people live in countries affected by fragility, violence, or conflict. A child living in a conflict-affected or fragile developing country is twice as likely to be undernourished as a child living in another developing country and nearly three times as likely to be out of school. No low-income fragile or conflict-affected state has yet achieved a single Millennium Development Goal (MDG).

The causes of intrastate civil conflicts are usually specific to the contexts where they occur, and the motives of attacks on education relate to the political, religious and ideological positions of the conflicting parties. Some of the main causes of armed conflicts include: poor economic conditions and unequal distribution of resources across different social groups; repressive political systems that deny civil liberties and fair representation in decision-making; ethnic divisions and monopoly of dominant ethnic groups in politics; societies that are making democratic transitions; struggles for control over natural resources and autonomist aspirations (Smith, 2004). In many of these contexts, education is also targeted for violent attacks because it is seen by the rebelling groups as a process of political socialization and a contributor to socio-economic inequalities. These inequalities and social injustices are reproduced through a biased system of education that maintains unequal access and outcomes in learning, imposes an exclusionary curriculum and non-native language of instruction, making it hard for children from minority groups to succeed in and through education (Novelli and Lopes Cardozo, 2008; Pherali, 2019; Smith and Vaux, 2003). There are also scenarios where non-state groups reject education which they consider antithetical to their cultural and religious values. For example, the Taliban's attack on state schools in Afghanistan and Boko Haram's disruption of education and abduction of girls in Nigeria are responses to an education that is perceived by the militant groups as a promoter of 'Western' liberal ideals and market-oriented educational goals (Burde, 2014; Human Rights Watch, 2016). In some cases, educational staff or institutions are viewed as affiliates of state or non-state groups and are treated as targets by both sides (GCPEA, 2020: 29). Teachers are threatened or sometimes killed for their involvement in teachers' unions and their activism and protests against privatization of education. In Nepal, the Maoist rebels' intrusion into schools was in order to expand their political base or to recruit young people into the rebel ranks (Watchlist, 2005).

Much of the literature on education and conflict focuses on either theoretical analysis of the duality of the education and conflict relationship (Bush and Saltarelli, 2000; Davies, 2005; Novelli and Lopes Cardozo, 2008; Pherali, 2016b) or the anecdotal reporting of assaults on educational infrastructure, teachers and pupils (O'Malley, 2007, 2010; UNESCO, 2011; Save the Children, 2013; GCPEA, 2020). Only a few seminal works draw on empirical knowledge and engage theoretically to provide a coherent analysis of the case studies of education and conflict (Burde, 2014; King, 2014). King (2014) examines the educational causes of horrific ethnic cleansing in Rwanda. She argues that the dominant perception that ethnic violence in Rwanda was caused by 'ethnic ignorance' is fundamentally flawed. Instead, her findings reveal that psychocultural factors such as 'categorization, collectivization and stigmatization' were synergistically operating within Rwandan society during the period following independence to cultivate a psychological rationalization of the proximate causes of genocide (18). She explains that 'exclusive categorization' of an ethnic group, which is then essentialized to eliminate individuality of the members in the category, served as the basis for a genocidal environment in Rwanda. Despite significant progress in securing stability, economic progress and promoting justice and reconciliation in the past two decades, the post-genocide government has become dictatorial and oppressive to its political opponents, and civil liberties have been denied (King, 2014). Authoritarian regimes are intolerant of criticism, maintain state fragility and cultivate insecurity and fear about the consequences of threats (Feldman and Stenner, 1997). They normally avoid investing in political succession and transformation (e.g. Cambodia, Zimbabwe and Syria), instead perpetuate narratives of historical catastrophes as a key deterrent to political opposition and as a strategy to remain in power. King (2014) paints a bleak picture of Rwanda's efforts to build sustainable peace through education as she argues that education in Rwanda today has yet again become a political tool that serves to promote conformity and national homogenization. However, more recently, Taka (2020) finds that learners in Rwanda find education to be cognitively rewarding and transformational as well as a facilitator of the rehumanizing process in the post-genocide period. Nevertheless, peace narratives taught at schools and narratives circulated in communities often contradict each other, and students do not always have the aptitude to challenge narratives that promote the genocidal ideology (Basabose and Habiyarimana, 2019).

Similarly, Burde (2014) provides some useful insights into the contentious role of education in Afghanistan's conflict over the decades, in which external interventions, particularly the US involvement, have been largely problematic. Her analysis of education in Afghanistan shows that undermining education as a basic humanitarian need or failing to recognize its interactions with underlying social, religious and political conditions can only leave 'important pathways to conflict open' (Burde, 2014: 6). She notes that

> the US government has never fully understood the role that education plays in Afghanistan or the importance it holds for most Afghans. US education policy in Afghanistan shifted from promoting 'jihad literacy' in the 1980s to 'education for stabilization' in the 2000s, and most official support for education was withdrawn in the intervening years. The use of education as a strategic tool – first to inculcate habits of war among the mujahideen in the 1980s and then to support the pacification of communities considered hostile to the US-backed Afghan government – has likely contributed to underlying conditions for conflict.

In a more critical tone, Novelli (2010) challenges the political and security interests of the donor countries in their educational support programmes in conflict-affected contexts. He argues that education aid in countries such as Afghanistan and Iraq has been hijacked by foreign military forces to win 'hearts and minds' of the people. This has led to blurring of the lines between humanitarian, security and development agendas, resulting in the emergence of 'securitization of education aid' (Novelli, 2011). The consequence is that aid workers are increasingly being attacked in conflict zones (Hoelscher, Miklian and Nygård, 2015) as the rebel groups see no difference between the humanitarian workers and armed forces who use humanitarian and development spaces to achieve their military goals. Along these lines, Whittall (2015) notes that humanitarian work is also being 'polluted' with Western political interests, and the relief aid in crisis contexts is increasingly becoming part of wider political goals of state-building, promotion of liberal democracy and the neoliberal market economy.

Interactions between Education, Conflict and Peace

Education has been found to be helpful in improving the impact of peace programmes on perceptions of peace, providing learners with knowledge and skills to deal with conflicts dialogically, and rehumanizing the minds that have been dehumanized by brutalities of war (Biton and Salomon, 2006; Gill and Niens, 2014; Kaufman, 2006; Taka, 2020). Yet, it receives negligible attention in conflict analyses and during peace negotiations (Novelli and Smith, 2011). King (2014: 5) finds that 'education is relegated to the margins' in studies that examine causes of violent intergroup conflicts. Where education is considered an important factor, it is analysed as a victim of conflict in terms of loss in educational funding and decline in enrolment due to increased military expenditures (Lai and Thyne, 2007), or as a pacifying force, minimizing the risk of conflict onset or reducing chances of rebel recruitment (Collier and Hoeffler, 2004; Oyefusi, 2008).

Specialists supporting education in conflict settings often make the mistake of attempting to resolve educational problems only by correcting 'educational politics' – that is, issues relating to rebuilding school infrastructure, distribution of textbooks, teacher recruitment, student enrolment and pass rates rather than critically engaging with the 'politics of education', which requires attention to societal factors such as gender inequalities, language of instruction and political economy of education that shape the fundamental structure of the education system (Novelli and Lopes Cardozo, 2008). So, the focus on 'politics of education' allows us to go beyond 'educationism' and to draw upon multiple disciplines, such as sociology, politics, cultural studies and peace and conflict studies to understand educational policies, distribution of educational resources and interrelationships between caste, gender, race, ethnicity and education. Nevertheless, education is mostly treated as a process of human capital formation and a vehicle for economic development (Barro, 2013; Becker, 1975; Schultz, 1961) – that is, it produces an employable workforce, innovators and business entrepreneurs. This idea assumes that poverty and deprivation are the major causes of conflict, and it can be prevented when people have the means to earn a decent living with the knowledge and skills gained from education and training. However, the exclusive emphasis on the economic logic of education undermines education's wider benefits and obscures the underlying structural inequalities that influence social outcomes across different sociocultural groups in society. Hence, it is crucial to recognize the nature of complex interactions between education and social change. As Novelli and Smith (2011: 7) note:

> Education is deeply implicated in processes of socialization and identity formation, which are vital for economic growth and individual and national advancement and can act as an important vehicle for social cohesion. On the

other hand, education can also undermine all these processes and, therefore, we need to ensure that it is delivered effectively and equitably and is a driver of peace rather than war. Crucially, education is not a marginal player in peacebuilding, but a core component of building sustainable peace.

Since the 1990s, education has received increased attention in debates about international development for several reasons. Firstly, education has been widely recognized as a human right but there are obstacles that reach beyond the challenge of access (McCowan, 2012). In addition to it being a basic right of children irrespective of their cultural, national or ethnic backgrounds, education is also an enabler of other rights such as freedom of speech, right to quality health, right to political participation and right to fairness and justice. Most importantly, educational systems are expected to uphold these rights even during conflicts. However, this is not always the case as McCowan (2012: 70) notes:

> Discrimination is strongly evident within both individual institutions and whole education systems. Well-known historical cases of discrimination include segregation of schools in the southern states of the USA. Furthermore, many if not most education systems display *de facto* if not *de jure* discrimination on the basis of socio-economic background, as well as ethnicity, religion, disability and gender.

As schools are microcosms of societal conditions, inequalities and prejudices that prevail in societies are also manifested in educational processes at schools. For example, attitudes towards refugee populations in host communities are likely to influence the way refugee children are treated at school by their teachers and fellow students from host communities. The practice of various forms of discrimination in society is often reflected in the way children from marginalized communities are treated in class or teachers' educational expectations of them.

Secondly, the Education for All (2000) movement has raised awareness about the importance of education across low- and middle-income countries, but almost 128 million primary- and secondary-aged children are still out of school in conflict and crisis settings (GPE, 2020). Significant progress has been made in recent years – primary school net enrolment ratio increased from 84 per cent in 1999 to 93 per cent in 2015 (UNESCO, 2015). According to UNESCO Institute of Statistics, the overall number of out-of-school children, adolescents and youth has decreased from 376.1 million in 2000 to 258.4 million in 2018 (UNESCO, 2019), which shows that the world is still far from achieving universal access to primary and secondary education. As almost half of the world's out-of-school children live in unstable and dangerous environments, they are doubly disadvantaged from access to education and training. More notably, contemporary conflicts are fought within civilian areas characterizing *undemarcation of the battlefields* – that the wars are no longer fought in designated geographical areas (Pherali, 2016b) and disrupting children's access to a normal educational routine. Schools and other public spaces are either deliberately targeted for violent attack or caught in the middle of clashes between conflicting groups (GCPEA, 2020). Hence, despite the campaigns on Education for All (EFA) and the current Sustainable Development Goal 4 (SDG4) on education, violent conflicts present major threats to global milestones on education.

Thirdly, young people are often caught in conflicts, either as passive victims who are abducted from schools, as combatants or soldiers in the battlefield or as activists or community organizers for peace and social change. The lack of access to education or employment excludes a vast number of youths from opportunities to meaningfully contribute to society and makes them vulnerable to manipulation by political parties or armed groups. However, it is also the case that war serves as 'a source of opportunities for children, who willingly join armed groups to obtain things – protection, a sense of family, education and training, power, money, or a sense of purpose, among others – denied to them in civilian life' (Wessells, 2006: 31). Various studies demonstrate that almost two-thirds of child soldiers join armed groups voluntarily (International Labour Office, 2003; Singer, 2006; UNICEF, 2002), but the distinction between 'forced' and 'voluntary' is not always clear (Andvig, 2006). Additionally, the invention of light-weight weapons and their accessibility across poor and usually unstable countries has increased young people's involvement in armed conflicts. Children as young as ten can be effective fighters with weapons like the AK-47 (Wessells, 2006: 19). Keeping children in quality education, providing them necessary social and employability skills and recognizing their broader 'socially and politically relevant roles' (McEvoy-Levy, 2006: 4) can minimize their chances of being recruited into armed groups.

Finally, globalization and neoliberalism have increased socio-economic disparities across the world to an extent that the top 1 per cent of the world's richest own 43.4 per cent of the global wealth, whereas the 53.6 per cent in the lowest tier of the global population hold just 1.4 per cent of the world's wealth (Credit Suisse, 2020). Market deregulation and the state's gradual withdrawal from providing public services such as education, health and other necessities have pushed the poor and vulnerable populations into deepening poverty (Harvey, 2007). Despite globalization's contribution in expanding economic opportunities and access to information and communication technologies, the world has become monstrously unequal with serious consequences for the poor to cope with economic pressures. The symbiotic relationship between capitalism and neoliberal ideology has benefitted global elites who monopolize economic gains by creating economic structures that favour policies of privatization and deregulation (Harvey, 2007). As a result, what has been observed is 'a pattern of predatory growth' in rapidly growing economies such as India where the poor face 'internal colonization' through confiscation of their agrarian land and loss of employment, while the privileged urban middle class reaps the benefits of market liberalization and foreign direct investment (Harriss, 2011; Walker, 2008: 559). Expounding on the case of India, Walker (2008: 565) notes that

> shaped by an unbridled market whose rules are fixed by capital aided by state power, the pattern of predatory growth ... has privileged urban India and sacrificed and exploited the countryside – which as the home to more than 70 percent of the Indian population still constitutes the fundamental base of the economy.

No doubt, the Maoist rebellion in several parts of India capitalizes on grievances of the rural poor who have suffered from feudalistic oppression at the local level and state-led expropriation for mining and industrial development (Harriss, 2011). In his famous work, *Capital in the 21st Century*, French economist Thomas Piketty argues that the world has produced wealth inequality to a level that could soon lead to an economic catastrophe unless some radical reforms are implemented (Piketty, 2013). He argues for the need of a new 'participatory' system of global economy that has socialist ideology at its core and proposes social property, education and equitable distribution of knowledge and power (Piketty, 2013). Piketty's arguments provide a powerful intellectual resource to work on potentially radical solutions to conflicts that have arisen from growing inequalities and an exploitative capitalist system.

Neoliberalism has intensified commodification of education through introduction of market mechanisms and logic in the education domain and facilitating competitions, liberalization and privatization of the education sector (Ball, 2007); inviting private providers whose primary motive is to make profits from educational enterprises and forcing education systems to import management techniques from the corporate sectors (Verger, Novelli and Altinyelken, 2012). Education has become a prominent global commercial sector with a growing flow of international fee-paying students and expansion of offshore university campuses. The expansion and standardization of educational qualifications is aimed at serving the global economic system by producing a workforce that is adaptable to market needs. To this end, education systems are homogenized through standardization of educational goals, content, language of instruction and pedagogies – a consequence of which is the destruction of diverse ecologies of knowledge located in the uniqueness of indigenous cultures. In many conflict-affected contexts, education of this type is being rejected where educational officials, teachers and students are targeted for violent attacks (e.g. Boko Haram in Nigeria, Taliban in Afghanistan, Maoists in Nepal and Malay Muslim separatists in southern Thailand) (GCPEA, 2014).

Evidence on Peace Pathways

In the peace and conflict studies literature, education is insufficiently featured as a domain of study (Burde, 2014; King, 2014; UNICEF, 2011). In a review of scholarly articles published in seven peace and conflict studies journals including the top-rated *Journal of Peace Research* and *Journal of Conflict Resolution*, King (2014: 6) found that slightly more than 2 per cent of articles referred to school or education. Those that focused on education mainly referred to peace education programmes giving particular attention to their role in improving 'perception of peace, the importance of grassroots education in overcoming weaknesses in peace agreements, the role of public education in addressing the emotional and symbolic roots of conflict and education's impact on one's propensity to forgive' (King, 2014: 6).

General understanding of the education and conflict relationship is that conflict causes damage to education. The well-known UN expert report, *The Impact of Armed Conflict on Children* by Graça Machel; the World Bank report, *Reshaping the Future: Education and Post-Conflict Reconstruction* and the Global Monitoring Report, *The Hidden Crisis: Armed Conflict and Education*, highlight some of the most debilitating and long-term impacts of violent conflicts on learners and education systems (Machel, 2001; Buckland, 2005; UNESCO, 2011). Some reports also compile information about an array of attacks on teachers, students and school infrastructures globally (UNESCO, 2007, 2010; GCPEA, 2014). The *Global Coalition for Protecting Education from Attack* publishes annual reports documenting attacks on education (GCPEA, 2020). These reports show that both rebel groups and state security forces are involved in inflicting violence on teachers, students and educational officials. One of the most gruesome effects of violent conflicts is mass displacement of vulnerable populations, which has severe impact on the educational life of children. At the end of 2019, violent conflicts and natural disasters have caused the forced displacement of 79.5 million people worldwide, of whom 24 million have been living as refugees (UNHCR, 2020). Around half of the refugee population is under the age of eighteen, of whom less than half have access to education. It is estimated that 37 per cent of primary-aged refugee children are out of school, whereas merely 24 per cent attend secondary schools.

The widespread loss of educational opportunities due to insecurity is a major barrier to the SDG4 on education in conflict zones. Lai and Thyne (2007) show that civil wars have devastating effects on a state's education system through the loss of its school buildings and personnel. When state budgets are drawn into funding military expenditures, less funding is made available for educational programmes. Secondly, forced displacement of communities including teachers, farmers, labourers and health workers and skilled people leads to the loss of a state's capacity to revitalize economic activities. Consequently, post-war situations are often fragile, and 'civil wars have a surprisingly high recidivism rate' (Walter, 2010: 1) forcing the conflict-affected countries into a 'conflict trap' (Collier and Sambanis, 2002). The chance of relapse back into conflict increases in situations where after a political settlement people's grievances (e.g. economic needs, security, social services such as education and health services) remain unaddressed (Collier, Hoeffler and Soderbom, 2008; Kreutz, 2010). Walter (2010) expands the conflict relapse theory, arguing that the majority of 'negotiated peace' situations return to violence, unless the government is committed and trustworthy enough. Another condition that minimizes conflict relapse is when the rebel movement is defeated outright by the government, but this may be a temporary scenario where root causes of conflict continue to prevail.

In educational terms, a cross-national analysis of regional inequalities and conflict onset in twenty-two countries in sub-Saharan Africa shows that the regions that have low levels of education are more likely to experience violent conflict (Østby, Nordås and Rød, 2009). The study reveals that education represents 'the recruitment costs' of conflict. In other words, providing access to education would increase the costs of recruitment in rebel groups, whereas less availability of learning opportunities would reduce the opportunity costs of rebel recruitment. Another widely cited work by Collier and Hoeffler (2004), focusing on male secondary education as the proxy for opportunity for rebel recruitment, shows that there is a positive correlation between low level of education and likelihood of conflict. They argue that the 'greed' of conflict actors has more power to explain the outbreak of civil conflict than 'grievances' such as poverty, exclusion and marginalization across social groups. In particular, availability of finance, mostly through primary commodities exports which create an opportunity for rebels to extort money, makes rebellion feasible and attractive (Collier and Hoeffler, 2004). Secondly, mountain terrains where populations are dispersed and possibly underprivileged in terms of their access to quality livelihoods facilitate guerrilla warfare. The analysis does indicate that 'ethnic dominance' in which minority groups are excluded can increase the likelihood of conflict, whereas social, ethnic and religious diversity, as long as monopoly of a single group is avoided, increases the cost of 'rebel cohesion', thereby reducing the possibility of armed conflict. However, the analysis simply explains the predictability of violent conflict under certain conditions and underestimates the conditions of grievances, thereby signalling strategies that could maintain stability rather than engaging with the problem of inequalities and the need for social transformation.

In contrast, Humphreys and Weinstein (2008) report on people's diverse motivations for participating in Sierra Leone's civil war. They provide an analysis of grievance theory, asserting that people who are deprived of economic opportunities, excluded from positions of power and alienated from mainstream political processes tend to mobilize against the state whereas 'members of ethnic groups that benefit from political power have stronger incentives to prevent a successful rebellion' (Humphreys and Weinstein, 2008: 441). However, from the 'selective incentives' perspective, people are likely to decide whether to join the resistance on the basis of comparative benefits they are likely to gain from involvement or refraining from participation in conflict. This could be explained in terms of security, financial gains or aspiration to secure individual or collective political power. Community membership can also explain the logic of participation, as argued, 'strong communities that can monitor individual behaviour and bring to bear a variety of social sanctions are essential for overcoming the free-rider problem that can limit participation in rebellion' (Humphreys and Weinstein, 2008: 442). In Nepal, indigenous peoples, women and Dalits who had been historically neglected in economic and social development had higher levels of participation in the Maoist rebellion (Lawoti, 2005; Leve, 2007). There were also widespread incidents of mass abduction of youth from villages and schools who were forced into the Maoist movement, suggesting that 'involuntary participation is a fundamental part of revolutionary mobilization and political violence' (Humphreys and Weinstein, 2008: 452). From an educational perspective, the case study of Sierra Leone showed that uneducated youth were nine times more likely to join the rebellion than those who had completed post-primary schooling. This might, however, have been due to lower opportunity costs to join the insurgency than to align with the status quo, increased insecurity in the community and forced recruitment by rebel groups.

Similarly, the youth bulge theory claims that countries with disproportionately large youth populations have an increased risk of conflict, and this risk increases as the level of education lowers (Barakat and Urdal, 2009; Collier and Hoeffler, 2004). In Nigeria, Oyefusi (2008) finds that low educational attainment increases the chances of rebel recruitment – that the completion of a key educational stage (e.g. from no education to primary education completion; from primary to secondary completion; from secondary to tertiary education) reduces the person's willingness to join a rebel group by 36 per cent (Oyefusi, 2008). Overall, the rebel recruitment thesis establishes that there is a strong pacifying effect of both primary and secondary male enrolment on likelihood of conflict onset. This argument is based on the notion that educational investment assures citizens that the government is responsive to their grievances, and secondly, it underpins educational pathways by gaining critical awareness about the causes of conflict and important skills such as dialogue, discussion and negotiation techniques that are key to resolving conflict peacefully. Even though a few studies examine the impact of quality and content of education on conflict, rebel recruitment theories largely assume conflict-mitigating effects of increased educational enrolments and overlook the risks of conflict-inciting educational contents that may promote extremist ideologies (Bar-Tal, 1998; Borchgrevink, 2008; Sullivan, 2007).

The reverse relationship with a causal direction from education to conflict is what Bush and Saltarelli (2000) call the 'negative face' of education. The notion of education as a 'perpetrator' of violence (Pherali, 2016b) scrutinizes the structure and content of education rather than simply pointing out the positive correlation between the lack or low level of schooling and increased chances of rebel recruitment and conflict onset (Collier and Hoeffler, 2004; Østby, Nordås and Rød, 2009; Oyefusi, 2008). Unequal access to education, linguistic and cultural repression in teaching and curricula, promoting hatred and intolerance through biased historical narratives and contents of textbooks characterize the negative face of education (Bush and Saltarelli, 2000). At the outset, the idea that education can create, harden and exacerbate conditions of violent conflict may be hard to process, acknowledge and enact for some peace negotiators, education policy makers and practitioners. As pointed out earlier in this chapter, the rebel recruitment thesis can provide some concrete policy prescriptions around quantity, content and quality of education – that expansion of educational opportunities can signal to youths that the government is committed to improving their life conditions and that education provides necessary knowledge and skills to deal with conflict and its legacies in a non-adversarial manner. However, the problem with this thesis is that it equates increased enrolments and completions in education to quality outcomes for peace (King, 2014).

Some argue that inequalities between groups, defined as horizontal inequalities (HI), as opposed to vertical inequalities (inequalities between individuals), can predict conflict onset (Stewart, 2010). Stewart (2010: 2) argues that horizontal inequalities have 'economic, social, political and cultural status dimensions, each of which contains a number of elements – some of which may matter to people in some societies, but not in others'. For example, economic horizontal inequalities relate to inequalities across groups such as castes, ethnicities, gender and so on in terms of access to resources and assets (Stewart, 2008). In Nepal, access to economic realms (e.g. employment in civil services, businesses, industries) has historically been monopolized by hill high-caste groups that also enjoy better access to education, health care and political positions such as the military, judiciary and government. In terms of cultural horizontal inequalities, the dominance of Khas-Arya culture, including Nepali language, customs, norms and practices, has suppressed regional, ethnic and religious diversity. Stewart (2010: 3) argues as follows:

> Any type of horizontal inequality can provide an incentive for political mobilization, but political inequalities (that is, political exclusion of particular groups) are most likely to motivate group leaders to instigate a rebellion ... By contrast, economic and social inequalities and those of cultural status are more likely to motivate the mass of the population. Moreover, cultural status inequalities bind groups together and thereby increase the salience of identity differences. Of course, political inequalities themselves may be partly responsible for other inequalities, for example as a result of clientelism and patronage, and decisions about the distribution of public services, as well [as] determining cultural status inequalities.

The horizontal inequalities theory draws upon Gurr's (1970) ideas of 'relative deprivation', arguing that 'while absolute poverty may lead to apathy and inactivity, comparisons with those in the same society who do better may inspire radical action and even violence' (Østby, Nordås and Rød, 2009: 303). There is growing evidence that intergroup conflict is more likely in societies where there are overt social, political and economic disparities between groups (ethnic, caste-based, regional, gender-based inequalities) (Cederman, Weidmann and Gleditsch, 2010; Stewart, 2008; Østby, Nordås and Rød, 2009; Wimmer, Cederman and Min, 2009). These inequalities may be reflected in political institutions, distribution of wealth and economic resources across social groups and formation of national identity. The mechanisms for conflict onset are: (1) 'shared group grievances' between groups, fuelling competition over political positions and ownership of sources of economic benefits; and (2) an increase in people's affiliation with their identities by further legitimizing their exclusion (King, 2014). Recently, Langer and Kuppens (2019) have highlighted 'education' as a key element of analysis in the HI theory. They argue that educational inequalities may:

a. engender severe grievances among disadvantaged groups which in turn could fuel (violent) group mobilization;
b. create, maintain or worsen existing socio-economic divisions and inequalities between groups;
c. both directly and indirectly worsen disadvantaged groups' access to political-administrative power and position as well as their perceptions of the prevailing objective political HIs; and
d. also contribute to conflict by failing to accommodate cultural diversity.
(Langer and Kuppens, 2019: 42)

In line with the above theoretical claims, a study by FHI 360 and UNICEF shows that the chance of conflict onset is doubled in countries with high education inequalities between ethnic and religious groups, whereas greater equality between males and females decreases the likelihood of conflict by as much as 37 per cent (UNICEF, 2016a). It shows a significant correlation between ethnic and religious inequality in education and likelihood of conflict, arguing that 'countries with higher levels of horizontal inequalities in terms of mean years of schooling have been substantially more likely to experience violent conflict' (UNICEF, 2016a: 3). Subnational educational inequality is a strong predictor of civil war, and marginalized and disadvantaged communities at the subnational level are more likely to experience conflict-related fatalities as compared to regions that are relatively better off.

Hence, the evidence is fairly strong to claim that increased educational access and improved equity in education across sociocultural groups have positive effects on peace and stability. Just the opposite is also valid – that the educational inequalities, inequity in provision of education and inequalities across various social groups can be complicit in production of conflict conditions. However, the quantitative analyses cannot sufficiently explain how the curricula and textbooks are produced and policies formulated; what are the power dynamics between different sociocultural groups; and how a particular type of identity is legitimized and promoted through education while diverse cultural identities are obscured; and what peace-promoting or conflict-fuelling messages are implicitly embedded in educational processes. The following section will make attempts to explore concepts and debates around education and peacebuilding.

Education in Emergencies and Peacebuilding

In recent years, three broad discourses about the role of education in peacebuilding have emerged: Firstly, *education in emergencies*, which primarily focuses on educational advocacy (e.g. policies, financing, professional development and evidence gathering) in times of humanitarian situations and protracted crises. Secondly, *conflict sensitive education*, a discourse that recognizes the 'negative face of education' in fuelling conditions of violence and therefore, the need that educational policies and practices should help reduce inequalities in access to and outcomes in education. The idea is that education should be inclusive in terms of language, culture and pedagogies and promote social justice. Third, *education for peacebuilding*, the notion that educational policies, programmes and pedagogical practices can play a positive role in peacebuilding by going beyond 'do no harm', and by 'placing a more explicit emphasis on social transformation' (Smith and Ellison, 2015: 4).

Education in Emergencies: Contributions and Tensions

Generally, the concept of 'education in emergencies' is featured in the works produced by the Inter-Agency Network for Education in Emergencies (INEE) and tends to include a broad range of themes that manifest different links between education, conflict and peace. 'Education in emergencies' refers to

> the quality learning opportunities for all ages in situations of crisis, including early childhood development, primary, secondary, non-formal, technical, vocational, higher and adult education. Education in emergencies provides physical, psychosocial, and cognitive protection that can sustain and save lives. Common situations of crisis in which education in emergencies is essential include conflicts, situations of violence, forced displacement, disasters, and

public health emergencies. Education in emergencies is a wider concept than 'emergency education response' which is an essential part of it. (INEE, 2018: 4)

The sub-field of education in emergencies (EiE) emerged in the 1990s as an international response to growing challenges around the provision of education in conflict and crises; and out of the realization that if the world was to achieve the Education for All goals, 'the particularities of the conflict/education relationship needed to be better understood and acted upon' (Novelli, 2019: n.p.). It draws on the scholarship in the broad fields of comparative and international education or development studies that focuses on access to quality learning in low- and middle-income countries. Academic studies around peace education and refugee education provide conceptual and analytical frameworks for research and policy analysis in this field. The INEE strategic framework aims (1) to provide thought leadership and global advocacy for education in conflict and crisis; (2) to strengthen capacity to deliver quality, safe, relevant and equitable education for all; (3) to provide, curate and organize knowledge to inform policy and practice and (4) to strengthen and diversify INEE membership (INEE, 2018: 13). The INEE has been instrumental in establishing EiE as a key agenda of the international humanitarian framework and in mobilizing its diverse membership to advocate for prioritization of learning in crisis contexts as well as to adapt the minimum standards of education in crisis settings. Education is seen as the most beneficial instrument for economic growth and poverty reduction; for protection and well-being of children during and after emergencies; a vehicle for peacebuilding and state-building; and a means to reduce risks from and build resilience to disasters and climate change (Winthrop and Matsui, 2013: 2). Despite these benefits, the practice of EiE faces several challenges, such as the lack of coordination between development, humanitarian, security and disaster risk reduction actors; low prioritization of policies leading to inadequate funding and insufficient attention to quality of learning (Winthrop and Matsui, 2013: 4).

Some scholars have recently voiced their concerns about the EiE field – that it has largely failed to challenge northern hegemonies and been co-opted by security interests of the donor countries (Brun and Shuayb, 2020; Novelli, 2019). Novelli (2019) points out that the field of EiE is silent about 'particular historical and socio-political conjunctures' such as the geopolitics of 'humanitarian interventions' in Iraq, Afghanistan and the Middle East; post-9/11 foreign policies of the United States and the 'war on terror' campaign; exaggerated claims about the role of Madrassas in radicalization and anti-West ideology; the use of education as part of the military strategy of counter-insurgency and the political agenda underpinning the support to refugees within neighbouring host countries so that they could be kept from arriving in Europe. Similarly, Brun and Shuayb (2020) argue that EiE does not deal with education's complex political problems in conflict and crisis settings. They note that

> leading actors, like UN agencies, overlooked the social, political and economic sanctions applied on most refugees, such as limited access to formal employment and higher education. As a result, refugees end up suffering two layers of injustice: the first results from having to follow the curriculum of the host country which is often not in their native language, nor contextualized to be relevant to refugees' lives, culture, history, and experiences. Secondly, they face injustice because they are being excluded from the right to participate socially, economically and politically. (Brun and Shuayb, 2020: n.p.)

Secondly, the EiE research and practices are usually 'apolitical', unclear about the long-term purpose of education and mainly deal with 'distributive' aspects and technicalities of educational provisions. The mainstream educational debates about injustices, inequalities and power relationships in education and tensions around curriculum and language of instruction are usually excluded (Brun and Shuayb, 2020: n.p.). Thirdly, EiE knowledge production is concentrated in the global North and funding is allocated to suit the donor countries' foreign policies rather than to empower refugee communities.

Conflict Sensitive Education

Conflict sensitivity involves a process of recognizing aspects of the education system or those of social domains that have been complicit in production of violent conflict, and if not addressed sensitively, may trigger, harden or reproduce conditions of instability or violent conflict. It requires a critical appreciation of the interrelationships between education, conflict and society and should follow a process in which the nature, causes and dynamics of conflict are systematically understood. Evaluations of the interactions between educational programmes and the conflict should be informed by the knowledge gained from a high-quality political economy analysis and then identifying opportunities through which education can promote peace. Essentially, a conflict-sensitive approach 'ensures that design, implementation and outcomes of interventions do not undermine peace or exacerbate conflict and contribute to peace where possible (within the given priorities)' (Goldwyn and Chigas, 2013: 10).

INEE (2013: 13) defines conflict-sensitive education as 'the delivery of education programmes and policies in a way that considers the conflict context and aims to minimize negative impact (i.e., contribution to conflict) and maximize positive impact'. As a process to implement conflict-sensitive education, they suggest three key steps:

1. Understanding the context in which education takes place;
2. Analysing the two-way interaction between the context and education programmes and policies (development, planning, and delivery); and
3. Acting to minimize negative impacts and maximize positive impacts of education policies and programming on conflict, within an organization's given priorities. (INEE, 2013: 12)

The first step involves conflict analysis, unpacking the history of the conflict; political, economic, sociocultural and environmental causes associated with the conflict and the role of education in it. This helps explain the root causes, escalating factors and triggers of the conflict; identifies the key actors, relationships and divisions between the groups participating in the conflict, and their positions, interests and needs and the dynamics of the conflict over a period. Conflict analyses do not necessarily investigate the interrelationships between conflict and education, so unless the analysis is conducted from an educational perspective, it would have little to say about how to adapt education for conflict mitigation.

In the past decade, aid agencies have been interested in political economy analyses of education to understand the causes behind unsatisfactory outcomes of education aid in conflict-affected and politically fragile contexts (Novelli et al., 2014). A political economy approach helps expose inequalities and injustices within and beyond the education system. These elements may range from historical processes of educational development, distribution of political and economic power across various sociocultural groups and effects of such power relationships on access, quality and outcomes in education to educational drivers of conflict and peace (Novelli et al., 2014; Pherali, Smith and Vaux, 2011). In this sense, 'conflict analysis is the foundation of conflict sensitive practice' and it 'can be conducted at various levels (local, national, regional or international) and seeks to establish linkages between them' (Gallagher et al., 2019: 8).

The second step of conflict-sensitive education involves the analysis of the two-way interaction between the conflict context and the education programmes and policies. Before the educational programme is implemented, it is important to consider when and how the programme will be delivered, when it would end and whether this would contribute to intergroup tensions. Questions around selection of target locations of the programme and diversity and inclusivity in staffing are also crucial. Resource allocations, partner selection and inclusion/exclusion of certain communities are areas that need to be considered carefully to avoid unintended complicity of interventions in fuelling tensions.

Finally, conflict-sensitive education should act to minimize negative impacts and maximize positive impacts of education policies and programmes on conflict (INEE, 2013). In this process, education must help mitigate grievances of those who are excluded from learning opportunities. However, it is also important to recognize that promotion of Western liberal values through education without fully appreciating local cultural dynamics can fuel tensions and conflicts. For example, supporting girls' education; excluding host community children from educational aid in refugee settings and empowering ethnic minorities and suppressed groups such as women to access equitable power and resources might fuel tensions unless there is an approach to equity, fairness and collective acceptance.

Education for Peacebuilding

As discussed earlier, education systems can be manipulated by authorities to create social divisions and antagonize societies (Bush and Saltarelli, 2000) but high-quality, conflict-sensitive education can be leveraged as an accelerator of positive change in political and socio-economic domains. Building upon the earlier work of Nancy Fraser (2005), Novelli, Lopes Cardozo and Smith (2017, 2019) propose a '4Rs' framework through which governments and education actors can enhance the role of education in peacebuilding. They argue that a policy of *redistribution* can facilitate equitable access to learning opportunities and resources for all. *Recognition* of diverse perspectives, identities, communities and individuals through relevant and adaptable learning opportunities can address grievances of minorities. This can be done through critical evaluations of policies on the language of instruction, and the inclusion of history, culture and geography representing different ethnic and indigenous groups, gender relations and citizenship in the curriculum. Improving equitable *representation* in the process of policy formulation with regard to fairness and transparency in representation and responsibility for educational decision-making and resource allocation can enhance a sense of ownership of change among teachers, parents, students and civil society. Education can promote *reconciliation* by redressing historical and contemporary economic, political and sociocultural injustices that underpin conflict and ethnic rebellion. It can amend educational practices that may fuel violent conflict and political uprisings (Novelli, Lopes Cardozo and Smith, 2017). The '4Rs' framework is a heuristic tool to examine different aspects of social justice and interactions between the four different 'Rs' – the levels of equity in access to educational services, resource allocation; participatory approach to educational decision-making; recognition of cultural diversity and the role of education in reconciliation (Novelli, Lopes Cardozo and Smith, 2019). These principles of social justice are applicable in the Nepalese context where children from Madhesi, Dalit and indigenous backgrounds have historically struggled to enjoy parity in educational access.

Empirical evidence around the effects of educational reforms on peacebuilding is meagre but some research has emerged out of UNICEF's *Peacebuilding, Education, and Advocacy Programme (Learning for Peace)* (2012–16) (Affolter and Valente, 2020). The programme was funded by the Dutch government and implemented in fourteen countries. Several case study reports point out that the 'Learning for Peace' interventions 'contributed to facilitating social integration, cooperation, inclusion, trust, and participation among citizens and citizen groups whose relationships were previously eroded' (Affolter and Valente, 2020: 223; UNICEF, 2015a). The overall message from this large-scale programme is that education is not 'neutral' in contexts where communities are divided along ethnic, political or religious lines, so educational interventions must be conflict-sensitive and geared towards addressing the grievances caused by social exclusion and structural inequalities. This could involve addressing issues such as unequal access to quality education, linguistic repression of minorities and monopoly of hegemonic groups in curricula, teaching workforce and educational decision-making. Parents and children can be key partners and agents of change therefore should be included as key actors in peacebuilding initiatives (Affolter and Valente, 2020: 234).

Burde (2014) argues that community-managed schools can improve educational access and can be more effective than state authorities in protecting students and teachers from violent attacks during acute conflict. When the insurgents are fighting against the state and its educational authority, community-led negotiations with insurgents could be a more hopeful way of minimizing educational disruptions. Additionally, restoring social services such as education in the aftermath of conflict provides not only a sense of achievement and hope for communities but also builds trust between the state and its citizens. By contrast, the top-down imposition of education (e.g. curriculum, medium of instruction, governance, teacher recruitment, etc.), ignoring local needs reportedly controlled by the Maoist rebels while state security forces remained confined within district headquarters. Parliamentary democracy was on the brink of collapse. King Gyanendra then dismissed the civilian government and imposed a state of emergency on 1 February 2005, expelling parliamentary parties and imposing direct rule, which led to the formation of a seven-party political alliance (SPA) against the royal regime. The royal assault on democracy was criticized by India and other European development partners who gradually withdrew their support from the royal government and aligned with the agendas of political parties that were sidelined after the royal takeover. However, public support for the resistance against royal takeover was insignificant as the people were hugely disenchanted by civilian governments' continual failure to deliver good governance. But the relationship between the king and the parliamentary parties deteriorated to the extent that the Nepali Congress, a prominent political party, abandoned its long-standing support for the constitutional monarchy, which would later have a historic repercussion in the abolition of the 240-year-old monarchy.

As the rebels' military strength gradually increased, the 'People's War' was reaching a state of power equilibrium with the government, and a military solution to the insurgency was deemed no longer viable. In this context, the SPA reached out to the CPN-M. This political alliance reinvigorated the people's movement against the royal regime, eventually reinstating the parliament and removing the monarchy from power. A Comprehensive Peace Accord (CPA) was signed between the government and CPN-M in New Delhi in November 2006, ending the decade-long violent conflict. The government and the Maoists agreed to invite the United Nations to monitor the peace process and manage the arms of both the People's Liberation Army (PLA) and the Nepal Army (NA). After nine years of political upheavals, a new progressive constitution was promulgated on 20 September 2015, which redefined Nepal's social, political and cultural identity. The new constitution paved the way for a federal system of seven provinces and recognized Nepal as a multi-ethnic, multilingual, multireligious and multicultural society.

Education Failing to Serve Social Justice

Schools remained at the forefront of the Maoist rebellion in which rebels extensively mobilized young people to expand their political and military influence. Education was also complicit in creating conditions for armed struggle increase in communist support in Nepal during the last fifty years as indicated by the election results, from 7.2 per cent of votes in 1959 to 33.15 per cent in 1994 (just before the 'People's War' was declared) and 56.98 per cent in the elections for the Constituent Assembly in 2008 (Lawoti, 2010: 6). In the general elections of 2017, the main communist parties won slightly more than 63 per cent of the directly elected seats in the federal parliament, forming a majority government but only to disintegrate again in July 2021.

While the 'People's War' emerged and escalated against a backdrop of widespread public dissatisfaction aroused by several post-Panchayat (1990s) governments, it surfaced in response to deep and historically embedded socio-economic divisions in Nepali society. The hill-based, high-caste Hindus (e.g. Brahmans, Chhetris and Newars) monopolized political, economic, social and cultural power and controlled resources, making it difficult for disadvantaged groups to benefit from economic opportunities. The economic liberalization in the post-1990 environment benefitted only the high-caste groups that overwhelmingly dominated the state apparatus, including political leadership, media, NGOs, commercial, policymaking and academic sectors (Neupane, 2000). Between 1995 and 1996 and 2003 and 2004, the poverty level among Brahman and Chhetri decreased by 46 per cent while it declined only 6, 10 and 21 per cent among Muslims, hill indigenous nationalities and Dalits, respectively (Tiwari, 2007: 7). Similarly, the gap between the poor and rich increased significantly over the period of one decade. It was found that the 'income share of the top 10 per cent of the people increased from 21 per cent in the mid-1980s to 35 per cent by the mid-1990s, while the share of the bottom 40 per cent shrank from 24 per cent to 15 per cent in mid-1990s' (Sharma, 2006: 1245). Agriculture, the backbone of the national economy, suffered negative growth due to inadequate development expenditure in the sector, the feudal land ownership system and increasing levels of poverty in rural areas. Hence, the ethnic and caste-based disparities, coinciding with degrading economic conditions, acted favourably for the Maoist struggle. The Maoists were able to garner support of the disadvantaged and marginalized populations and indigenous nationalities by promising socio-economic transformation of the state.

The massacre of almost the entire royal family by Crown Prince Dipendra in June 2001 led to the surviving Prince Gyanendra's accession to the throne. When the newly crowned king Gyanendra embraced tough measures to crush the insurgency, it rather 'exacerbated the political instability and allowed the conflict to spiral out of control' (Shields and Rappleye, 2008a: 91). By 2004, the country was engulfed by violent conflict; almost 80 per cent of the territory was

CPN continued to demand elections for a Constituent Assembly to establish a republican state and was outlawed from 1952 to 1956, allegedly for inciting violence and associating with other armed groups in the country. Even though their primary demand was elections for a Constituent Assembly, the CPN participated in the parliamentary elections held in 1959, securing four seats (out of 105) in the parliament. King Mahendra later dismissed the elected government on 15 December 1960 and banned multiparty politics to introduce a partyless Panchayat system on 5 January 1961 that would last for thirty years. This consisted of a national assembly of representatives elected by the people and a four-tiered structure of governance – national, district, town and village Panchayat committees, while the king remained above the constitution. The national identity comprised three pillars – monarchy, Hinduism and Nepali language, invoking the slogan of '*Ek Raja, Ek Bhesh, Ek Bhasa, Ek Desh*' (One King, One Dress, One Language, One Nation). It was presented as a home-grown indigenized democratic model, as opposed to Western-style liberal democracy and the USSR's communist system. King Mahendra argued that it was the most suitable political system for Nepali society.

The subsequent years of Panchayat polity were punishing for political parties, including the CPN, as many of their members were imprisoned or forced to flee to India. In the following years, the CPN underwent ideological splits facing 'a chronic problem of factionalism', resulting in as many as a dozen communist parties (Lawoti, 2010: 5). Meanwhile, the splinter factions continued to be active clandestinely in different parts of the country even during the Panchayat era. As Hutt (2004: 3) argues: 'opposition to the Panchayat system grew – partly because of its increasing exclusivity and unaccountability, partly because it was patently failing to deliver the "development" (*bikas*) that had become one of its watchwords, and partly also because of the manner in which, latterly, it tried to suppress dissent, even among adherents of the system.'

The first communist armed rebellion was launched in 1971 by some youths in the East of Nepal who, inspired by the Naxalite Maoist movement in West Bengal (India), killed several civilians – the 'class enemies'. The movement was crushed brutally by the Panchayat regime, but the left ideology continued to thrive among the grassroots. Even though this communist faction transformed to become the Communist Party of Nepal (United Marxist and Leninist), adopting principles of liberal democracy and becoming the largest party in the parliamentary elections in 1994, another communist faction, the Communist Party of Nepal-Maoist (CPN-M), exploited the long-established radical communist base in the western mountains and declared the 'People's War' in 1996. There has been a dramatic

3

Educational Development and Conflict in Nepal

This chapter mainly focuses on the historical backdrop of the 'People's War' with reference to the processes of educational development in Nepal. The analysis will concentrate on Nepal's processes of nation-building and the ways sociocultural diversity and relationships between different ethnic and cultural groups and issues around inequalities and exclusion of ethnic minorities, Dalits and indigenous communities have been addressed or excluded. In particular, the long-standing social injustices and marginalization of ethnic and indigenous communities in the pre-1990 period will be analysed to locate the historical antecedents of the 'People's War'. This chapter will also touch upon the history and development of communist movements prior to the declaration of the 'People's War' in 1996 and will argue that education largely remained as a service available to the privileged, with most ethnic and indigenous groups deprived of access to quality education.

The Political Context of Armed Conflict and Transition to Peace

The violent communist rebellion in Nepal was not an unanticipated incident. The onset of the communist movement harks back to the birth of the Communist Party of Nepal (CPN), officially launched in Calcutta, India, in September 1949. The CPN was against the restoration of the monarchy after the end of the Rana oligarchy in 1951, and therefore denounced the 'Delhi Compromise' agreement between the king, the Nepali Congress and the Rana regime in that year, which marked the first steps towards a more democratic government. The of unemployment among Black populations continue to pose the greatest threat to social cohesion and peacebuilding in South Africa.

Where prosocial justice reforms are undertaken within the education system, they are usually limited to 'redistribution' of educational resources while overlooking the other dimensions such as involvement of disenfranchised groups in educational decision-making, inclusion of diversity in the curriculum and educational processes and implementing changes to support reconciliation between divided communities (Smith, Datzberger and McCully, 2016). Drawing upon case studies of education in conflict-affected Pakistan, Myanmar, South Africa and Uganda, the authors reveal that education sector plans primarily focus on economic goals rather than social development, inclusivity and promotion of an equitable society. Education is hugely underfunded, limiting the needs-based adaptation of educational processes. Additionally, policies aimed at equity, social cohesion or reconciliation often face a political economy challenge in which the country's dominant political class is usually manipulative or resistive to changes. Most crucially, there is 'a striking absence of donor and multi-lateral policy strategies' that 'foster implicit and explicit peacebuilding' (Smith, Datzberger and McCully, 2016: 11). Hence, the educational process broadly fails to acknowledge past and present grievances.

Generally speaking, the research is thin when it comes to reporting micro-level experiential dimensions of education and conflict such as how teachers and school leaders experience and navigate through both physical and psychological threats and assaults on schools and trade off their survival in the contexts of protracted conflict. Hence, the purpose of this book is to present the analysis of experiences of teachers, school leaders and pupils during Nepal's Maoist insurgency (1996–2006). What emerges from this analysis is the prevalence of a disproportionate focus on conventional forms of schooling during conflict without calculating the risk of potential attack from armed groups, which may be counter-productive in terms of children's safety, learning and their social and emotional development. As the onerous pressure to keep pupils safe during crisis ultimately falls upon teachers and school leaders who face direct violence against their schools and communities, their voice needs to be taken into account in educational reconstruction and post-war reconciliation processes.

and preferences, can be counter-productive to peacebuilding goals. Providing necessary financial and technical support and enabling communities to take ownership of the process of educational development has positive effects in bringing communities together and reducing grievances. However, it is crucial to recognize that decision-making may be highjacked by a few local elites, and the prevailing power dynamics, discrimination and exclusion of certain groups may be reproduced even within locally managed education provision. So, educational reforms must tackle these difficulties sensitively (UNICEF, 2011). This could help identify students and social groups that need targeted support, potentially increase representation of excluded social groups in educational decision-making and promote an inclusive educational practice by reducing 'elite capture' of the opportunities (Pherali, 2012).

When educational reforms are introduced, it is vital to prioritize policies that protect girls (Smith and Ellison, 2015), children from poor families and those with disabilities while changes around broader issues such as inequity, exclusion and segregation along the lines of ethnicity, religion, geographical location and language are set in motion. Even though peace-promoting educational reforms have been initiated in some contexts, the impacts of such programmes have been limited. A study in Uganda shows that investment in *hard inputs* designed to strengthen equity of access to school resources, such as infrastructure, teachers and fees, has limited success (UNICEF, 2015b: 32). The high school fees and the low opportunity costs of attending secondary education undermine equity in education. The investment in *soft inputs* such as peace education, creation of dialogic space and mutual learning to mend traditional identity fault lines generally have limited impact. This is mainly because discussions about peace and social transformation are outside the formal curricular contents and instructional processes of school. Thus, collectively, the prevailing political and economic divisions between the urban South and rural North in Uganda are continuously reproduced rather than reduced (UNICEF, 2015b: 33). Similarly, in South Africa, 'race continues to be the predominant group identity marker in the country, despite substantial ethnic (tribal and linguistic) heterogeneity', where race-based and class-based discrimination, including the use of language and class-size norms, prevents Black or poorer learners from attending the formerly white schools (UNICEF, 2015c: 2). The failure of the post-apartheid governments to transform socio-economic structures and improve the living conditions of the vast majority of poor Black and coloured South Africans has preserved the apartheid era systemic discrimination and inequality. For example, the de facto residential segregation between racial communities and high levels by failing to promote equity in access, quality and outcomes across castes, gender and ethnic divisions, which reinforced social injustices (Pherali, 2011; Shields and Rappleye, 2008a, 2008b). Even though public education was available to all, it largely served the traditionally privileged social groups, primarily hill-based high-caste males from three dominant castes: Brahman, Chhettri and Newars. For example, over 80 per cent of the leadership positions in key social and political domains such as administration, judiciary, security institutions, media and voluntary organizations were occupied by these social groups that represent around one-third of the national population (Neupane, 2000). A recent Nepal Social Inclusion Survey also uncovered that the exclusions linked to linguistic, caste, ethnic, religious, regional and gender identity persisted long after the Maoist insurgency ended and these exclusions were also based on disadvantages including the areas of social capital, participation in governance and sense of agency (Gurung, Pradhan and Shakya, 2018). Dalits continued to experience untouchability despite the legal ban on such practice.

The unequal outcomes in and through education contributed to perpetuate the existing social order and the grievances of the social groups that struggled to gain upward social mobility. In higher education, particularly girls, members of suppressed low castes and neglected ethnic groups such as Dalits, Madhesi and indigenous nationalities are hugely underrepresented (Bhatta et al., 2008). Teachers and school leaders, most of whom belong to high-caste groups, neglect children from Dalit, Madhesi and indigenous communities or have low educational expectations of them (Bhatta et al., 2008). For children from marginalized social groups, the education system failed to nurture their academic potential and disregarded their continued underachievement and dropout from school. Bourdieu (1977) describes this as 'symbolic violence' which is 'gentle', 'invisible' and often goes unrecognized but is more powerful than physical violence. It imposes and legitimizes the discriminatory social structure. This nuanced but toxic role of education was never challenged seriously throughout over half a century of educational development.

Attacks on Education

Education in Nepal has been at the epicentre of civil conflict, both as a problematic institution that failed to promote equity and social justice and also as the major battleground during the war (Caddell, 2006; Pherali 2011, 2016a; Vaux, Smith and Subba, 2006). During the conflict, pupils and teachers were frequently abducted by the Maoist rebels in order to engage them in 'revolutionary training programs' (Pyakurel, 2006: 55) or were forcibly recruited into the Maoist militia (Watchlist, 2005). The Maoists imposed mandatory donations on teachers across the country, and schools were frequently forced to close down (Simkhada, 2006: 64). Private schools were particularly threatened (Caddell, 2006) and the student wing of the CPN-M demanded closure of all private schools, accusing them of being merely commercial ventures rather than serving the broader social good.

It was reported that more than seventy-nine schools, one university and thirteen district education offices were destroyed by the Maoists between the period of January 2002 and December 2006, of which thirty-two suffered bomb explosions and at least three schools were caught in the crossfire between the rebels and security forces (INSEC, 2007). On the other hand, security personnel arrested, tortured and even killed teachers and schoolchildren suspected of being Maoist activists or sympathizers (Amnesty International, 2005). These extrajudicial actions by the state were justified through the broad agenda of 'combating terrorism' and the belief that state terror was the most 'cost-effective' response to the 'resistance to elite domination' (Sluka, 2000: 31). The emergence of a new Maoist state in the periphery meant that teaching and learning at schools in that area was controlled by the Maoists, and some elements of the national curriculum were barred from being taught. For example, Maoists banned the teaching of Sanskrit, and teachers and school heads were assaulted or murdered for non-compliance. On the other hand, security forces targeted teachers accusing them of being Maoist sympathizers. The total number of teachers killed by the Maoists and the state reached 145, while 331 pupils were murdered during the ten-year period of violent conflict (INSEC, 2007). The number of children abducted and tortured by the warring parties was reported to be several thousands.

Overview of the Education System in Nepal

Nepal's modern education system has a history of just over seven decades. The end of the Rana oligarchy in 1951 and the beginning of an egalitarian political system created an opportunity to introduce universal access to education. Education was then perceived to be the right of liberated people, and therefore a Board of Education was established in 1952 to review the existing situation of educational provision and set a course for educational development that was needed for the modernization of Nepal. The National Education Planning Commission (NEPC), with financial and advisory support from the United States, was tasked to study existing educational initiatives and propose a homogenous national education system that would promote unity, democratic values and national pride.

The first Five Year Plan for Education in Nepal (1956–61) emphasized 'national' characteristics in the education system by adopting a national curriculum for the primary level, compulsory teaching of the Nepali language in all schools and categorically barring the learning and teaching of other indigenous languages. The NEPC report recommended that Nepal's modern education be geared towards restoring historically ignored 'essential characteristics' – 'national pride, virility and individuality' (Pandey, K. C. and Wood, 1956: 74).

The royal coup of 1960 and the establishment of the Panchayat system added a new theme of *rajbhakti* (service to monarchy) to education and placed a greater emphasis on national unity and solidarity (Onta (1996) for an analysis of making of the national history in Nepal). The National Education System Plan (NESP) was announced in 1971 with an aim to meet the social, political and economic needs of the nation and again to solidify the project of nation-building through the educational process. The main objective of the NESP was to produce a citizenry loyal to the Crown and Panchayat political system as well as to develop scientific and technical human resources (HMG, 1971). All schools were nationalized under the Ministry of Education and a national curriculum was made compulsory to instil Panchayati values through teaching and learning across the country. The United States and other donors viewed this plan as a 'ploy' by the palace to legitimize royal supremacy and solidify the Panchayat system. As a result, the education sector lost substantial international funding.

The expansion of education during this period was simply a 'psychological adornment' rather than a national strategy to produce citizens capable of contributing to the economic development of the nation (Ragsdale, 1989: 15). Hence, the education system was developed as a tool for nationalizing the diverse Nepali society, favourably disposed to the monarchy and the ruling elite (mainly representing hill high castes) (Lawoti, 2007) who were in control of the state apparatus. Even though two major political changes have occurred since, the legacy of the Panchayat education system still prevails. Apart from the idea of monarchy as a unifying force, the influence of Panchayat ideology is deeply entrenched among the dominant political class even today. The notions of Nepaliness defined monolithically along the linguistic, cultural and religious monopoly of Hindus; the centralized rent-seeking mechanism of the state that is controlled by hill high-caste males; unease at federalism and pluriversality and continued marginalization of cultural, ethnic, regional and religious minorities characterize the captivity of the Nepali psyche and sociopolitical conditions of the Panchayat legacy. Therefore, it is important to analyse these historical antecedents in order to fully understand why, despite a huge amount of investment, Nepal's education has failed to produce the intended outcomes.

The Nepalese school system has three main types of schools: community schools (supported by the government but may be aided or unaided by state funding), institutional schools (supported by parents and trustees and privately managed) and religious schools (MOE, 2016). Out of a total of 35,055 schools, 27,728 are community schools and 6,206 are registered as institutional schools that are funded privately (GoN, 2018). A small proportion (1,121) are registered as religious schools, a majority of which are Madrasas (Islamic schools). There are also many unregistered religious schools that do not receive any grants from the state. In 2001, the Seventh Amendment of Nepal's Education Act 1971 paved the way for community transfer of state-funded government schools. Community schools have three sub-categories: community-aided (fully supported financially and managed by the government), community-managed (supported and funded by the government fully but managed by the community) and community-unaided (getting either partial or no support from the government). Under the School Sector Reforms Plan 2009–2016 (SSRP), a new structure of school education was introduced, converting the primary and lower secondary level of education to a combined structure of one-year early childhood education, 1–8 grades of basic education and 9–12 grades secondary education (MOE, 2009). An overview of the school system is provided in Table 3.1.

The most significant change in the new system has been the merging of primary and lower secondary level structures into a single basic education from grades 1 to 8. This change can be perceived as a strategic move by the government in order to receive international funding up to grade 8 as part of the global strategy for universal basic education. Even though this aspect can be viewed as a positive step forward, Nepal's education faces a range of structural challenges that work against the goal of educational equity.

Education and Social Disparities

Despite the significant expansion of education during the last few decades, there exist ethnic and caste-based disparities in access and attainment. Even

Table 3.1 The Structure of the School System in Nepal

Age	Grade	Types of School System	
		Old System	New System
16	12	Higher Secondary Education (Grades 11–12)	Secondary Education (Grades 9–12)
15	11		
14	10	Secondary Education (Grades 9–10)	
13	9		
12	8	Lower Secondary Education (Grades 6–8)	Basic Education (Grades 1–8)
11	7		
10	6		
9	5	Primary Education (Grades 1–5)	
8	4		
7	3		
6	2		
5	1		
4			Pre-Primary Education/Early Childhood Development
3			

in 2001, a full decade after multiparty democracy was restored, equal rights were spelled out in the new constitution and educational 'development' efforts intensified, disparities existed. Literacy rates among Brahmans, the upper caste, was 70 per cent as compared with 10 per cent among the several low-status caste groups that constituted 9 per cent of the country's population (Central Bureau of Statistics, 2003). Socio-economic status is strongly correlated with access to private education – 44 per cent of students from the richest quintiles were enrolled in private schools as compared to 7 per cent from the three poorest quintiles (Central Bureau of Statistics, 2004). Those who have access to English medium education in private schools are more likely to succeed in the modern job markets such as the business sector and the evergrowing number of non-governmental organizations. The wealthiest quintile benefits from the social and political networks of the privileged and is likely to gain easier access to economic opportunities. This kind of social reproduction (Bourdieu, 1984) is difficult to break through project-based interventions and the caste-based social order continues to be reproduced. The prevalence of inequality across ethnic groups is closely linked with the systemic hegemony of Nepali-speaking hill high-caste Hindus who have dominated the political system since the formation of the Nepali state (Phyak and Ojha, 2019; Pradhan, 2020).

One of the earliest studies by Stash and Hannum (2001) shows that the early stages of educational expansion failed to narrow the gaps across caste and gender. Examining the 1991 Nepal Fertility, Family Planning and Health Survey (NFHS), the authors report that even in highly educated high-caste households, gender discrimination continued to prevail, while boys in urban areas disproportionately benefitted from the increased educational opportunities. Additionally, 'caste affects both selection into and attrition from primary school', suggesting that historically defined low-caste groups continued to be left out or underachieve in education (Stash and Hannum, 2001: 376). Providing a more nuanced intersection between caste and gender, the authors note:

> High-caste Brahmins – including Brahmin and Chhetri castes – in the fulfilment of their social and religious roles as the priest caste have long prized literacy skills; however, high-caste women were traditionally denied any access to these skills. Social norms setting expectations for women are commonly considered to be more restrictive among high than low castes. Moreover, the activities of high-caste women beyond the home can be severely circumscribed, particularly in more remote or socially conservative regions of the country. High-caste groups tend to be socioeconomically advantaged, and households with greater resources may be better able to implement stricter standards governing women's activities and interaction with men. (Stash and Hannum, 2001: 359)

Similarly, an education sector analysis by the National Institute for Research and Training (NIRT) and American Institutes of Research (AIR) reports that 'girls consistently perform less well than boys and are more likely to dropout and repeat across all grades' (NIRT, 2016: vi). The literacy rate across different caste/ethnic groups is also worryingly disparate and children whose mother tongue is other than Nepali have lower learning outcomes (UNICEF, 2015). For example, only 23.1 per cent of Tarai Dalits and 35.4 per cent of Muslims are literate as compared to 80 per cent of Tarai Brahmans/Chhetris and 78.5 per cent of hill Brahmans (NIRT, 2016: 66). Children with disabilities, mainly those who are girls living in rural areas, are the most marginalized in terms of access and completion of school education, while almost one-third of female children are engaged in child labour (UNICEF, 2015).

Neupane (2017) also shows that girls from Dalit and indigenous groups perform significantly lower than those from high-caste Brahman and Chhetris. She further reports that students' school attainment is predicted by household head's level of education, land sufficiency, student/teacher ratio and local caste/ethnic composition. Children particularly from the lowest quintile of historically marginalized communities, such as Madhesi and Muslim, are more likely to drop out of education before they reach the secondary level and are affected disproportionately by high-repetition rates (NIRT, 2016). These problems of inequity in education highlight not only the failure of the education system in addressing inequalities both in access and outcomes across gender, caste and ethnicity but also expose how education has been complicit in reproduction of social hierarchies in Nepali society. The political domination and cultural hegemony of the hill high-caste males contributed to normalization of these educational disparities, creating favourable conditions for armed rebellion.

Economic Relevance of Education

Globally, returns on investment in education are significantly higher than those achieved through investments in other areas. A recent analysis of returns to education shows that the private average global rate of return to one extra year of schooling is about 9 per cent and over the years, the returns to higher education have also increased significantly (Psacharopoulos and Patrinos, 2018). Low-income countries like Nepal gain higher returns through investment in education as compared to high-income countries, and women accumulate higher rates of returns than men do. In Nepal, one extra year of schooling leads to a 6 per cent increase in earnings and there are huge earning disparities across gender and private/public education (Akanda, 2010). Also, since social returns to education are as high as 10 per cent, it is crucial to invest more in girls' education and ensure equity in access to higher education so that educational outcomes do not harden socio-economic inequalities (Psacharopoulos and Patrinos, 2018).

Even though education is viewed as a 'good thing', it is not necessarily valued as a tool for guaranteeing a secure economic future for the majority of rural populations. Employment opportunities are scarce, and nepotism and favouritism are rampant. Almost one-third of the Nepalese youth population is currently employed in unskilled jobs in the Gulf States, Malaysia and Korea. Since 1993, there has been an unprecedented growth of labour migration to the Gulf Corporation Council (GCC) countries and Malaysia for temporary employment. In the fiscal year 1993/94, the Department of Foreign Employment approved 3,605 foreign labour permits which peaked at 519,638 in 2013/14 before declining to 236,208 in 2018/19 (GoN, 2020). A small minority of the migrant workers are female (8.5%), who are employed in the domestic work sector, where they are vulnerable to abuse and economic exploitation (Bajracharya and Sijapati, 2012; Guichon, 2014). In the year 2017/18, almost two-thirds of the Nepalese labour migrants were engaged in low-skilled work and yet made a contribution of 8.79 billion USD to the Nepalese economy, which is 68.5 per cent of the total foreign exchange earnings (GoN, 2020).

The exponential growth in the number of low-skilled labour migrants expressively reveals serious problems in Nepal's education system, economic policies and governance. The temporary foreign employment of a large youth population has resulted in precarious economic growth without sustainable economic structures in the country. Therefore, educational development needs to relate more to local level economic activities in order to better establish the relevance of education in young people's lives.

Educational Progress in Numbers

The *Dakar Framework for Action* identified six key Education for All goals which also include 'Ensuring that by 2015 all children, particularly girls, children in difficult circumstances and those belonging to ethnic minorities, have access to and complete free and compulsory primary education of good quality' (UNESCO, 2000). In Nepal, there has been significant progress in access to education over the last sixty years. The literacy rate among the adult population (fifteen years plus) has increased to 67.91 per cent, and 92.39 per cent of the youth population (fifteen to twenty-four) are literate (UNESCO Institute for Statistics, 2018). From the situation in 1951 when there were 8,505 students in 321 primary schools and a mere 1,680 students in 11 secondary schools, there are currently 3,942,354 students studying in 15,091 primary and 1,840,772 students in 8,968 secondary schools across the country with a total number of 5,783,126 students enrolled at basic level (grades 1–8) of education (DoE, 2016). In the last sixty years, the numbers of primary and secondary schools have increased by more than 102 and 661 times, respectively. Despite these achievements, 101,223 children were reported to be still out of school; 481,015 of 15- to 24-year-olds are illiterate and 17.62 per cent of children failed to transition to secondary schools in 2018 (UNESCO Institute for Statistics, 2018).

Gender-based disparity in terms of access to education has almost ended, with girls making up 50.8 per cent of children enrolled at the basic level of education (GoN, 2015). However, there is still a large gender disparity in the teaching workforce. For example, only 17 per cent of teachers in secondary schools are female (GoN, 2015). A significant improvement in Dalit and Janajati participation in basic education has been achieved with an average of 17.9 per cent Dalits against the national share of their population of 12 per cent and 35.7 per cent Janajatis against 40 per cent (GoN, 2016).

However, the quality of education remains low, while repetition and dropout rates are high. While the pass rate in the School Leaving Certificate (SLC) examination in 1991 was only 24 per cent, it reached 68.67 per cent in the year 2010. Following the eighth amendment and implementation of the National Education Act 1971, the SLC examination has been renamed as Secondary Education Examinations (SEE) with the introduction of a new grading system. However, the nature of the exam system and approach to assessment mostly rewards memorization rather than creativity, critical thinking and independent learning. Discussions with teachers and students in rural districts revealed that the SEE results can be questioned due to poorly managed exams, and irregularities such as external cheating, guidance by teachers in the exam halls and copying among students still remain pervasive in most SEE exam centres in rural areas (Pherali, Smith and Vaux, 2011). While Nepal is proud of its progress in the global race on reporting educational statistics, standards, quality and relevance of education seem to have received less attention. Therefore, the education system is blamed for not serving the labour market well (World Bank, 2001). Nevertheless, education makes a significant contribution to the national economy – that 1 per cent change in primary enrolment rate leads to 39.17 per cent of increase in GDP and completion of secondary education and tertiary or higher education expands the economy by 71.36 per cent and 11.43 per cent, respectively (Nowak and Dahal, 2016).

Transition to Local Autonomy: Ethnic and Indigenous Agency

It has been argued that the 1990s has been an era of 'ethnicity building' (Gellner, 2007: 1823) as opposed to the Panchayat era of nation-building (1960–90), during which discussion of ethnic identity and interethnic disparities was perceived by the state as a threat to national unity. While Nepali still remains the official language, the Constitution of Nepal 1990 restored the right to have primary education in the mother tongue. Subsequently, the Constitution of Nepal 2015 has also recognized all mother tongues spoken in Nepal as the national languages. Even though Nepali is the language for official business, individual provinces have been granted the authority to nominate one of two additional languages spoken by the majority to be used for official purposes. The Curriculum Development Centre (CDC) under the Ministry of Education has developed curricula in various local languages: for example, five books for grades 1–5 have been developed in the Maithili, Bhojpuri, Awadhi, Tamang, Limbu, Bantawa Rai, Chamling Rai, Sherpa, Gurung, Magar and Nepal Bhasha languages (CDC, 2010). The CDC (2005, 2010) also made the provision of an additional subject that could be developed by the school to address the local need and also be delivered in the students' mother tongue. However, there has been a lack of meaningful engagement with local communities in the process of design and development of mother tongue materials and, more importantly, the limited capacity of the existing workforce to teach in local languages has not been fully recognized. This process is yet another top-down intervention, prescribed by international agencies without adequate preparedness of the actual beneficiaries (Shields and Rappleye, 2008b: 269). Subedi (2018: 66) found that 'teachers lack an adequate knowledge and skill in designing the local curriculum' and hence, 'the mandatory provisions of local curriculum in primary schools remained on policy only as a nonfunctional intervention to promote the local knowledge.' Hence, many schools have adopted English language as an additional subject instead.

The 40-point demand of the CPN-M before the declaration of the 'People's War' included a point on education in the mother tongue – 'all languages and dialects should be given equal opportunities to prosper. The right to education in the mother tongue up to higher levels should be guaranteed' (Maoist Statements and Documents, 2003). An ethnic and indigenous right was one of the prominent slogans and a uniting force of the Maoist movement that expanded its power base among ethnic groups and indigenous populations. Therefore, not surprisingly, the majority of Maoist activists and People's Liberation Army members were young people from 'indigenous nationalities', down-trodden castes and marginalized ethnic groups (Lawoti, 2005). During the conflict, the Maoists also structured their 'new state'[1] based on the ethnic majority population in local areas and were still advocating for the same until the second Constituent Assembly elections in 2013. However, their poor results in this election gave no support for this agenda, and a compromised model of federal territorial restructuring was eventually produced.

Presently, the Constitution of Nepal 2015 guarantees local autonomy in educational governance, which provides an enormous opportunity to redress educational disparities across ethnic, caste, gender, regional and religious communities. Despite the constitutional provision that bestows powers on local municipalities to formulate contextually relevant education policies,

---

[1] The CPN-M used the term the 'new state' to refer to their political control and the 'old state' to the existing state mechanism. They were still running their own judicial system, education, taxation and traffic registration in some rural parts of the country until 2008, when these structures were dissolved.

the institutional culture is constricted by the legacies of centralization, neopatrimonialism and dependency on the power centre in Kathmandu. The 'persistence of old institutions' and the 'lack of capacity' to function autonomously serve as the major barriers to local agency, formulation and implementation of local education policies (Shangraw, 2019).

Private versus Government Schools

Even though most Nepalese children attend state schools, 24.63 per cent in basic education (1–8) and 17.76 per cent in secondary level (9–12) are currently receiving education in privately managed schools (GoN, 2018). Recent statistics show that 17.3 per cent of Nepal's basic education schools and 34.79 per cent of secondary schools (9–12) are under private management (GoN, 2018). As noted earlier, a small proportion of children in basic education (1.12%) attend religious schools. Private schools in Nepal do not receive government funding, nor are their teachers provided professional development training or monitored by the state in the same way the state schools are. These schools charge fees from the parents and offer the curriculum in English. Private schools have historically performed significantly better than government-funded schools in the SLC examinations (Thapa, 2015). For example, 89.8 per cent of the students in private schools passed the so-called iron-gate SLC examination in 2014/15, whereas only one-third of public school students succeeded in their first attempt (Office of the Controller of Examinations (OCE, 2016). Consistent with findings in other contexts (Kingdon, 1996; Goyal, 2009), Nepal's case also shows a positive association between private school attendance and higher learning outcomes. This does not necessarily predict social outcomes of private education, nor does it guarantee students' success in higher education. More importantly, private schools predominantly serve the populations with high socio-economic backgrounds – in 2009/2010, 56 per cent of students in private schools came from the richest quintile while their counterparts from the lowest quintile made up only 5 per cent (Dahal and Nguyen, 2014). Joshi (2019: 66) notes that the expansion of private education was 'fueled on the demand side by parental preference for private schools, linked to poor perception of public schooling quality and due to social prestige reasons; and on the supply side by providers that are accommodating their clientele's ability to pay'.

Much of the debate about the proliferation of private education focuses on failure of public schools to provide quality and relevant education to students, lack of accountability, corruption and teachers' professional dereliction of duty (Pherali,

2017). There is very little constructive dialogue within the policy circle about possibilities of mutual learning from educational practices between the public and private sectors, other than the fact that public schools in some places hastily adopt English as the medium of instruction. The lack of policy debate on the overall educational provision partly contributes to a systemic disengagement of national policymakers from some of the effective practices in private education provisions, limiting the reforms in public schools to local management and governance, rather than, for example, formalizing the best practice of parent–teacher interactions on children's academic progress in private schools (Bhatta and Budathoki, 2013).

During the Maoist insurgency, private schools were forced to make mandatory donations; their properties were vandalized or destroyed and many, particularly in the rural areas, were forced to close (Caddell, 2006; Pherali, 2011). In 2001, the government imposed a 1 per cent service tax on private schools and provided powers to District Education Offices to monitor their educational affairs (Bhatta and Budathoki, 2013). Since 2006, a series of new regulations have been introduced: free scholarships for 10 per cent of students including 2 per cent of those from the families that were victims of the Maoist movement – 2006; suspension of school fee increase by Supreme Court order – 2012; and minimum standards on infrastructure, curriculum and school – 2013. However, the private schools, backed by their union, have refused to implement these directives; instead, they 'view the government's treatment as primarily antagonistic' (Bhatta and Pherali, 2017; Joshi, 2019: 66). As Joshi (2019) notes:

> On paper, the government has made revisions, clarifications and expansions on the standards that private schools have to adhere to, given equity considerations and the evident growth in private schooling. However, on their part, the private sector actors yearn to be acknowledged for providing education and employment opportunities, and an assessment of their needs and challenges as they also educate the citizens of the country. (Joshi, 2019: 66)

The general perception that all private schools in Nepal have a sound financial situation is debatable. A large number of private schools outside the Kathmandu valley struggle to survive, teachers prefer to work in the capital city and more importantly, affordability of private education in smaller towns and rural areas is low. However, teachers in many private schools are reported to have been exploited, as private school owners ignore the government regulations (Poudyal, 2017). Even though government regulation requires independent schools to spend a minimum of 60 per cent of their total income on teachers' salaries, a recent evaluation conducted by the Department of Education shows that teachers in some private schools are paid significantly less, whereas the founders and principals were drawing much higher salaries than the basic salary fixed by the government (DOE, 2016; Dhungana, 2019).

Despite these dynamics, private education, particularly at the higher secondary level, is growing rapidly. There is very little or no control over the fees charged by these private institutions, whose 'quality' and 'standards' are heavily publicized in both print and electronic media. As there is no 'general consensus regarding what constitutes quality' (Bhatta, 2009: 4), these institutions have created a public perception of their 'superiority' (Bhatta and Budathoki, 2013) in which quality is determined more by modern infrastructure and the use of English as a medium of instruction than by improved creativity, critical thinking and innovations in teaching methods. Crucially, English as the language of instruction in private schools fuels the private/public divide, given that international development agencies and the private sector in Nepal value English-speaking employees who can supposedly meet the global economic and development needs. For parents, the English-medium education, despite its higher costs, is instrumental for increasing their children's employment opportunities in these sectors. In this process, parents in rural areas and those who represent the lowest quintile of the population are unable to pay the high education premium and hence, are stuck with a lower chance of achieving social mobility. Research shows that higher levels of private education spending increase both wage dispersion and the education premium, leading to hardening socio-economic inequalities and undermining the role of public education spending in lowering income inequality (Huber, Gunderson and Stephens, 2020).

Hence, private education contributes to reproduce existing socio-economic structures in Nepali society, which are often argued as the major cause of the communist rebellion. A large majority of educated parents including schoolteachers, government employees, politicians and social workers, who are generally the privileged social class, can afford to send their children to private schools and for them, the poor quality of public education is not necessarily a pressing issue that needs urgent action.

Politics of Language and Cultural Identities

The Maoist rebellion and diverse ethnic and social movements have challenged the 'state-centric' and assimilationist approach to nation-building in which education has played a complicit role for several decades (Burghart, 1984; Hutt, 2012; Malagodi, 2013). Even during the post-1990 liberal politics, efforts around inclusion in education mainly focused on access to schools for all with some tokenistic reforms relating to mother-tongue instruction, scholarships for girls and Dalit children, and campaigns for girls' education (Shields and Rappleye, 2008b). The fundamental ideology and values embedded in education were only challenged by the Maoist movement that demanded transformative change in policies alongside a new vision of Nepali society. The Maoist rebellion as well as the struggles of indigenous nationalities and Madhesis have asserted 'people-centric' inclusive notions of 'Nepaliness' and legitimation of the language, history and lifestyles of diverse cultural, social and regional communities in the national space (Gellner, 2016; Lal, 2012; Lawoti and Hangen, 2013). The education system needs to be transformed to ensure that inclusion is not just at the level of access but also in outcomes and processes such as the curriculum, pedagogies, language of instruction, teacher recruitment and teachers' professional development. However, it should be recognized that the processes of social interactions at the grassroots levels do not exist completely separated from the hegemonic nationalism and newly reclaimed or celebrated ethnic identities. Rather, educational spaces harbour what Pradhan calls 'simultaneous identities' which individuals oscillate between. In her ethnographic study, she reveals that

> the students … did not choose between their ethnic identity and national identity, they discursively positioned 'ethnic identity' as 'national identity'. The everyday language practices complicate the neat compartmentalization of identities. Contrary to the ideas of difference espoused in ethnic activism and assimilationist ideas of homogeneity articulated in nationalist discourse, students made simultaneous claims to more than one social identity, which were considered neither incompatible nor binary opposites. (Pradhan, 2020: 15–16)

It would be difficult to claim that 'simultaneity' of identity manifestation could be observed across all educational spaces and geographical regions, especially in Madhes, where the state has neither seriously sought assimilationist outcomes nor allowed ethnic identities to thrive in the past. However, from a conflict perspective, acceptance, legitimation and nurturing of 'simultaneous identities' through educational processes in which students are enabled to develop a sense of national pride as ethnic/indigenous communities could potentially help mitigate grievances around language and identity that have played a negative role in Nepal's violent conflict. The challenge is that schools are not the only places where learning happens. Local histories, community members' everyday narratives and lived experiences of learners at home and in their neighbourhoods are also influential spaces of learning, and these spaces are often dominated by emotive and biased cultural and political discourses.

Education and a Critique of International Development

Discourses about education and international development tend to focus on issues around educational access, improving literacy rates, and more recently quality and equity. However, concerns around societal barriers that deny educational access to most children are less rigorously tackled in the education literature. These barriers require engagement with the political economy and the need for rebalancing power through equitable representation of disenfranchised communities and wider recognition of cultural diversity (Novelli, Lopes Cardozo and Smith, 2017, 2019). In Nepal, there is a disconnection between the global agenda for educational reforms and the deficit in capacity, ownership and applicability of externally driven prescriptions for educational change (Regmi, 2017). The disjuncture lies not only in the overly economic logic of education and its prescribed curriculum but also in the philosophical underpinnings about what constitutes learning, relevance and the object of education in local ecologies. In other words, the imported models of education, irrespective of limited efforts to incorporate local content, fail to speak to the peculiarity of local needs. The education systems in the economically advanced societies were developed over decades along with the changing needs of their societies. Attempts to replicate these systems as a panacea, without appreciating contextual complexities, will 'succeed in transforming neither education nor broader society and its development' (Paulson, 2011: 13). From a conflict perspective, such educational interventions can only rupture local development patterns and increase dependency on foreign aid and policy prescriptions. This has led to a decline of aid effectiveness and to disjuncture between development trajectories and local needs, ultimately contributing to conflict (Rappleye, 2011).

Rappleye (2011: 88) provides a useful theoretical and conceptual discussion laying out five different categories of 'conflict and development' theories, their presumptions about progress and relevant implications for education: neoclassic development, moderated classic development, failed development and conflict as development success. He presents the case of Nepal to problematize what is generally an uncritical image of development as a cure for poverty and violent conflict. Drawing on the case of the Rapti Development Project in Nepal supported by USAID, Rappleye (2011: 88) uncovers the negative face of 'development', the unintended outcome of which contributed to spark 'collective action by oppressed groups' in the form of the 'People's War'.

Educational goals and priorities are also influenced by the discourse of 'development', producing a so-called educated workforce that is unemployable in the local market. In addition, development aid destroys its beneficiaries' confidence and gradually reduces their ability to utilize indigenous solutions to their local problems (Ferguson, 2006; Rahnema and Bawtree, 1997). The imported models of development and market economy cause serious economic imbalances; increase dependency on foreign aid and destroy local economies in the name of becoming 'developed' or like the West. Ultimately, the divorce from external support becomes almost unthinkable for national governments whose survival is largely dependent on international aid. This 'trap' of development which Shrestha (1997: 50) calls a 'modern-day intoxicant' leads to a violent rebellion, through which the victims of this false 'development' rhetoric engage in a collective action against the structures nurtured by 'international development'.

Conflict-affected countries or those prone to civil disorder are often labelled 'fragile states' in development terms. Bengtsson (2011: 34) notes that the concepts of 'fragility' and 'fragile states' are rather 'fuzzy' – yet have become 'buzz-phrases' in the development sector including, with regard to, education in emergencies. Nepal has been labelled as one for several years given the protracted civil conflict and subsequent ethnic uprising in the Madhes region. Concepts bearing negative connotations such as 'poor governance as identified by a lack of political commitment and/or weak capacity to develop and implement pro-poor policies' (Rose and Greeley, 2006: 1) and persistently dysfunctional economic policies and institutions (Chauvet and Collier, 2008) often stereotype these nation states. These labels are imposed on rather than negotiated with so-called fragile nation states based on the criteria developed by external agencies. In addition, the term 'fragility' is used inconsistently or ostensibly with prejudice to refer to 'underdeveloped' countries, while developed countries can also exhibit 'uncontrollable' civil disorder (Bengtsson, 2011). The meaning of 'fragility' is generally subjectively determined, which Bengtsson argues can be 'detrimental' in aid interventions to these countries. The inconsistent labelling of 'fragile states' followed by corresponding policy prescriptions often lead to a development monopoly in the form of external patronage, which is likely to be resented by these nation states, often jeopardizing the effectiveness of aid.

Education as one of the main social services has been affected adversely as a result of such development sector politics.

The expansion of modern education may be seen as a 'development success' (Rappleye, 2011) in Nepal, in that by providing critical awareness of the unjust political and socio-economic realities despite the hegemonic education policies, formal education played a critical role in creating a mass of frustrated youths. Many of them found a sense of hope in the armed rebellion against various forms of injustices as well as the rhetoric of modernization and development (Pherali, 2011). These theoretical trends are not only useful in better conceptualizing the education-conflict development nexus but also for understanding assumptions and hypotheses about the causality of modern-day violent conflicts. Developing an awareness of this process can help identify an effective role of education in building sustainable peace.

To sum up, the expansion of education after the 1950s and the rapid growth of private schools in the 1990s did not lower the educational gap even though it did appear that the increase in the number of schools across the country was aimed at providing universal access to education. In reality, the early phases of educational development (1950s and 1960s) were primarily championed by the dominant social groups in society who were able to maximize their own potential to benefit from modernity and the opportunities created by liberalization of the political and economic spheres. Many of the schools in this early phase were established in the areas that were inhabited by traditionally privileged groups. As the state failed to make progressive advances to address the historical gaps between the dominant high-caste groups and historically marginalized communities, inequalities persisted. The education system promoted the hegemony of hill high-caste communities by systematically undermining cultural and linguistic diversity. Hence, this type of educational development legitimized social divisions along cultural lines, offering a comparative advantage to the traditionally privileged while reproducing structural barriers for non-Nepali speaking ethnic and indigenous nationalities.

4

Impact of the 'People's War' on Educational Professionals

When the rebels expanded their stronghold, the state administration started to cripple. You might have seen the wire fence around Liwang town. The Maoists could very easily arrive close to the area outside the fence at any time. The security situation was quite tense and all of us at school were scared. One day, the Maoists exploded on the route to school. I cannot remember the exact date, but it blasted at 4.00 pm that day. Some students were walking along that route on the way back home but those who had lessons until 4.00 pm were still at school. Some of the teachers had already left the school for home and the others were still at school. When the bomb went off, those students who had reached near the explosion area returned to the school. Then, the police arrived at the school. The situation was tense. The police made all children to stand in a queue. Just across the river, some children who had gone past the explosion site were hit by the launcher and killed. (Head teacher from a secondary school in Rolpa)

After that crossfire and massacre of children at school, the chief district officer formed a school reconstruction committee, appointing members from the district and the local agencies. I was persuaded to serve as the coordinator of the committee despite my fear of those people [Maoists] who might give me trouble. I have served in this school for twenty-six years. We needed to repair the school buildings that had been damaged by the bullets here and there and needed to build two new blocks. After that dreadful incident, the school was closed for many days with dead bodies lying on the ground for eight days. Students and teachers were scared to visit the school. We decided to hold Bhagwat Puran [a Hindu ritual to purify the place] as people thought it would help the soul of all those who died rest in peace and free the school of haunting souls.

Immediately after the work was completed one morning I was at home, it was morning. Three people came to my home and they said they were from the 'army' and wanted to know if there were any Maoists, I said we did not know. Then, they went away but their commander of this area called Agni arrived after ten minutes. He asked me to give him my mobile. I said I did not have a mobile. He said 'no, you have one. All the activities here are immediately reported'. I said, 'You can check both my homes and you won't get anything'. He said, 'you are lying! get up'. Then, he and other two persons who came later started beating me up with sticks lying around. After that I fell unconscious. The women at my house started crying and the people in the village were scared that the same thing would happen to them. Then the Village Head told them that I had never done anything wrong in the society and if they wanted to kill someone, they could kill him instead. After that they left. My whole body was swollen, and there were blood formations and after 20–22 days the formation burst. The two in the legs burst out but the one in the waist didn't so, I went to a hospital in Dhangadhi and the doctor there told me it would cost Rs 50,000 to drain the blood which I could not afford. So, I kept on enduring that pain as I could not go anywhere. Later Dr Paudel in Dhangadhi operated on me.

Even today if I don't take medicine, it hurts me in the intestinal region, if I walk or talk for more than fifteen minutes, I suffer from serious pain. I have to eat very little amount of food because of that. I grew very weak recently after the problem got worse. After an endoscopy the doctor told me that there is a wound in the intestine. That's why I don't talk or walk around much. (A teacher in Doti)

Civil Wars and Education under Attack: A Global Scenario

Educational institutions should be safe spaces for learners, educators and communities that are involved in creating a better future for their societies. However, in conflict-affected environments, schools and universities are frequently targeted for violent attacks, and the impact of violence is not limited to disruption of educational routines and loss of children's learning. The experience of direct violence and constant fear for life have long-term physical and psychological effects. The Global Coalition to Protect Education from Attack (GCPEA) defines attacks on education as 'any intentional threat or use of force – carried out for political, military, ideological, sectarian, ethnic, or criminal reasons – against students, educators, and education institutions' (GCPEA, 2020: 86). These attacks may be perpetrated by both the state security forces, including the police, armed forces or paramilitary or militia groups on behalf of the state, and non-state armed groups that are resisting the state to gain control of state power (Human Rights Watch, 2021).

For example, over forty-five attacks on education by Islamist armed groups were reported in Burkina Faso in 2020, where the armed groups killed, abducted, beat, robbed and threatened education professionals; intimidated students and parents and burned and looted fifteen schools; in Mali, armed groups continued to recruit children as soldiers in 2019 and carried out fifty-five attacks on schools; the Saudi-led coalition forces were responsible for killing 222 children and attacking four schools in Yemen; ongoing conflict in Syria continues to destroy schools and health facilities and 217 schools were reportedly abandoned due to clashes in Idlib between December 2019 and March 2020; schools and educational facilities in Ukraine continue to be damaged by shelling, small arms and light weapons fire (Human Rights Watch, 2021). The education sector experienced the highest number of attacks in Afghanistan, Palestine and Syria during the 2015–2019 period – in Afghanistan, over a hundred schools were targeted with arson and explosive devices in 2018 alone; and almost 40 per cent of Syria's schools were damaged between 2013 and 2019 (GCPEA, 2020). These are some of the most recent records of attacks on schools, teachers and students.

Since the publication of the UN report, *Impact of Armed Conflict on Children* by Graça Machel, effects of violent conflicts on educational communities have been scrutinized by the international humanitarian community (Machel, 1996). One of the first reports, *Education under Attack* authored by Brendon O'Malley focused on targeted violent attacks carried out for political, military, ideological, sectarian, ethnic or religious reasons, against students, teachers, academics, education trade unionists, education officials and all those who work in or for educational institutions such as schools, colleges and universities (O'Malley, 2007). Since the GCPEA was formed to address the problem of targeted attacks on education in 2010, it has been regularly reporting on details of violence against the education sector globally. In a recent report, GCPEA has documented over 11,000 attacks on education or military use of educational facilities globally between 2015 and 2019, in which over 22,000 students, teachers and education personnel were reported to have been harmed' (GCPEA, 2020). The nature of these attacks ranges from destruction of educational infrastructure to assaults on members of the education community: threats and harassment of students while going to and from school, forced participation of students and teachers in ideological or militia training, forced labour, sexual violence, targeted killings, and forced recruitment of children into the rebel ranks. Additionally, school and university premises are increasingly being used by military forces, and attacks on university students have also been reported.

In Nepal, Human Rights Watch (Watchlist, 2005: 5) reported that in the first six months of 2004, 54 children had died from bomb blasts, crossfire and other forms of violence and 99 children were injured, 77 arrested and 6,689 were abducted by the Maoist rebels. Teachers were targeted for intimidation, taxation and violence which contributed to teacher absenteeism due to fear for their life. One of the many incidents reported in the study is described below:

> In 2002, a gun battle between Maoist and government forces in the Mahabir High School in Chainpur, Siraha district, during school hours caused panic and fear in the school and in the wider community … Subsequently, the school was closed for ten days and many children were afraid to attend after the school reopened. During and after the incident, some teachers were detained and abducted, which caused irregular class scheduling. (Watchlist, 2005: 23)

Education is also a root cause of conflict in many contexts (also discussed in Chapter 2 generally and in Chapter 3 more specifically in the case of Nepal) due to unequal access across different social and cultural groups, the issue of the medium of instruction and curriculum offered (Smith and Vaux, 2003). Teachers are often threatened and killed in Colombia because of their involvement in teachers' unions, resistance to neoliberal policies and social activism (Díaz-Ríos, 2021). In southern Thailand, the Malay Muslim separatist groups attack teachers in state schools who are viewed by the militants as representatives of the Thai state that represses the former's cultural and religious identity, whereas security forces raid Islamic schools and carry out arbitrary arrests of teachers and students on suspicion that their activities promote separatist ideology (Liow and Pathan, 2010; UNICEF, 2014). Teachers may be viewed as sympathetic to a non-state group's political cause and the entire education system may be seen as a process of cultural assimilation that threatens either of the conflicting groups' 'societal security', the essential character of the society (Waever, Buzan and Kelstrup, 1993). The physical spaces of educational institutions also serve for 'tactical purposes' that are occupied as 'bases, barracks, fighting positions, prisons, interrogation or torture centres, or they may place barricades near them' (GCPEA, 2020: 16). In several authoritarian regimes, critical academic scholarship, popular education and social movements led by academics and university students may pose a threat to the political authority's monopoly of power. This may result in university academics and students being arrested, displaced and persecuted (Pherali and Millican, 2020).

Analysis of the motivation for attacks on schools, students and teachers demonstrates that the nature of the conflict, geographical features and sociopolitical factors determine the reasons behind an array of attacks on education. In Nepal, when the Maoists expanded their area of control, known as *adhar ilaka* (base territory), the state security posts were withdrawn to the district headquarters. By the year 2002, the war had spread across the country, engulfing seventy-three out of seventy-five districts, claiming the lives of approximately eight thousand people and causing enormous economic losses (Kumar, 2003). Schools were one of the few state institutions that remained in the areas that were controlled by the Maoists, and the state resources that continued to reach schools were largely in the form of teacher salaries. As a peasant-led popular movement, the 'People's War' needed both funding to mobilize its fighters and educated cadres to expand their political base in their base territories. So, *chanda atanka* (terror of donations) and *rajanitik prakshiksan* (political training) became some of the popular and petrifying vocabulary among teachers in rural schools. Teachers would face *bhautik karbahi* (physical action) unless they extended their loyalty to the Maoist campaign by attending their political education programmes or regularly donated a significant proportion of their monthly salaries to the 'great people's revolution'. The use of these concepts in the rebellion discourse manufactured what Sluka (2000: 22) calls 'a culture of terror' among teachers and using threats, assaults and humiliation, Maoists 'institutionalized a system of permanent intimidation'. Meanwhile, when the teachers encountered the security forces, they were often accused of being Maoist sympathizers or colluders and hence harassed, threatened and sometimes detained.

Relevance of Education in the Onset of Conflict

There is an increasing body of literature dealing with the problematic role of education in the emergence and duration of violent conflict. The analysis in Chapter 3 also highlighted that educational development in Nepal since the advent of a democratic system in 1951 has been implicitly influenced by key political events as well as the prevailing sociocultural conditions of Nepali society. Interviews with teachers, head teachers and educational officials in Nepal reveal that the effects of conflict on schools and educational actors need to be understood from the perspective of the 'negative face' of education which is often overlooked in educational discussions (Bush and Saltarelli, 2000; Novelli and Lopes Cardozo, 2008).

Teachers' Perceptions of the Economic Relevance of Education

The dominant theme emerging in the data in relation to education's complicit role in conflict is about its relative failure to provide employability skills to young people, producing a mass of youth with qualifications but without the necessary skills to secure a stable livelihood. A teacher from Kathmandu claimed that education 'definitely contributed to the conflict':

> Unemployment problem is widespread in the country making people feel frustrated. If education only produces unemployed people, they are bound to be upset, and will be annoyed with the government and to vent their ire they would be compelled to get involved in the revolt. That is why until the education policy becomes employment-oriented, frustrations will persist. (Teacher from a public school in Kathmandu)

Similarly, another teacher in Sankhuwasabha mentioned:

> The education is not people-oriented, scientific, nor applicable to the lives of people and hence, schools have become a hub for producing educated unemployment. (Teacher from a public school in Sankhuwasabha)

The problem of educated unemployment could be viewed as both the failure of the government to create a vibrant economic environment that creates jobs and an inability of the education system to produce graduates with relevant skills for the job market. The production of the 'educated person' in Nepal rather concentrated on the idea of conditioning the learner with a sense of national pride linked to the history of valour and bravery of the ancestors (Onta, 1996; Skinner and Holland, 1996) and the transformation of the 'self' as a Westernized modern citizen (Pigg, 1992). This educational ethos considerably hardened Nepali nationalism but did little to advance knowledge and skills for economic development. Despite limited economic outcomes, the idea of education is widely understood as the process of moving towards the 'light' of consciousness from the 'darkness' of ignorance. In this sense, political resistance symbolized both the by-product of educational consciousness and critique of the existing social, political and cultural order. As mentioned above, Rappleye (2011) calls this 'conflict as development success' – that development outcomes could be that the general masses become critically aware of the prevailing social injustices and inequalities and organize to transform the old social order through a radical political change.

The Educational Divide

Many participants in the study noted that the tiered education system had contributed to the creation of two types of citizens with unequal economic potential. This relates to the idea of cultural and academic capital (Bourdieu, 1986): that young people from diverse social and economic backgrounds are raised in unequal educational and economic environments, which reproduce hierarchical social class. Private schools, predominantly based in the capital Kathmandu or outreach urban settings, serve urban populations who are relatively privileged in economic terms and could afford to pay for private education, while a vast majority of children in the rural areas receive a poor-quality state education. An education officer observed:

> Socio-economic disparity and caste differences are the reasons for the advent of the conflict. These problems that plagued our society also created a divide in the education sector, for example, government school is for the poor and the private education for the well off. Because of this, it has been apparent that the education system has been producing two types of educated workforce. (District Education Officer from Doti)

While the education system may be generally questioned for its deficient alignment with the economic needs, private education has expanded the economic potential of the growing middle class based in Kathmandu (Liechty, 2003) and helped them to keep influencing the way that national governments interacted with global neoliberal policies, ignoring the fundamental needs of rural populations, and widening the gap between the rural poor and urban elites. A society that has been deeply unequal along caste, gender and ethnic lines has now increasingly adopted the prerequisite of Western modernity, simply to revalidate these hierarchies along the notions of social class. As Liechty (2003: 8) noted, 'class has increasingly come to be the framing paradigm for many people in Kathmandu, encompassing (though by no means eliminating) the social valence of caste.' He further notes that 'as more and more of everyday life revolves around the social imperatives of the money/market economy, the moral (and economic) logic of caste is subordinated to the economic (and moral) logic of class' (Liechty, 2003: 8). Private education has played a key role in driving social change along these lines in the last three decades, which were challenged by the Maoist movement whose political base was predominantly the rural peasantry.

However, teachers in public schools felt that state education was better at providing knowledge that was socially and culturally relevant to Nepali children, unlike the private curricula that focused generally on the Western form of knowledge. A teacher from a private school in Kathmandu shared a similar view and maintained that the English-medium education promoted 'pro-Western' modern values and lifestyles, which are generally 'away from dominant social and cultural realities of Nepal' (Interview with a teacher from private school in Kathmandu). Even though there is a perception that private educational providers offer a better quality of education, some teachers in government schools argue that private schools emphasize rote-learning which best suits the current system of assessment. As a teacher from a government school mentioned:

> Students graduated from government schools are socially, politically and culturally educated and develop a better understanding of our local society whereas private schools educate children for the Western economic market. Simply because private school graduates know better English and can perform better in the SLC exams, it should not be understood as a measure for quality education. (Nepali subject teacher from a secondary school in Kathmandu)

Another teacher in the East highlighted that the provision of a two-tiered system of education in the country was complicit in fuelling violent conflict. He elaborated that

> existing education system is of two types: the education imparted in government schools is received by poor people, whereas those who can afford to pay for an English medium education send their children to private schools. Difference in the type of education has also contributed to conflict. (Teacher from a public school in Sankhuwasabha)

The Maoist agenda against privatization of public services, including education, put private schools at direct risk of attacks during the insurgency (Caddell, 2006). Private education also symbolized the neoliberal policy pursued after the 1990s (Regmi, 2017) and fuelled the already existing socio-economic disparities (Thapa, 2015), consequently making the entire educational sector a domain of elite reproduction.

Equity in Education

There was a strong sense in teachers' perspectives that education had failed to create an equitable society by providing equal educational access to all social and cultural groups. One of the respondents mentioned that

> they (low caste groups) were dominated and pushed to the bottom. Brahman and Chhetris were cleverer and were able to maintain their superior positions in society. Other castes such as Magars, Gurungs and others gradually got involved

in the armed conflict. Dalits particularly, joined the rebellion. (Teacher from a public school in Kathmandu)

Teachers noted that the education system with a mandatory use of Nepali as a medium of learning and teaching created a linguistic barrier for children from non-Nepali speaking ethnic or indigenous groups. Even though there was an opportunity to participate in education, the educational structures (e.g. medium of instruction) played against their linguistic backgrounds, which systematically led to their underachievement. The Khas-Arya groups (particularly Brahman and Chhetris from the hilly region) had long monopolized the state power by enforcing the Nepali language and Khas culture in the formal curriculum (Pherali, 2011). The political hegemony and legacies of unjust educational processes in the previous decades continued to shape socio-economic disparities even during the periods of democratic government. Analysing the politics of education in the Panchayat era, Lokranjan Parajuli concludes that the long-term damage of the 'defective' education system

> not only kept on reproducing the social inequality but also exacerbated it by creating such situations where the students from relatively poor and disadvantaged communities could either not have access to education or even if they did, they could not graduate to the next level. It is therefore no surprise that the social composition of Nepali public life even today reflects this dynamic; it is the preserve of those who are resourceful – caste and class wise. (Parajuli, 2019: 409)

Ragsdale (1989) also argued that the imposition of the Nepali language as the medium of instruction significantly disadvantaged a large number of children whose first language was other than Nepali. Hence, the right to education in the mother tongue was one of the fundamental demands of the Maoists before they declared the 'People's War' (Maoist Statements and Documents, 2003).

Education for Revolution

Another problematic aspect reported by most participants was the lack of education among the rural populations, who were easily attracted to the communist slogans and political narratives. This did not necessarily mean that a lack of education meant a greater level of manipulation by political groups but it did indicate that there was less rigorous debate and dialogue at local-level political gatherings, and the process of 'popular education' might have instead become top-down political socialization or indoctrination. The socio-economic reality of the poor and disenfranchised populations and the long-standing neglect of their basic needs by the state made it easier for the Maoists to connect with the grassroots populations. Another teacher revealed:

> Uneducated people would not normally challenge any political view. It is not within their capability to advocate for educational, social or economic future of the country as they were deprived of education. The 'People's War' received the maximum support from and involvement of the rural uneducated people who found the Maoist ideology attractive … and those who were knowledgeable, they used those people to fulfil their self-interests. (Teacher from a public school in Sankhuwasabha)

The idea that the rural population was largely 'deprived of education' seemed to indicate that they were unable to exercise their agency in conversations about politics and the justification for the 'People's War'. The Maoist political campaigners also entered school premises to expand their organizational structures among students as well as teachers through formation of school committees of their respective unions. Schools had historically been part of political production as envisioned by the Panchayat regime, through the nationalization of community schools in the early 1970s and the reshaping of education largely to inculcate Panchayat ideology in the young people and communities (Ragsdale, 1989). Ironically, despite the Panchayat's strict political control, some teachers and students were organizing against the regime and promoting counter-hegemonic narratives to assist the democratic forces (Parajuli, 2019). Teachers became the most influential political agents in the rural areas and therefore various political groups would compete to garner their support. The end of the Panchayat system in 1990 and beginning of the multiparty polity intensified competition among political parties to expand their base among teachers and students. Hence, educational settings became sites of political activity and participation of school actors including young children became commonplace. The CPN-M capitalized on this political culture to gain support for their rural-based movement. Teachers as prominent members of local communities possessed significant social capital and they had influence not only on rural populations but also on students who could be mobilized for political rallies and cultural performance during mass meetings. A teacher in a private school in Kathmandu lamented that

> politics entered the education sector enormously. And from the point of view of small children, it is not worthwhile because they were forced into political involvement. (Teacher from a private school in Kathmandu)

Another teacher from Doti revealed that

> our school always experienced direct political interference. All the political gatherings during local and national elections usually took place within the school premises which led schools to close down during these events. This trend greatly affected our teaching and learning. (Teacher from a public school in Doti)

The post-1990 political environment observed a growing culture of teachers' open involvement in party politics and use of students and school premises for mass meetings, which allowed the Maoists to seize schools for their political campaign. A widespread practice of political use of schools was essentially the facilitator of the school-based political violence in subsequent years of the Maoist uprising. Another teacher in Doti claimed that the massacre that took place in his school was precisely linked with the unrestricted culture of using educational spaces for political activities. He lamented:

> Cultural programmes had been organized by political groups in our school on several occasions in the past but on that fateful day, the army raided the cultural programme of the rebels in which six of our innocent students lost their lives including four young members of the Maoist group. Had there been no practice of performing political programmes in the school, the crossfire would not have taken place on that horrific day. (Teacher from a public school in Doti)

Teachers in the Revolution

Most participants indicated that the security forces were suspicious of teachers and often arrested and tortured them, accusing them of being Maoists or their sympathizers. This assumption was largely reinforced by the fact that the Maoist leadership predominantly consisted of former teachers. A teacher who explicitly claimed his political affiliation with the CPN-M mentioned:

> If you look at the background of CPN-M leadership now, you will see most of the leaders coming from teaching backgrounds. The leadership understands the ground reality of [education] in this country. The state was aware of the fact that the 'People's War' was being commanded by the education sector who had access to the grassroots level workers such as peasants, labourers, and other low level working groups. Those who were working in the education sector were

aware of the failures of Nepal's education system and therefore got involved in the rebellion with the aim of changing it. (Teacher from a public school in Rolpa)

Here the respondent implicitly recognizes that the education system in Nepal was ostensibly used to impose political hegemony of the ruling class but also produced political leadership that propelled an armed rebellion. For example, the Maoist leader, Pushpa Kamal Dahal (Prachanda) was born in an upper-class Brahman family and gained a university degree before working as a secondary schoolteacher. Similarly, Dr Babu Ram Bhattarai, the vice chairperson of the UCPN-M, studied in a missionary school in Gorkha and obtained top grades in the SLC examination. Later, he went to Jawaharlal Nehru University, one of the most prestigious institutions in India, to gain his doctorate in Regional Development and Planning. He was a top achiever throughout his academic and political career and is widely respected as an 'always first' man in Nepal. Interestingly, the average Nepali teacher is aware of these facts and thus understands the connections between education, discrimination, development and the conflict (Pherali, 2011: 140). Hence, the 'People's War' was planned and launched not by those who were deprived of access to education but by a small group of ideologues who had been highly educated and thus came to seize the political opportunity of insurgency to topple 'the feudalistic structure of the state' (Bista, 1991). That is, the idea of the 'communist revolution' in Nepal was born in the minds of generally educated people who mainly came from privileged backgrounds. They supposedly knew how to convert people's latent discontent, engendered by long-standing state negligence, into the driver of rebellion. As one school principal argued:

> The 'People's War' was declared and led by some of the highly educated people. But, you must be aware that the 'People's War' began from Rolpa, a remote underdeveloped district. Why did it begin from Rolpa while the political movements in the history have started from urbanised or developed cities? Firstly, the dominant population of this region is Magar. Historically, the Magars have been always oppressed by the Brahman oriented state structure of this country. This caste [Magar] is deprived of having opportunities to progress and has always been down trodden. The people from this caste are socially, politically and educationally deprived. They are very naive and easily persuaded by other people. Secondly, Rolpa is much behind in educational development as compared to other districts in Nepal. Out of five districts in Rapti Zone, Rolpa has been the least performing district in educational development. People would not have abilities to critically analyse, explain and look into political propaganda and therefore, would easily be manipulated. (Head teacher from a school in Rolpa)

Living as Teachers in the Middle of War

The experiences of conflict as reported by schoolteachers, head teachers and education officers indicate that living as educational professionals during the armed conflict was the most distressing experience of their lives. Such horrific experiences of conflict were consistent throughout the country both in the rural and urban areas.

Direct Violence on Schools

Many private schools suffered physical attacks by the Maoists during the conflict. These schools suffered permanent closure or destruction of their property, such as school buses that are used for everyday transportation of schoolchildren. Among many, a reputable school in the heart of the capital saw its property set on fire and a school building blown up by the rebels. One of the interviewees reported that even meeting the Maoist demands of mandatory donations did not protect their school from being attacked:

> **Interviewee:** They exploded a bomb in the principal's office and set fire on the school bus.
> **Q:** Was that because you didn't pay them?
> **Interviewee:** No, nothing of the sort. It was just a message to the rest of the private institutions that if you go along with us, it's okay, otherwise these are the consequences you might have to face.
> **Q:** What do you actually mean by 'go along with them'?
> **Interviewee:** Do what they say. Pay what they want.
> **Q:** So, the blast was because you didn't pay ...
> **Interviewee:** No, no. We had to move along whatever they said. We did move along with them. But it was just a message to the rest of the institutions in the country.
> (Teacher from a private school in Kathmandu)

It appears that the private schools were doubly disadvantaged during the conflict. Firstly, the Maoists would extort money from these institutions to fund their war, which was resourced from public donations and extortion largely from private institutions. Secondly, the CPN-M had an ideological objection to the provision of private education that was used as a justification for their action against these establishments. There was no choice but to comply with their demands of donations but still, there was no guarantee of security.

There were explosions and crossfire unpredictably everywhere across the country. Explosions in civilian areas would often cause loss of innocent lives, and the news of attacks on schools and teachers created a perpetual state of fear across the entire education community. For example, a teacher in Kathmandu reported that he was horrified to read the news about the kidnapping of a schoolteacher by the Maoists in Okhaldhunga district, who was later murdered barbarically by breaking his limbs (focus group discussion with teachers at a private school in Kathmandu). The news of such violent incidents spread across the country making even relatively peaceful areas psychologically vulnerable. It was not only the individual experiences but also the general narratives of violence, brutality and 'demonstration killing' that created fear among teachers and schoolchildren (Lawoti and Pahari, 2010). Teachers in rural areas commonly witnessed violent incidents within and around the school premises. Teachers in Rolpa reported that they would hear explosions and crossfire during school hours almost every day and were fearful about being caught in the middle. They mentioned that bullets went past over the school hostel almost every night (Teachers from a private school in Rolpa). Another teacher from a different school in Rolpa mentioned:

> A political leader affiliated to the Nepali Congress was shot dead near the school, which terrorized young children who were in the school when the incident took place. (Teacher from a public school in Rolpa)

Elsewhere in Kathmandu, a teacher described how Maoists enforced an anti-Sanskrit campaign in the school:

> On the day of exam, a group of Maoist supporters forcefully entered the school premises and burnt the question papers of Sanskrit [a pro-Brahmanism subject taught in the school curriculum]. (A teacher from a public school in Kathmandu)

Elsewhere, violence occurring in the school surroundings disrupted school routine. During the communal riots in Kapilvastu in 2007, schools faced some of the most dangerous situations. As a teacher describes the horror of the riots:

> As many as 300 houses of Pahadi communities were burnt down and 25 people killed. Schools in the Southern parts of Kapilvastu were closed for up to four weeks. Bhuwaneshwori secondary school was closed for two months. Similarly, 120 vehicles were set on fire and hotels and shops of Pahadi people were looted. (A teacher from a public school in Kapilvastu)

The participants revealed that these incidents had a profound impact on their physical and emotional well-being, and it was difficult to express those emotions in words. Distress, discomfort and trauma were frequently displayed by the respondents during the interviews, which indicated that the impact of conflict was deep, sustained and continued to affect their professional as well as personal lives.

Forced Participation in Political Activities

In rural areas, the Maoist cadres forced many schools to refund the school fees paid by the students and often conducted their political education programmes in the schools, forcing teachers and students to attend. School buses were often forcefully used to ferry their cadres to the meeting venues. After the state of emergency was lifted briefly in 2001 and the Maoists joined the peace negotiations with the government, Maoists conducted a drive for membership expansion, and teachers were compelled to join the party. When the Maoists withdrew from the peace negotiation and the state of emergency was declared again, many of those teachers who took membership or participated in the Maoist mass meetings were arrested and tortured by the security forces (Teachers from a private school in Udaypur). A head teacher in Rolpa pointed out that teachers could trust neither the Maoists nor the state for their security during conflict. The state was neither interested in protecting teachers from the Maoists nor did it allow them to negotiate their own safety within the 'base areas' controlled by the rebels. Instead, it harassed, threatened and detained teachers, accusing them of operating against the state and colluding with the Maoists.

General Strikes

For the political parties including the Maoists, a general strike was the most common tactic of political resistance. Generally known as *banda* in Nepali, the national or regional strikes would enforce complete shutdown of all businesses including schools, making it difficult for schools to complete the syllabus within the academic calendar, which affected students' exam results. During emergencies, teachers in private schools often walked long distances to get to work or else they would lose their salary. A teacher in Kathmandu lamented that 'We [teachers] had to work even during the curfew. We attended school risking our lives.'

State 'Terror'

Teachers in most districts reported that the security forces often treated teachers disrespectfully. During the *Kilo Sierra 2* operation in Rolpa and Rukum districts, the security forces carried out indiscriminate arrests, interrogation and torture of anyone suspected of Maoist affiliation (A teacher from a public school in Rolpa). Teachers in Sankhuwasabha also reported that the security forces mistreated teachers and students and carried out lootings in civilian homes (Teachers in Rolpa and Sankhuwasabha). The Maoists and royal army personnel would visit villages in each other's disguise to obtain information about their enemies, and ordinary villagers who reported the truth would later be accused of spying on or supporting the opposite side and assaulted, arrested or sometimes killed (Teachers from public school in Doti). In Rolpa, a teacher described as follows:

> A powerful bomb exploded near the school several times. On one occasion, Maoist rebels who were allegedly dressed in the school uniform attacked the police checkpoint located near the school. Then the army entered the school and mishandled all teachers and students. Most of us were beaten badly. The security forces prevented learning and teaching for twenty-two days. (A teacher from a public school in Rolpa)

Teachers' narratives of violent conflict show that schools were targeted equally by government forces who arrested, tortured and even killed teachers and schoolchildren (Amnesty International, 2005; Dhital, 2006). The violation of human rights and atrocities caused by the state was far higher than those caused by the Maoists (INSEC, 2007). As noted earlier in this chapter, the Maoists engaged in 'demonstration killing' of teachers and school principals to terrorize anyone who opposed their movement (Lawoti and Pahari, 2010: 309). Many victims' families still do not know why their kin were abducted, disappeared and murdered and are waiting for the truth. For example, the barbaric murder of Muktinath Adhikari, a school head teacher in Lamjung,[1] featured in the documentary *Schools in the Crossfire 2004* by Dhruba Basnet, which captures the traumatic experiences of Adhikari's colleagues at school, of students who resisted his abduction and of orphaned family members. This was defended by a Maoist leader in the documentary, who maintained that 'those who stand against the "great" "People's War" are class enemies and therefore not spared. We [Maoists] turn cruel to them'. However, in the absence of a Truth and Reconciliation Commission, it is largely unknown what Muktinath Adhikari as well as hundreds

---

[1] Some of the ideas presented in this chapter were published previously in: Pherali, T. (2016). 'School Leadership during Violent Conflict: Rethinking Education for Peace in Nepal and Beyond', *Comparative Education*, 52(4): 473–91.

Muktinath Adhikari was seized by the Maoists and taken from his school while delivering a lesson on 16 January 2002. He was killed within an hour of abduction. His dead body was found tied to an alder tree.

of other teachers, parents and children did to 'stand against' the Maoist movement. Similar incidents were reported elsewhere by teachers during the interviews.

> They killed my school's headmaster. We were together and the Maoists and students were preparing for a political programme for the next day. The school was closed that day and someone called him [the head teacher] and took him away. Later, they walked him along the side of Lankhua river to a jungle and sheared his neck and killed him. The next day his body and head were brought to the village and we saw the gory scene. However, the Maoists have not officially taken the responsibility for the killing and therefore it is still a mystery. But unofficially they say they killed him, which indeed they did. And in that situation the school was in disarray and I was obligated to run the school as the villagers offered me the role of headmaster based on seniority and I had to take the responsibility despite my unwillingness. During the course of my work a lot of incidents like that happened. In some cases, because after that the Maoist activities intensified, they banned the practice of charging fees from students, not even the examination fees which had to be paid by the school. This put us in a very difficult situation. (A teacher from a public school in Sankhuwasabha)

Teachers in their interviews reported that they were trapped in the middle of the conflict, which resulted in loss of professional motivation, as their prime concern during the conflict was how to survive. Furthermore, teachers in the area of Maoist control suffered a dilemma of whether to implement the new 'Maoist curriculum' or to continue teaching the government-prescribed 'national curriculum'. In some rural areas, the Maoists enforced their own academic calendar and replaced the national anthem with a revolutionary song.

In rural areas, schools provided young recruits for the insurgency and school premises were often captured as shelters by both warring parties (Watchlist, 2005). In some places, school buildings were turned into military barracks, preventing teaching and learning in the school. By 2004, an estimated 3,000 teachers had been displaced from schools in the rural areas, directly impacting an estimated 100,000 students' education (Thapa and Sijapati, 2004). A significant number of displaced teachers were still living in the district headquarters two years after the conflict had officially ended and some of them cited insecurity as the reason for not being able to return to their designated schools (Interviews with teachers in Rolpa and Sankhuwasabha).

Teachers and children were also caught in actual crossfire between Maoist rebels and security forces. In one incident in October 2003, eleven young people, including four local students, were killed in Sharada Secondary School, Mudbhara in Doti, when security forces opened fire indiscriminately at the

Maoist cultural group who had gathered in the school to perform a cultural show as a part of their political campaign. The school soon turned into a battlefield and then graveyard. Even five years after this traumatic incident, teachers and children were still struggling to recover from the trauma.

Q:	Where were you, Sir, when the incident took place?
A Male Teacher:	I was in the school, hiding behind a cabinet when the army and the Maoists were firing the bullets. Later, a fellow teacher came and asked me to come out, and while we were walking out of the room we heard the army shout at us. They were saying: 'We will kill you, we will shoot you.'
Q:	And where were you, Miss?
A Female Teacher:	We were also here [in the school]. We came out when we heard the cry: 'Shoot! Shoot!' They said, 'Shoot from the roof.' We were so scared when they asked us to put our hands up that we could not even lift our hands. They fired despite seeing the students in their school dress … they arrived and opened fire instantly.

Teachers reported that their professional 'morale and motivation' almost collapsed due to the stressful experiences during the conflict. In a group interview, teachers in a community school in Doti said: 'Our enthusiasm and energy have run out of steam. During the conflict, they were virtually non-existent in us. You never knew what would happen and when, and the mental pressure diminished our interest in teaching.'

These findings are also corroborated by similar observations made by Ezati and colleagues in the post-war context of Northern Uganda (Ezati, Ssempala and Ssenkusu, 2011). The authors reported that the post-conflict impact of violence among teachers was largely manifested in the lack of professional motivation (Ezati, Ssempala and Ssenkusu, 2011). When the primary motive of life becomes escaping from physical violence, professional motivation, creativity and aspirations become largely paralysed.

The State of Fear and Psychological Trauma

Schools remained at the centre of attention for both conflicting parties for a number of benefits they provided to the armed struggle. For example, schools offered a mass of inquisitive young people, who could be persuaded more easily than adults and trained to take part in the movement. Secondly, gaining support of schoolteachers would mean that their social influence on the rural populations could be exploited in favour of the rebellion and expanding their support base. The increasing influence of the Maoists in rural areas, particularly on schools, provoked increased surveillance of schools by the security forces. As a result, security incursions on school premises and unlawful arrests of teachers, school heads and students became pervasive. The school head teachers were traumatized but equally ensnared in their moral responsibility to protect teachers and pupils from violent attack while maintaining learning and teaching at school. One head teacher lamented:

> During the conflict, I lived in a state of terror all the time. I would not know who would summon me and where they [Maoists or security forces] would ask me to go or something else. Life was completely uncertain. (A head teacher in Udaypur)

The news of 'disappearance', 'abduction', 'arrests', 'torture' and 'murder' of schoolteachers and students often became front page headlines in the national dailies. Teachers and pupils were caught in frequent clashes between Maoists and security forces or violent attacks on civilians in the surrounding communities (Pettigrew, 2003). The 'culture of terror', as explained by anthropologists such as Green (1995) and Suárez-Orozco (1987), becomes widespread as the violent incidents become ubiquitous around the communities. Frequent encounters with violence, either in person or obliquely through the media, get people 'to accommodate themselves with terror or fear' but the 'low intensity panic remains in the shadow of waking consciousness' (Green, 1995: 109). Hence, living in a state of terror causes considerable psychological and psychosomatic damage.

The military aerial attacks on school premises during mass meetings often made no discrimination between venues or people attending the programmes, which often resulted in civilian casualties. The most distressing experience of the school heads was their inability to prevent the abuse of their school premises and abduction of teachers and pupils. These experiences eroded their capacity to manage teachers and be accountable to parents and education authorities. Their psychological and emotional well-being deteriorated significantly. Consequently, the social intimacy between school and community gradually waned and educational quality and pupils' aspirations became insignificant compared to the need to cope and survive during conflict. Green's (1995) notion of 'routinization of terror' also illuminates the way terror impacts on social relations. She explains that 'routinization of terror is what fuels its power' and allows people to live in a chronic state of fear with a façade of normality at the same time that terror permeates and shreds the social fabric (Green, 1995: 108). The head teachers frequently mentioned how the experience of violent incidents caused them psychological trauma during conflict.

> The security forces arrested me despite their knowledge that I did not have any involvement and I was working with the district security chief when Holeri [a small town in mid-west] was attacked. Yet, they accused me of colluding with the Maoists in carrying out that attack. (A head teacher in Rolpa)
>
> One of them was sporadically showing his gun on his waist to intimidate me. Then, another rebel put his gun on my head, I was so numb and I thought that was it. After I was released, I fell ill for several days. (A head teacher in Sankhuwasabha)
>
> After the massacre in my school, all the eleven dead bodies of the children including those of the Maoists were lying in front of the school building. I did not know what to do. I was so scared but went to inform the District Education Office about the incident. I was too scared to return home so, I went to Mahendranagar [a bigger town away from the school] for a few weeks. When the situation cooled down a bit then only I returned. (A head teacher in Doti)

The head teachers were traumatized by both 'visible' and 'invisible' (Zur, 1994) violence. The 'visible' violence was manifested through military arrests, abductions, physical assaults or even 'public executions' of educational staff who were frequently accused of spying or collusion. The everyday news of attacks on and abduction of teachers and schoolchildren maintained the prevalence of 'invisible' violence. Anonymous phone calls and letters demanding mandatory donations to the 'People's War' (Pherali, 2011) continuously caused distress and fear of death. As Gounari (2010: 184) argues:

> Fear generates an uncritical acceptance of anything and makes people deterministic and cynical about the future. Horror of violence prevents us from thinking and therefore it is used to paralyze thinking. It mobilizes feelings of fear, but one would have difficulty connecting the feeling with a theory that is able to explain its underlying cause.

The head teachers' role increasingly became more like a political broker struggling to protect their teachers, students and themselves from the ongoing insurgency and its brutal encroachment on the school system. Schools often received letters from Maoists, requesting teachers' participation in political education programmes. These requests were mandatory and head teachers were obliged to send representatives from their school. As attendance at these programmes was life threatening, nominating individuals for this task was morally painful for head teachers. School heads often faced a Catch-22 situation, as dishonouring the Maoist 'orders' would invite attacks on schools but attending their programmes would equally risk being caught in crossfire or facing arrest and torture by the security forces.

Alongside its ideological apparatus, the Maoist rebellion mobilized 'fear' as a controlling mechanism. The insurgents turned merciless on anti-Maoist elements and imposed the discourse of 'revolution' and 'great People's War' on all domains of society, including education. Schoolchildren were used for 'spying' (Watchlist, 2005), and teachers' freedom to interpret and critically discuss ideas about democracy, social values, history and culture were severely constrained. Teachers in all districts mentioned that they were fearful about being labelled as rebel supporters or anti-revolutionists, based on teaching or discussing these subjects. A head teacher in Sankhuwasabha lamented that armed soldiers regularly walked around his school and eavesdropped on teachers' lessons. Educational activities were under strict surveillance by the state, whereas rebels systematically targeted schools for representing the hegemonic ideology, curricula and ethos of dominant social groups. The teaching of Sanskrit, a language that symbolically epitomized Brahman male domination, was banned in schools. The biographies of royals who were viewed as the 'chiefs' of feudalism and historical oppressors were also prohibited in the school curriculum. Teachers reported that schoolchildren in their districts were forced to tear out the portraits of the monarchs from their textbooks and in many places, the students affiliated to the Maoist student wing All Nepal National Free Students Union (Revolutionary) burnt the books. A head teacher in the southern district of Kapilvastu described: 'During the exams, the CPN-M led groups of students entered the school and set fire to the exam papers as a protest to boycott Sanskrit from the school curriculum and subsequently vandalized the school offices and then exploded a grenade in my office. It was a horrifying incident.' Rebel aggression on schools would subsequently be followed by police and military intrusion, resulting in widespread arrests of students as Maoist suspects. The damaging effects of these incidents would permeate not simply the school system but the entire community.

Not only the teachers but also education officers in the district education offices were trapped in the middle of the escalating conflict. Educational authorities were helpless in terms of influencing security-related actions that would often violate the education code of conduct. A district education officer described his experience of being abducted as the following:

> I had been held hostage while I was the Paanchthar district's DEO. The Maoists kidnapped me and held for twenty-five days to get the government remove the military camp from the local school premises. The Royal Nepal Army had occupied the school's compound and they checked teachers and students every morning when they arrived at school. The Royal Army had taken full control of the school. The student wing of the CPN-M sent me a letter asking for immediate removal of the army from the school. I put the matter before the security committee in the district but the army ignored the request. (The DEO from Sankhuwasabha)

The above comment, 'the army ignored the request', resonated in other districts such as Rolpa where a head teacher revealed that educational authorities including the district administration officer were powerless before the military's interventions in the civilian space. Most frustratingly for school actors, the state failed entirely to provide security to educational staff while expecting them to follow government regulations in the rebel-controlled areas.

Teachers, Politics and State Oppression

The All Nepal Teachers Organization (ANTO), the CPN-M affiliated teachers' union, resisted the government's flagship education policy on educational decentralization which was being supported by the World Bank. Maoists were opposed to government attempts to 'disengage from the direct financing and supervision of the country's public schools' (Carney and Bista, 2009: 197). Teachers' and university students' unions often declared strikes and forcibly closed down educational institutions to undermine the government control over the education system.

Nepal's teaching workforce is often accused of being highly politicized despite the state's failure to protect their personal and professional well-being during the conflict, blaming teachers for the broader systemic failure in the education system. Carney and Bista (2009: 205) indicate that the broader social and economic conditions of the schools and 'the lack of living wage and intolerable working conditions' of the teachers are often inadequately considered when teachers' accountability is debated. During focus group discussions, teachers in Udaypur highlighted that they have always played a critical role in

Nepal's struggle for democracy and social change. Their role as 'transformative intellectuals' was evidently reflected both in their direct participation in social and political movements against unjust regimes as well as in their resistance to privatization of education. Hence, the donor-induced discourse that denigrates teachers as political activists (e.g. World Bank, 2001) fails to explain the critical question about teachers' historical role in promoting social justice and their struggle against neoliberal reforms in education.

The progressive agenda of the Maoists, relating to social equality, political inclusion and grassroots empowerment, attracted many teachers to join the rebellion. Most importantly, the Maoist leadership that consisted of former teachers mobilized moral, intellectual and financial support from teachers to expand the influence of rebellion. The general perception of intimacy between teachers and progressive agendas influenced the security forces' negative attitudes towards teachers. By 2005, the state authority's influence had shrunk within the district headquarters while over three quarters of the country was controlled by the Maoists. The only means of survival as a teacher in rural areas was by extending unconditional support to the 'People's War'. A head teacher in Rolpa mentioned how the district security chief responded to head teachers who asked him to provide security from the rebels:

> In response to our demand for security to enable us to work in rural schools, the security chief frankly replied: 'We cannot secure your lives. You are the representative of the state in the rural villages. If you realize that you cannot secure your life in the village, migrate to the district headquarters for your safety and security. Otherwise, you take necessary measures in your discretion to survive and run the schools. Please do not go to the areas that are susceptible to crossfire and battles. Please do not expect anything from us.' (A head teacher in Rolpa)

This situation reveals the total failure of the state authorities in their capacity and willingness to protect teachers during conflict. The educational community was abandoned to face violent incursions on schools while children's right to education and well-being fell in serious jeopardy.

The declaration of the state of emergency in November 2001 suspended all civil rights, declaring Maoists as terrorists and concentrating powers in the then Royal Nepalese Army. The military deployment across the country resulted in reduced mobility of people around the village (Pettigrew, 2003) and substantially increased military hostilities in schools. The school heads who had managed to protect their schools by complying with the Maoist demands (e.g. attending their political programmes, paying donations and allowing their political training at schools and in some cases, agreeing to temporarily store ammunitions and food stuff for the rebels, etc.) were now arrested and tortured for their 'collusion' against the state. The head teachers' cooperation with rebels, which was a survival strategy in rebel-controlled areas, was now criminalized by the military state that was only accountable to the autocratic monarchy. Several teachers in the interview revealed that they were often abused and harassed by security forces at checkpoints on the way to and from school. As Rummel (1994) argued in his work on the dynamics of state violence, the increased state violence on Nepal's civilian populations can only be explained by the arbitrary power which was seized by declaring the state of emergency. He notes that 'the more power a government has, the more it can act arbitrarily accordingly to the whims and desires of the elite, and the more it will make war on others and murder its foreign and domestic subjects' (Rummel, 1994: 1).

'Terror' of Mandatory Donation

'Chanda aatanka' (the terror of mandatory donations) was reported to be the most widespread form of 'terror' that engulfed schoolteachers during the conflict. The mandatory donation, as it implies, would also dictate the amount one had to pay, leaving little or no room for negotiation. The Maoist donation campaign also led to the escalation of state surveillance on teachers' everyday life. Security forces would view it as financing terrorism irrespective of the conditions under which such donations were made. A head teacher in the western Tarai lamented:

> They [Maoists] demanded [money] from me but there was some negotiation and finally they came to a compromise. I was able to reduce the amount they had initially demanded. They started visiting my home regularly and threatened to kill me. I simply could not take any chance by not paying them. (A head teacher in Kapilvastu)

Schools would receive letters indicating the details of donations, including the amount and deadline for payment. Analysis of these letters reveals that the messages were often written in an extremely intimidating tone and made death threats to the head teacher. This caused psychological distress and drastically paralysed their ability to manage the school affairs. A letter below which was sent to a head teacher in Sankhuwasabha exemplifies such a gruesome tone:

Dear [Name supplied] Sir,

We received your letter. Are you always drunk? You have been told several times previously that you could send the money to the letter bearer unless you could come yourself. Do you really feel like living in a safe place? Why do you give trouble to our people? Is your intention to trick us? Now, you will be solely liable for all the money from teachers in your school since 2002, in addition to your liability of NRS 50,000. You will not be excused if it does not happen after this letter. Why do you force us to be cruel? … there are rumours that you collected the money and embezzled in funds. What is going on? You better explain.

Area In-charge,

CPN-M

Head teachers were responsible for dealing with the donation requests and had no choice but to take risks by working clandestinely to fulfil rebel demands. The teaching workforce, although portrayed as a victim of the conflict, was rather a contentious entity which was fragmented through individuals' covert political affiliation with the conflicting parties. Some teachers were sympathetic to the cause of 'revolution' and voluntarily extended their financial contributions in support of the 'People's War' while others unwillingly heeded rebel demands in exchange for their own physical safety. Head teachers were continuously involved in secretive dealings with the Maoists, negotiating with their teachers and parents, and publicly maintaining neutrality in order to protect their schools from attack.

The privately owned schools had to either pay high donations to the Maoists in order to survive or face permanent closure. The issue of private education as a Maoist target has been explored elsewhere (Caddell, 2006; Watchlist, 2005) but rather interestingly, it was found that private schools faced enormous pressure from the parents, who either questioned school principals for not meeting Maoist demands, thereby inviting threats to their children's lives, or strongly opposed the idea of financing the Maoist insurgency with the money which had been paid for their children's education. Either way, the school leadership was caught in the middle.

Relational Disequilibrium: An Excruciating Misery

As the entire country became a war zone, the ordinary population was trapped inside the violent confrontations between the rebels and state forces. The military deployment during the emergency period created a high risk of fatal skirmishes in villages, endangering civilian lives and their properties. School premises were strategic locations for both the warring parties in providing a space to stay in during their mobilization. For Maoist rebels, schools were ideal sites for political education and expanding their support base across young students and teachers. Head teachers often engaged in negotiating these mandatory requests that, whether heeded or opposed, would equally put them at risk. The two head teachers below revealed:

> The army and the armed police would frequently visit the school and enquire about the Maoist activities [in the village] or the information about the rebel hideout. We could not possibly give information as the Maoists would kill us after the army has left. Mostly, we would not know any information but the army would use force to make us report on Maoists whether we know anything or not. (A head teacher in Kapilvastu)

> I was frequently forced to provide food and shelter for the Maoist rebels. My house is located near the military barracks and the soldiers would also visit my house repeatedly. I was caught in the middle and my life during the conflict became like 'hell'. (A head teacher in Sankhuwasabha)

The state authority neither provided security to schools nor did it tolerate schools' self-negotiated peace with rebels which would allow them to continue teaching and learning. In rural areas, head teachers mentioned that maintaining a balanced relationship between the Maoists and security forces was painfully stressful. As the head teachers from Doti and Kapilvastu mentioned:

> I had to allow the Maoists to perform their cultural programme in my school on the one hand and cooperate with the security forces in their search for rebels on the other. (A head teacher in Doti)

> Armed forces entered my school and arrested one of my students. I had to cooperate with the armed soldiers despite the fact that what they were doing was wrong. Later, I received pressure from the Maoists to facilitate the release of this student. I went to the military camp to hold several negotiations. (A head teacher in Kapilvastu)

In many districts, the head teachers' relationship with the education authorities also collapsed. Head teachers faced contesting authorities, the old but crumbling state and the dangerous emerging 'new state'. The only way to survive was by maintaining relational equilibrium between the two. Elsewhere, Makkawi (2002: 51) analyses similar complexities of living in conditions of protracted crisis in which Palestinian teachers in Israel continuously struggle to balance the pressure from the Jewish state and 'cultural and national expectations of their own community and students without putting their jobs in jeopardy'. However, in some cases in Nepal, the fear created by the Maoists worked as a corrective to the inefficiency of the state bureaucracy. An education officer shares such an experience:

> When the conflict was at its peak, I was working in the remote district of Dolpa. What I observed in that period was that the fear of Maoists improved teachers' absenteeism and punctuality in their duties. The Maoists had circulated a warning to the teachers in the district that they would be physically punished unless they performed their professional duties with integrity. This approach worked really effectively and I felt that fear was perhaps necessary in maintaining discipline. (An education officer in Kathmandu district)

However, teachers in all focus group discussions agreed that the fear of persecution worked at one level but it was rather transitory and the teachers' low performance was rather underpinned by broader structural problems in the education system which involved issues such as fragmented education policy, dysfunctional assessment system, lack of educational resources and inadequate teachers' salary. Teachers' professional motivation and passion for educating children cannot be maintained amidst fear and physical threats; these would rather lower their morale and make them indifferent to their profession.

Addressing the Effects of Conflict on School Governance

Schools are essentially complex ideological and political battlegrounds that offer both opportunities and threats to conflicting groups. Either way, educational spheres are likely to come under attack during violent conflict, and the global campaigns for protection of schools during crises are far removed from the grassroots reality and the roles teachers, head teachers and pupils play during conflict. The major problem is that the international community has repeatedly failed to hold armed groups and armed forces accountable for their indiscriminate attack on education. In April 2014, 276 schoolgirls were abducted from Chibok, Northern Nigeria by Boko Haram militants who consider modern education to be a cultural invasion incompatible with their Islamic beliefs. In August 2014, Israeli drones attacked UN schools in Gaza, claiming ten lives and leaving dozens wounded. The ensuing pressure of attack on pupils and schools is greatest for school leaders and teachers, whose voice does not always feature

Figure 4.1 Liwang town, Rolpa.

in the debates about planning or rebuilding education in emergencies. While children are understandably at the centre of concern in a crisis, the traumatic experiences of teachers and school heads are equally important for reimagining an effective educational provision.

5

Young People as Victims of Conflict and Political Actors

During the Maoist insurgency, children suffered continuous harassment from the security forces and were abducted by the Maoists to participate in political campaigns or in some cases forcibly recruited into the rebel army. Children were an integral part of the Maoist cultural wing that promoted progressive ideology through popular art media – songs, dances and soap opera. The Maoist rebellion had a strong component of political education that was underpinned by a progressive ideology, providing a moral justification for violence. Young people were often exposed to a discourse about exploitation of the poor, ethnic and caste-based discrimination, unequal land distribution and injustices on marginalized populations, which instilled a feeling of resistance in young people who willingly plunged into the movement. Hence, as this chapter will argue, children and young people were not only victims of the conflict but also active participants in the Maoist movement.

At the time of research, the young people who participated in the study were studying either in the 10th (15–16 years) or 12th (17–18 years) grade of school education, which meant that all their educational life had occurred during the 'People's War'. Students were given a narrative writing assignment titled 'The Armed Conflict and My Experiences'. In total, 240 students representing eight schools from six geographically diverse districts – Doti, Rolpa, Kapilvastu Udaypur, Sankhuwasabha and Kathmandu – participated in the study (Figure 5.1).

Researching Children's Experiences in Conflict: A Methodological Note

Researching into young people's experiences of violent conflict is methodologically challenging as interviews might not always be the best tools

Figure 5.1 Balkalyan HS School, Rolpa.

to capture their stories. Narrative researchers who mainly rely on interviews or other forms of data do not generally use narrative writing tasks as a method of data collection. However, this innovative tool was deemed to be culturally suited and was the most effective method of obtaining young people's experiences of the conflict. My extensive research on young people's role in communities in the past and project work with youth in rural Nepal (Pherali, 2007) shows that young children from rural areas in Nepal can express their ideas and feelings more eloquently in writing rather than in formal interviews. This method also allowed for a possibility to obtain a range of different stories with a large group of young students.

Polkinghorne (2007: 471) notes that narrative research is the 'study of stories' and 'narrative researchers study stories they solicit from others: oral stories obtained through interviews and written stories through requests'. This makes narrative research 'both phenomena under study and method of study' (Clandinin and Connelly, 2000: 4). Narrative inquiry is a useful method of 'capturing experience' and 'developing modes of analysis and interpretation that provide explanatory power for understanding "experience"' (Hendry, 2007: 492–3). The process of analysis and interpretation is actually 'an act of colonization, of violence', which tends to distrust the storyteller and their empirical narratives. However, stories are just extracts of the broader social context and the partial representation of social reality. Stories have a purpose. So, the storyteller is often selective and partial about their experience. To challenge the idea of doing justice to the participants' narrative as argued by Hendry (2007), I try to glance beyond the superficiality of the story in order to explore multiple questions (e.g. Why? What if? How? What else?) that often have answers outside the respondent's story and also to put the story to the test within the context of untold but relevant stories that exist out there in different forms. In this chapter, I therefore engage actively with what the students narrated about their experience of conflict to provide a more balanced picture of education and conflict dynamics from the children's perspectives.

As Hendry (2007: 495) notes, 'through telling our lives, we engage in the act of meaning making'. She further argues – 'we are our narratives. They [narratives] are not something that can be outside ourselves because they are what give shape to us, what gives meaning'. However, the object of narrative research is to extract, analyse and interpret the 'narrative truth' with an assumption that 'the stories are constructed around core facts or life events, yet allow a wide periphery for freedom of individuality and creativity in selection, addition to, emphasis on, and interpretation of these "remembered facts"'' (Lieblich, Tuval-Mashiach and Zilber, 1998: 8). In trying to understand young people's narratives about conflict, I was able to combine my own understanding of the education and conflict nexus that was gained through interviews with teachers and parents to give voice to the young people through a 'less exploitative research method than other modes' (Hendry, 2007: 489). This allows for considering not simply the stories in isolation, but the context where these stories have been conceived and narrated, as an effective way to understand the lived experiences of these participants.

The students were asked to write about what they had experienced at school, on the way to and from school, at home or in their communities in relation to the violent conflict. The task provided detailed guidelines and flexibility to write their stories in any style or structure they wanted. These stories included narratives of conflict-related incidents, which these young students had become part of or witnessed, read or heard about. The following questions were prompted to facilitate their structure of the stories:

- What incidents took place? Write in detail. Were they about you? Were they about teachers, children, parents or education offices?

- Did they affect you? If 'yes', how?
- What was done about it?
- How do you feel about them now?
- What changes do you intend to see in school education (topics you should study, methods of teaching, learning, life at school, etc.) in relation to the experiences you described?

The students were assigned the task to be completed at home and returned the following day to the researcher. The completed tasks provided vivid descriptions of young people's experiences, explaining their relationship with the Maoist movement and the effects of violence on their personal and student life.

Children in Crisis: A Global Scenario and Relevance to Nepal

Children are the greatest victims of civil wars. Save the Children's *Stop War on Children* report highlights some of the most gruesome stories of children who live in conflict zones (Save the Children, 2019). With 420 million children – one-fifth of children worldwide – living in conflict-affected countries today, the child population in conflict zones has doubled since 1990. Since 2010, 'grave violations' of children's rights in conflict settings have almost tripled, and the debilitating effects of war on food supplies, health systems, water and sanitation have caused deaths of hundreds of thousands of children globally. The *undemarcation* of the battlefields in civil wars (Pherali, 2016b) has brought violence around civilian homes and schools, increasing the risks of children being caught in clashes and indiscriminate attacks. Secondly, armed conflicts are increasingly protracted and have become part of global geopolitical tensions and proxy wars, and education has become an integral part of security and military strategies (Selenica and Novelli, 2021). Thirdly, schools have also become tactical targets of both state and rebel groups. On an average, four schools or hospitals were attacked or used for military purposes each day in 2016 worldwide (UNICEF, 2016b). For example, the Somali militant group al-Shabaab attacked Garissa University College in Kenya on 2 April 2015, killing 147 people, mostly students (Gettleman, Kushkush and Callimachi, 2015); Russian forces have frequently targeted schools and hospitals in Syria (Wille, 2020); the Saudi Arabia-led coalition has indiscriminately attacked civilian and non-military targets in Yemen (Sengupta, 2016) and in Gaza, Israeli Defence Forces were responsible for eleven attacks on schools in 2020 (UN, 2021).

Protracted violent conflicts in countries such as Afghanistan, Myanmar, Somalia and Syria have led to a mass exodus of civilian populations, resulting in the largest refugee crisis since the Second World War. At the end of 2020, 82.4 million people were forcibly displaced worldwide as a result of conflict, violence, persecution and human rights violations, out of which 26.4 million are refugees (UNHCR, 2021). Over fifty million children who have been uprooted because of protracted armed conflicts in their countries are in desperate need of education (UNICEF, 2017). Refugee children are five times more likely to be out of school and currently, only half of the primary-aged refugee children are enrolled in school, while female refugee children are 2.5 times more likely to be out of school than their male counterparts (UNICEF, 2017). Children are more easily manipulated to become soldiers and suicide bombers and because of their physical and cognitive vulnerability, they are an easy target for rebel groups. The impact of conflict on children is more severe in terms of their physical well-being, mental health and emotional and psychosocial development (Save the Children, 2019).

The United Nations Convention on the Rights of the Child (UNCRC) was adopted on 20 November 1989 and has since become the most widely ratified human rights treaty in UN history. The Convention contains the idea that children are not just voiceless objects whose lives and futures are decided by their parents or other adults but they are human beings with their own voice, rights and agency. Covering the rights of young people under the age of eighteen, the Convention mandates international communities, nation states and everyone concerned to allow children to grow, learn, play, develop and flourish in their lives with dignity. For instance, Article 19 focuses on protection of children from violence, abuse and neglect; Article 22 deals with the rights of refugee children; and Article 38 sets the standards for young people's participation in armed conflict. More importantly, Article 39 notes:

> States Parties shall take all appropriate measures to promote physical and psychological recovery and social reintegration of a child victim of: any form of neglect, exploitation, or abuse; torture or any other form of cruel, inhuman or degrading treatment or punishment; or armed conflicts. Such recovery and reintegration shall take place in an environment which fosters the health, self-respect and dignity of the child. (UN, 1989)

There are six possible categories of human rights violations against children: killing and maiming of children, abduction, forced recruitment as child soldiers, sexual violence mainly on girls, violent attacks on schools and deprivation of humanitarian aid during conflict and protracted crisis (UNICEF, 2020). The first UN report on children and armed conflict noted that millions of children were caught up in conflicts as targets of the warring parties. It highlighted that

> [children] fall victim to a general onslaught against civilians; others die as part of a calculated genocide. Still other children suffer the effects of sexual violence or the multiple deprivations of armed conflict that expose them to hunger or disease. Just as shocking, thousands of young people are cynically exploited as combatants. (Machel, 1996: 5)

During the decade-long armed conflict in Nepal, children's experiences also reflected much of what the UN report had highlighted. However, unlike some of the violent conflicts elsewhere, the 'People's War' in Nepal was justified by Maoists as a progressive protest movement, built on people-centred political ideology, in which children's involvement represented their political empowerment. Humanitarian agencies aligned themselves with the global discourse of 'children as victims' and viewed children's involvement in the Maoist movement as a violation of children's rights. However, some of the children's stories collected as part of this research reveal that children were well informed about the political rationale of the Maoist rebellion – that their narratives reflected maturity of critical consciousness about economic, political and social injustices in Nepali society. Those who had participated voluntarily were inspired by the idea of 'revolution' for progressive change that could bring about fairness, equal opportunities and social justice to the people. Indeed, there are grave violations of children's rights in conflict-affected environments, but the research and advocacy programmes that simply portray children as helpless victims of conflict whose rights must be protected might be undermining children's right to take part in political struggles for social transformation. This chapter will focus both on an array of effects of conflict on Nepali children and the way that young people exercised their agency and took part in political activism.

Failing Quality in Education and Young People's Frustration

With a backdrop of failing education and economic stagnancy, youth frustration particularly in rural areas found comfort inside the rapidly growing political and social movements in the early 1990s. While most young people's social and economic mobility was limited by the traditional power structures, a large number of rural youth saw the emerging rebellion as the only available option that could offer a respectable and collective purpose in life. All this happened simultaneously with some remarkable educational achievements. For example, primary enrolment increased at the impressive rate of 20 per cent per decade compared to the 2 per cent literacy recorded in 1951. As a measure of its success in expansion, Nepal had achieved 92 per cent primary enrolment and adult literacy had grown to 49 per cent, which included 70 per cent of the youth population (15–24 years) (World Bank, 2001). However, one must ask whether the rise in access represented gains in the 'quality' of education and served the interests of the country at large. As discussed elsewhere, there is a pervasive feeling that education largely provides theoretical knowledge and young graduates mainly gain certificates without any substantial employment skills, a perspective that is often hidden by the statistics proffered by development agencies working in this sector. Instead, there is mounting evidence that rather than reasonably contributing to the economic life of individuals or the nation, the increase in enrolments without either (1) improvements in quality or (2) adequate employment opportunities for those 'lucky' enough to graduate, only fuels frustration and conflict (Pherali, 2011: 141).

The movement underpinned by Maoist ideology (Lawoti and Pahari, 2010) needed to mobilize the masses, including young people, who got trained and inspired by the narratives of 'revolution' and the promise of social transformation (Bhattarai, 2003). In this context, schools provided multiple benefits to the rebels while primarily serving as centres for political education (Watchlist, 2005, 2007). van Wessel and van Hirtum (2013) argue that schools in Nepal's Maoist rebellion were 'tactical targets' rather than indiscriminate victims of attacks. They provide four broad explanations to why Maoists as well as security forces were using schools as their strategic sites during the conflict. Firstly, schools offered much-needed reasonably large physical spaces where the conflicting parties could gather people for mass meetings and take shelter during mobilization. Secondly, schools represented 'normality and a sign of a functioning state' and taking over their affairs would provide Maoists with a sense of control over a key domain of state authority. Thirdly, schools were useful sites for political socialization through which the Maoists could recruit young militants and gain political support from teachers. Fourthly, the rebels could extort much-needed financial resources from teachers. Except for the first one which provided equal tactical benefit to both the Maoists and security forces, the last three were mainly valuable to the rebels. However, the security forces targeted schools in order to sabotage the links between schools and rebels in these three areas so that they could reduce the Maoists' influence.

The interactions between education, children and armed conflict need to be examined not only from the global perspective of children's rights to a stable life and education, but also by considering what this link means within the sociopolitical context and nature of the conflict. Children's participation in the Maoist rebellion has formally been denied by the Maoists but informal conversations with Maoist leaders reveal that children were viewed as an integral part of the 'people's revolt' in which everyone spontaneously rose to the need for a political change. While the United States had listed the Communist Party of Nepal-Maoist (CPN-M) in their list of terrorists and the Nepali government also followed suit, the CPN-M consistently claimed that the Maoist movement was an organized people's resistance against the feudalistic monarchy and century-long structural inequalities. As they were keen to gain international legitimacy as a political organization, they were, at least rhetorically, inclined to respect international human rights laws and the call for Schools as Zones of Peace (SZOP). However, children and young people reported several incidents in which they had been victims of violence. Most of the students who shared their stories had witnessed some degree of violence but everyone felt its effects. The sections below will discuss these issues in detail.

Abduction and Disappearance

In many schools across the country, students and teachers were taken by force to attend mass meetings or political training which were often organized clandestinely outside the reach of security forces. The locations of these events would often be far from communities and schools, so children would have to make long journeys, sometimes overnight, to get to the destinations. Political education was part of the Maoists' mass mobilization strategy, so some students would join voluntarily after the training events and others would be forced to join the movement. An estimated 32,000 schoolchildren were abducted either for political campaigns or recruitment in the rebel army during the conflict (Thapa and Sijapati, 2004). One student from Sankhuwasabha revealed:

> On 25 May 2004, when we were studying in the class, five Maoist cadres entered our school and announced that they would like students from classes 9 and 10 to go with them. We all started crying. There was no chance of denying the Maoists. So, we accompanied them. I lost all my hope for life. I felt devastated for not being able to bid a goodbye to my parents before leaving. We were taken

to a distant village called Yafu and on the way, we were allowed to sleep in the group of six and one person had to be a sentry guard carrying a heavy rifle in hand at a distance of half an hour walk. We could barely sleep during the night. Thankfully, I was released later on as there was a big group of soldiers who were going to Khotang district, and they could not take everyone with them for logistical reasons. When I arrived home, my parents could not stop crying for me. (A nineteen-year-old female student in Sankhuwasabha)

Similarly, another student in Kapilvastu also reported her experience of being abducted by the Maoists:

It was not only we, students but also our teachers were abducted by the Maoists. This happened frequently. There was no one else as a replacement when the subject teacher would be kidnapped by the Maoists. We could not do anything to prevent it. The whole school would remain tense after the abduction. The teachers could not fail us because they were aware of the consequences of such incidents, but the quality of education was badly affected. (A nineteen-year-old female student in Kapilvastu)

Children and young people reported that they did not have a choice when Maoists asked them to come to attend political gatherings. The Maoists referred to the existing education as a bourgeois system, which was irrelevant and did not prepare young people for intellectual and economic prosperity, so the armed rebellion had become necessary to reform the state structures, including the education system (Maoist Statements and Documents, 2003). From their perspective, at a time when the 'great People's War' was being fought for radical political change, 'bourgeois' education was insignificant, and students and teachers needed to join the rebellion to serve this 'great mission'. Some parents also agreed with this narrative about education. As one of the parents revealed:

The existing bourgeois education produces young people who cannot be employed. We do not have the foundation for professional and scientific education that produces independent thinking youth. It consists of songs and praises of kings and places ... it does not teach children how to move forward and change society. (A parent during a focus-group discussion in Sankhuwasabha)

It appears that parents who held socialist views disagreed with the present system of education and implicitly argued that the Maoist movement was a legitimate response to the systemic failures in education. Despite the risks associated with joining the resistance, they believed that the sacrifice was worthwhile for a wider cause.

Table 5.1 Forced Disappearances during the People's War

SN	Organization	Cases Registered
1	National Human Rights Commission (NHRC)	2,800 cases (900 cases remain unresolved – 600 disappearances and 300 abductions)
2	International Commission of Jurists (ICJ)	209 cases (195 disappearances and 14 abductions)
3	Advocacy Forum	417 cases
4	Informal Sector Service Centre (INSEC)	933 cases (828 disappearances and 105 abductions)
5	The Society of Families of the Disappeared	1,162 unresolved cases
6	International Committee of the Red Cross (ICRC)	3,000 disappearances, of which 1,127 cases remain unresolved

Many children reported that they had lost either family members or close relatives to the armed conflict. Some of them had joined the Maoists or were serving in the security forces. Children also wrote about their family members being killed during the war, while some were arrested or kidnapped by either Maoists or the security forces and families did not know their whereabouts. It is estimated that over three thousand people were victims of forced disappearances in the period 1996–2007 (International Commission of Jurists, 2009). As Table 5.1 shows, several organizations had documented cases of forced disappearances, many of which are still unresolved:

The Watchlist on *Children in Armed Conflicts* also highlights that there was a widespread pattern of disappearance in Nepal when the government launched a counter-insurgency strategy (Watchlist, 2007). One student in Udaypur described the disappearance of his uncle as follows:

> My uncle was the head teacher in a local school. One day in 2002, he was summoned by the District Education Office in the district headquarters of Okhaldhunga. When he went to see the DEO, he was arrested by the police and charged with being a Maoist activist. My auntie was then notified by a letter that he needed some clothes in the police custody. When she hurriedly visited the district headquarters the following day and wanted to see her husband, the administration told her that he was transferred to Rajbiraj [the regional administrative office]. Then she anxiously went to Rajbiraj where she was told that he was no longer there and perhaps transferred to Kathmandu. We could not get any information about his whereabouts. The family broke down economically and emotionally. The eldest son went to the Gulf for employment and the youngest joined the 'People's War'. The government disclosed only in

2007 that my uncle was beaten ruthlessly and killed soon after being arrested in 2002. (A fifteen-year-old boy in Udaypur)

In addition to the horror of ethnic riots (discussed in the next section), children in Kapilvastu had also experienced abduction and forced recruitment into the Maoist ranks during the decade-long civil war. One student reported how she escaped from the Maoist abduction as follows:

> We could hardly study in peaceful situations in the school. There was always fear of being abducted by the Maoists. One day while we were studying, some Maoist rebels arrived in our school and asked us to go with them. We did not know where they intended to take us but we did not have any choice. So, we followed them. On the way, I deliberately walked slowly and acted being left behind and then ran away from them. I did not go to school for one week and soon moved to another school. (An eighteen-year-old female student in Kapilvastu)

Many children described their fear and trauma after experiencing violence or having lost their relatives to the conflict. One young girl in Kapilvastu revealed that her brother-in-law was killed in front of her when his house was caught in the crossfire between the Maoists and security forces. She revealed that she fell unconscious for hours. When the brother-in-law's friends protested against the death, the security forces accused them of being Maoist supporters and killed twelve of them during the protest (An eighteen-year-old female student in Kapilvastu). Another student wrote:

> When I was thirteen years old, several vehicles were set on fire in Chandrauta market and violence started spreading. Then, we fled to the lentil farm and stayed the whole night for our safety. When I was fifteen years old, heavily armed Maoist rebels attacked the police barrack near my house one night. The heavy bombardment and constant firing between the rebels and the police force was so scary that we took sanctuary in our neighbour's house and saved our lives. Last year, we were attacked by the Muslims. (A nineteen-year-old female student in Kapilvastu)

The above quote indicates how young people vividly remember their violent experiences and reveal their frustration about being repeatedly victimized despite their innocence. Children and young people in Kapilvastu displayed serious concerns about ethnic and religious hatred, even after the peace agreement had been signed and national politics had taken a new turn.

Additionally, the Maoists used various tactics to recruit children such as 'kidnapping of children; abduction of large groups of children from schools; and use of propaganda campaigns to attract children as "volunteers"' (Watchlist, 2007: 5). A human rights organization in Nepal recorded that 33,160 schoolchildren were abducted from schools for political campaigns (INSEC, 2007), many of whom were subsequently released, but some were killed in the crossfire or the aerial attack by the state army while 'others joined the movement voluntarily or under pressure' (Lawoti and Pahari, 2010: 310). Watchlist (2007) estimated that there were between 3,500 and 4,000 child soldiers in the Maoist ranks, who mainly served in local militias. However, many children also served in the Maoist core military wing 'People's Liberation Army', where they were trained in how to use modern heavy weapons, including 'socket bombs' (Watchlist, 2007: 4). The Child Workers in Nepal Concerned Centre (2004) reported that an estimated 475 children had lost their lives within the first six years of the conflict while 562 sustained injuries either in the crossfire or in explosions. Hence, schoolchildren were victimized by the state as well as by the Maoists. It was only in February 2010, four years after the Comprehensive Peace Accord (CPA), that nearly three thousand minors were released from the People's Liberation Army (UN, 2010b).

Abduction of children from school is one of the common tactics of armed groups in conflict-affected settings. Examining the case of children's kidnapping by Boko Haram in Nigeria, Ibrahim and Mukhtar (2017: 140) argue that the effect of the abduction on children and parents is 'memorably traumatic', more so for parents who lose contact with their children during the period of abduction. Similarly, Freeman (2006: 29) reports that parents of abducted children often have thoughts of 'extreme violence' and some feel depressed and ill as they find themselves in a situation of helplessness and are caught in the fear that they would lose their children forever. Landau et al. (2015) examine the effects of children's exposure to violence in Israel in various socio-ecological settings such as family, neighbourhood, schools and political conflicts. Their analysis shows that experiences of violence generally have traumatic effects on children resulting in aggression, violence, fear, sleep disorder, revenge seeking, depression, poor academic performance, panic and involvement in criminal activities (Chinwokwu and Arop, 2014). It is therefore pertinent that psychological recovery of children who have experienced violence is necessary to minimize the long-term impact on their social and cognitive development (Machel, 1996). As Amusan and Ejoke (2017) argue:

> Any traumatic event influences an individual's total wellbeing (school children and their parents) as their inability to match thoughts and memories of trauma

would result in nightmares and if not timely managed, can lead to a psychiatric case. Kidnapping has both long-term and short-term effects on individuals, families, society, and the state at large, as it is one of the most psychologically damaging crimes of all. Victims of kidnap often take many years to heal from the psychological wound inflicted upon them while others never completely recover. Kidnappings cause deep emotional and mental scars that leave victims to battle through issues of trust, independence, love, sex, respect, and a litany of others. (Amusan and Ejoke, 2017: 53)

Displacement and Victimization

Several reports reveal that the Maoists committed atrocities against civilians who did not support them (INSEC, 2007; Watchlist, 2005), which often led to a massive scale of internal displacement, mainly people fleeing to the district headquarters or to the capital Kathmandu. The displacement of families caused financial pressures and seriously disrupted children's right to education. Almost five years after the Maoists signed the peace agreement ending the decade-long conflict, 50,000 people reportedly remained displaced, and due to the ethnic conflict that erupted in September 2007, a year after the end of the Maoist insurgency, approximately five thousand were forcibly displaced from the Tarai/Madhes region (Internal Displacement Monitoring Centre, 2011).

The families and relatives of personnel serving in the security forces, including the military and police, were often the first targets of the Maoist rebels in rural areas. A sixteen-year-old girl in Udaypur noted that her families were 'threatened and maimed to recall [their] serving members' from the army. She further revealed that her family was forced out of their home and locked out by the Maoists as her father was serving in the army and her 'uncle and auntie were kidnapped and heartlessly tortured by the Maoists'. Shakya (2011) also reported similar findings in her study, drawing upon her extensive fieldwork relating to human rights violations during conflict. Experience of violence in the communities and school surroundings was a common phenomenon. A student in Sankhuwasabha wrote:

> During conflict, a violent incident took place between the army and Maoists in Makalu village. Later, we found out that two Maoist rebels had been killed. It was only when we saw the dead bodies, they were my two uncles. A couple of years later, my own friend decided to join the Maoist Red Army. She also tried to convince me but I did not want to give up my study. A few months later,

she was killed in a battle in Tehrathum. (A nineteen-year-old male student in Sankhuwasabha)

Hart (2001: 28) mentions that children who joined the 'People's War' often did so 'with the encouragement or example of parents, especially, of older siblings'. He further notes that children's participation in the rebellion was closely related to their parents' ideological affinity with the movement and the attractive Maoist ideology (Hart, 2001). In addition, the cultural norm for Nepali families of children's obedience to elders also explains children's attitudes towards the 'People's War'. An additional dimension relates to children's attraction to the Maoist cultural troupe that accompanied the People's Liberation Army (PLA) and political wings of the party. Similar to the 'struggle *yangge*' (*douzheng yangge*), the musical art form that was used by the Chinese Communist Party (CCP) 'as a political tool to influence people's thinking and to disseminate socialist images' (Hung, 2005: 82), the CPN-M also used revolutionary songs, invigorating dances and emotive soap operas that carried powerful messages of the struggle. Hung (2005: 87) argues that the significance of these musicals is in constructing 'a narrative history through rhythmic movements – that is, using *yangge* to weave recent CCP developments into a success story about the communists coming to power, the gallantry of the PLA, the staunch support of the Chinese people, the correct party leadership and a bright socialist future for the country'. The progressive songs and cultural performances promoted

> the radical rhetoric of social justice: equal rights, free from discrimination both in terms of caste and gender, liberation of oppressed, ensure identity, language and culture rights of the underprivileged and marginalized and children found the elegant Maoist parades and musical programmes that condemned feudal lords fascinating. (Shakya, 2011: 560)

Security forces often targeted schools on the suspicion that Maoists were present at schools to organize political training or cultural programmes. One of the most shocking incidents of this kind occurred in Doti in 2003 in which security forces raided a secondary school where the Maoist cultural groups were preparing for musical performance. Security forces suddenly surrounded the school and opened fire indiscriminately. One student who was caught in the crossfire explained:

> In October 2003, the armed security forces attacked my school. On that day, a group of Maoists had organized a cultural programme in our school. They were not particularly armed. In fact, these artists were students like us who were

brought from another school to perform a cultural show at our school. But they were members of the Maoist cultural groups. The Maoists made all students stay and enjoy the cultural performance. They would not let anyone leave the school premises without their permission. Before the show began, there was an explosion near the school. Suddenly, armed soldiers surrounded our school and started shooting at us intensely. Two of the children who were on their way home were killed on the spot. Other three children were shot inside the school. I was also hit on my leg and fell on the floor inside the canteen. I screamed for water but there was no one around. The soldiers who had gone mad locked all others inside the classrooms, shooting randomly at everyone who was found suspicious. Eleven young people were killed during this attack and of the dead, six were my friends. I fell unconscious. When I opened my eyes, I found myself on the hospital bed. I realized that I was later airlifted to the regional hospital. Despite the long treatment, doctors could not take the bullet out of my leg for several months. My leg will not be recovered, and I walk with this bamboo crutch. (A seventeen-year-old male student in Doti)

For secondary schoolchildren in the outlying regions, it was virtually impossible to remain 'politically neutral' as the conflict escalated, even if they managed to escape being recruited by the rebels or being used by security forces. Young students who experienced these risks revealed that the mounting conflict resulted in despair in life and the futility of going to school (Pherali, 2011). Students reported that the traumatic experience of being caught in the crossfire had made a long-term impact on their lives. Another student from Doti corroborated the incident which occurred in their school:

When the army entered the school playground, they started shooting recklessly. They started firing at us madly and indiscriminately despite our telling them that we were students from the school. Some students managed to escape but others started running back into the classrooms. Suddenly, I was hit by a bullet on my right hand and fell unconscious. I was airlifted to Kathmandu for treatment where I stayed for two months before returning home. I can no longer write with my right hand so I had to learn to use my left hand. I cannot concentrate properly and often get disturbed by the memory of the violence. (A nineteen-year-old female student in Doti)

The above narrative of violent encounter and the effects of being attacked by the security forces reveals potentially long-term impacts of conflict on children. Drawing upon stress response theory, Amusan and Ejoke (2017) highlight a broad range of potential psychological impacts on children. These may include: cognition (intrusive thoughts; impaired memory; denial; flashbacks and confusion), emotional (shock and numbness; fear and anxiety; helplessness), anger at anybody (perpetrators; themselves and the authorities), depression and anhedonia (loss of pleasure in what was initially pleasurable) and social withdrawal (isolation; irritability and denial) (Amusan and Ejoke, 2017: 53).

Learning While Trying to Survive

The fear generated by the violent conflict also altered the way in which people moved around in their communities (Pettigrew, 2003). Clearly, public mobility suffered from self-imposed restriction as an understandable precaution against being caught in a sudden occurrence of violence in the village. This was more so for teachers and students in the mountainous areas, where travelling to and from schools risked being caught in the crossfire (Pherali, 2011). Parents of teenage children would always be worried about their children's safety while they were at school. Watchlist (2007: 2) reported that a large number of young children had been forced to flee their homes 'to avoid recruitment by the Maoists, or to seek better lives away from already impoverished communities further damaged by the conflict and the government's brutal responses'. Some parents in Kapilvastu district reported that they were compelled to withdraw their boys from school and send them away for foreign employment hoping that they would at least be protected from forced recruitment in the rebel army. As one parent lamented:

> The soldiers in the camps would observe our children play on the school playgrounds with their binoculars. Anyone who was able to jump and looked physically fit would be arrested as a Maoist suspect. (A parent in Kapilvastu)
>
> We were extremely terrorized by the risk of our children being nabbed by the armed groups on their way to and from school. I could not live with the everyday fear of losing my son. So, I took him out of school and sent him to Malaysia for work. (Another parent during a group discussion in Kapilvastu)

As revealed in the above quote, parents evidently prioritized their children's safety over the latter's educational future and aspirations in life. It also shows the parents' desperation in making these choices despite being aware of the hardships, demanding manual work and dire working conditions in the Middle East or Malaysia. Here, 'losing' one's young son temporarily by sending them abroad was described as a more intelligent decision than potentially having to lose them permanently to the conflict at home. This, however, would often lead to family disintegration and abandonment of the long-term dreams of success through education that parents and children collectively saw for themselves.

Security forces also arrested students suspecting them of maintaining secretive connections with the Maoist student wing All Nepal National Free Students' Union Revolutionary (ANNFSU-R), which was also labelled a 'terrorist group' by the government. Students were usually stopped and interrogated on their way to school and back. As the soldiers would mistreat and even assault people on suspicion during their patrolling, young students were hugely intimidated by the presence of heavily armed soldiers in their villages and school surroundings. One student in Sankhuwasabha described the experience of her friend being hassled by security forces during her overnight stay in her rented accommodation:

> On 31 October 2004, I was staying at Bhanjyang to complete my high school study. One day, one of my friends arrived from Dhankuta where she had been to take her entrance exam for a nursing course. The following morning when she was leaving for home, she had an encounter with the soldiers at a shop outside my rented house. The soldiers stopped her and started interrogating. As she was scared, she lied about her visit to Dhankuta and pretended that she was a student in my school and shared the house with me. But they quickly found out that she had already completed her secondary level education. They came to my room and pointed a gun on my chest and repeatedly asked me if she was a Maoist, which I consistently denied. Later, she told the truth but the soldiers arrested her and took her to the army barracks. She was released after a month when her brothers stayed as her guarantors. (A nineteen-year-old female student from Sankhuwasabha)

Elsewhere, 'children were mobilized by the Maoists to create student unions in schools to influence their peers to understand their ideology and political rhetoric, and the importance of being part of the insurgency' (Shakya, 2011: 560). A young boy in Sankhuwasabha revealed that security forces would turn brutal against Maoist suspects and their sympathizers. He stated:

> On 23 January 2003, the Royal Nepal Army raided my uncle's house and inhumanly tied my cousin's hands and legs and blindfolded him before dragging him outside the house. They beat him mercilessly and arrested him. We later found out that he had distributed membership of the Maoist-affiliated student union to other students in his school. (An eighteen-year-old boy from Sankhuwasabha)

In Rolpa, the origin of the Maoist insurgency, most children seemed to have negative perceptions about the police and army. Even before the 'People's

War' was declared, a large number of people in this region were arrested and charged with false cases (Maoist Statements and Documents, 2003) for their political affiliation with the United People's Front, a political party that later converted into CPN-M. Most people in this district viewed the state authority as a violent oppressor. Many students from Rolpa mentioned in their writing that every time a conflict-related incident occurred in and around the village, the security forces would normally target teachers and students. As one student explained:

> I was a student in grade 8. Once, the police and army surrounded our school while we were taking English lessons. We had the impressions that the army and police often tortured and killed people for no reasons. When I saw armed soldiers outside our classroom, I started shivering with fear. The soldiers got all senior students to stand in a queue on the playground. They started interrogating everyone. They beat up some teachers and students heartlessly. (A seventeen-year-old female student in Rolpa)

The above was one of the many illustrations of how students experienced the conflict. As Shakya (2011: 560) noted, 'schools were not the "zones of peace" that they were promoted to be but were rather "zones of war" as both the armies of the conflicting parties violated the rights of children' under the UN convention. Another student in Rolpa witnessed a horrific scene of attack on civilian homes from her school. She explained that she had experienced 'so many events of violence' in the past few years. She stated:

> Once we were taking an exam, suddenly we saw the Royal Army setting fire on two houses in the village next to our school. The soldiers threw a seven-year-old child into the burning house. Suddenly there was gunfire, and a bullet went through the left hand of our teacher who was invigilating the exam. (A nineteen-year-old female student in Rolpa)

These findings are consistent with various reports highlighting human rights abuses and indiscriminate intrusion of the conflicting parties into schools and violence against teachers and children (Amnesty International, 2005; Shakya, 2011; Sharma and Khadka, 2006; Watchlist, 2005). Often targeted at children and young people (Machel, 1996), these violent incidents severely affected children's education and the quality of their lives. Mounting experiences of these kinds led to a rise in forced migration of families, uprooting children's normal routine and life chances through education.

Ethnic Violence and Children in Kapilvastu

The ethnic violence in Kapilvastu began after the assassination of Mohit Khan, a local landowner and Muslim leader, by some unknown persons on 16 September 2007. Mohit Khan was a former member of the pro-monarchy vigilante group called Pratikar Samuha[1] (OHCHR, 2008). Muslim/Madhesi communities that Khan belonged to, accused Pahadi groups of his murder and started retaliatory attacks by burning homes and businesses owned by Pahadi people. The hostilities between the Pahadi and Madhesi groups spilled over to neighbouring districts and lasted for five days, resulting in the killing of fourteen people; displacement of six thousand to eight thousand people of Pahadi origin to the North; an estimated four thousand people in the Internally Displaced Persons (IDP) camps; and more than three hundred buildings damaged or destroyed including five mosques and two hundred houses (OHCHR, 2008).

Children who participated in the study in Kapilvastu reported that the entire village felt like a war zone for almost a week. It was mentioned that the September 2007 riots were more horrific than what they had endured during the decade-long armed conflict. This was due to the explicit nature and intensity of violence in a short period of time. As one student described:

> The communal violence that erupted on 16 September 2007 forced my family and neighbours to flee our homes. It was a festive occasion of Teej and all our sisters, aunties and mothers had gathered to celebrate the festival. Suddenly, hundreds of armed Madhesi people entered the village attacking the villagers and setting fire on their homes. Then, they attacked our neighbour and shot him in front of my eyes. We heard that they were raping women in the village. Suddenly, they set fire on our house and we somehow managed to escape to the nearby forest. It rained heavily all night. There were pregnant women and new-born babies and young children who suffered from hunger all night. When we returned to the village next day, the village was all wrecked and young girls of fifteen to sixteen years had been raped. There was no one to pick up the scattered dead bodies. We picked up some left-over belongings from homes and fled to Sundaridada [a village in the north] where we stayed for one month. We were moved to another place for a few more months before finally the political parties and the government assured

---

[1] Pratikar Samuha were pro-state self-defence groups that were active in some Western Tarai districts during the armed conflict. They were mainly set up by some anti-Maoist Madhesis who saw the Maoist movement as a Pahadi-initiated and led political struggle. They were reportedly protected, supported and allegedly trained by the then Royal Nepalese Army to counter the Maoist influence. There was no formal decommissioning of such groups and they continued to possess arms long after the peace agreement was signed.

that it was now safe to return to the village. Not everyone has been able to return though. (An eighteen-year-old girl of Pahadi origin in Kapilvastu)

The above narrative of a young girl represents the common experience of children and families during the ethnic riots in Kapilvastu. The description of overwhelming experiences of forced displacement paints a harrowing picture of children's struggle to survive the violence. It can be argued that ethnic violence of this type contributes to reinforcing of individuals' collective identity more firmly and stereotyping the 'other' as a criminal, cruel and rival ethnic group. This can create a longer-term challenge for community cohesion. Similarly, another student wrote:

> The following day 'Nepali' people came to our village and burnt down Muslim people's homes. They also set fire on two tractors. All Muslims from our village fled to India. We also took refuge in our relatives' house. Villagers took turn to guard the village at night and young girls and women often hid in the sugarcane farm and fields to be safe from rioters. (A nineteen-year-old Tharu girl in Kapilvastu)

It was interesting to observe how this young girl uses the term 'Nepali' to refer to the people of Pahadi origin. This demonstrates deeply rooted divisive identity markers that portray a particular type of ethnic traits associated with Nepali national identity and non-recognition of Madhesi, Muslims and Tharu ethnic groups as authentic 'Nepalis' (Pherali and NEMAF, 2021). The cultural hegemony of hill-based, high-caste groups (Brahman-Chhetri) and their language (Nepali) has systematically undermined the cultural, religious and indigenous identities of the other ethnically diverse populations of Nepal (Lawoti, 2005). Education in this situation systematically contributes to the process of reinforcing or reproducing these cultural prejudices (Apple, 2004; Bush and Saltarelli, 2000; Davies, 2004). As Gellner (2007) also notes, schools and government organizations propagated a highly exclusionary national identity that neglected the sentiments of lower castes, ethnic groups (Janajatis, including Tharus in the Tarai), religious minorities (Buddhists, Muslims and now increasingly Christians) as well as Madhesis living in the economically crucial southern plains of the country. The recent rise in ethnic politics challenges the state-sponsored repressive traditions against minority ethnic and indigenous nationalities and problematizes the notion of 'Nepali' as the only unifying national identity. A mural on the wall of a busy Kathmandu street reads 'Down with the idea of national identity that requires Nepali language and daura-suruwal-topi.'[2] This indicates that the ethnic

---

[2] National dress that has been traditionally promoted as national uniform.

violence in Kapilvastu has its roots in social and political exclusion of various cultural and religious groups in the district.

When Mohit Khan was murdered in Kapilvastu, his supporters asked the police to stay away and began to take revenge against the Pahadi community (OHCHR, 2008), which they viewed as being protected by the state and security forces. Since the security forces are dominated by people of Pahadi origin, for Madhesis there has always been a problem of trust in the state institutions (Pherali and NEMAF, 2021). So, the riots that followed need to be examined from the perspective of ethnic grievances rather than only as a chaotic mobocracy. The literature on riots and mobocracy is also increasingly suggesting that 'when people riot, their collective behaviour is never mindless. It may often be criminal, but it is structured and coherent with meaning and conscious intent' (Radburn and Scott, 2019: n.p.). The analysis of rioting in England in August 2011 also indicates that 'it was those who identified as anti-police that mobilized onto the streets', and the targets of their 'collective rioting were not random, but focused predominately on the police, symbols of wealth and large retail outlets owned by big corporations' (Radburn and Scott, 2019: n.p.). Reicher and Scott (2011) also argue that the 'social identity approach' provides a more rigorous and nuanced understanding of riots behaviour and crowd action. This approach 'rejects the pathological and decontextualized analysis' of crowd action during riots and 'points towards the pressing need to interpret those crowd actions as a meaningful and symbolic reaction to the subjective and material realities of the participants' social context' (Scott and Drury, 2017: 12).

Most children in Kapilvastu reported that their homes, grain and cattle were set on fire by the rioters. A student mentioned that his younger brother lost his sense and developed mental health problems because of the attack on their home (An eighteen-year-old male student in Kapilvastu). He also lamented that there was no support provided by the government nor did any NGO or INGO extend meaningful support during the crisis. Schools in the region were reportedly closed for up to two months due to the fear of a return of violence. Particularly, teachers from Pahadi ethnic backgrounds felt insecure about returning to schools, which adversely impacted on teaching and learning (Figure 5.2).

Children's Participation in the Maoist Movement

The reasons for children's participation in the political and armed activities of the Maoists are not dissimilar to those relating to adults. For many children, the

Figure 5.2 Children on the way to school – Sharada HS School, Doti.

Maoist movement provided a sense of meaning and purpose in life that they were able to be part of a significant mission of sociopolitical transformation. The idea that it was war by the people for equality and social justice and against caste, gender and ethnic domination appealed to young people's sense of duty to their nation. Many children had a family member or relatives who were involved in the rebellion and children were constantly exposed to conversations about the importance of the struggle within their families and communities. These exposures served as the basis of children's political socialization and formation of their political identity. Children also participated in the rebellion in spite of their parents' wishes (Hart, 2001). For some, taking revenge may have been the primary motivation whenever someone in their family would be detained, tortured or killed by the security forces, whereas others were attracted to the power and sense of pride that came from serving in the Maoist militia. As Hart (2001: 24) notes, the student wing of the CPN-M offered 'a kin-type network in potential competition with the traditional family'. Young people in rural areas were conscious about the bleak prospects in life even if they completed their school education – job opportunities were scarce, and nepotism and favouritism was rife in the public sector. Children from low-caste groups, ethnic minorities and girls struggled to see a positive and fulfilling future through the generally poor-quality education. Hart (2001) presents an account of a female teenager who challenges the prevailing patriarchal exploitation and gender discrimination and sees involvement in the Maoist movement as a way of addressing these societal problems:

> Before the initiation of the People's War, I did not know anything about politics or parties. But after the initiation [of the armed struggle] one of my relatives suggested I take part in the local cultural group and asked me to go to their rehearsal. I didn't tell my mother or father about this – I only told my older brother who said 'Go ahead if you want to die … Can you carry a gun on your shoulder?' I replied 'You didn't give me a chance to study and now I am eager to solve the problems of the people and the nation. I want to fight for liberation. If you won't allow me to go I will rebel.' (Hart, 2001: 28)

Given that the young people who took part in this study were still at school, almost all of them had avoided being recruited as regular members of the rebel army. Some of them wrote about having contributed either voluntarily or by force to Maoist activities. However, they wrote quite extensively about their friends who had joined the movement and the frightening incidents they had experienced during the conflict. In the aftermath of the conflict, teachers' and students' involvement in party-based political activism became pervasive and children were participating regularly in mass demonstrations. Many students were involved voluntarily in mass demonstrations and rallies as part of the programmes organized by their student unions. During my fieldwork in Liwang, Rolpa, I was able to observe one such political action led by schoolchildren:

> This is my third day in Rolpa district. As usual, I went to my research school in the first hours. When I reached the school, pupils from class six to ten had marched out from school to the town centre and teachers were chatting in the staff room. When I asked teachers about the empty classrooms, they explained that children were voluntarily taking part in a 'political cause' and the teachers had no authority to stop them from marching out. Suddenly, around 200 children, aged between 10 and 16 years appeared up on the main road demonstrating and chanting slogans against an NGO that worked for education and welfare of children in the district. The programme manager of the NGO was accused of abusing his position and spreading his party's political ideology among the youth in exchange for the support he provided through the NGO. The children blamed that he would only take the programmes to the school if the children supported the political party of his affiliation. As the protest was

likely to be tense, the district administration deployed police to safeguard the NGO's office from possible vandalism by the young protestors who demanded dismissal of the programme manager and closure of its programmes in the district. The furious children blocked the road for several hours by burning tyres and confronting with the police. Finally, the protesters were invited by the district administration officer to negotiate who assured that the matter would be thoroughly investigated. Finally, the children withdrew their strikes and went back to school while their leaders engaged in negotiations. (Research diary excerpt from Rolpa district)

The above excerpt shows that schoolchildren are not merely vulnerable entities waiting to be educated at school; they are active agents of change who carry out political actions against prejudice and discrimination. However, young pupils in post-conflict Nepal are also manipulated by adults with trivial and selfish political motivations that undermine the real opportunity for learners to critically engage in social issues that impact upon their lives. Teachers and students tend to have parallel domains of political actions which are linked to their respective identities, but their political positions at the macro level do converge as affiliated to respective sister organizations across different parties. However, Nepalese schools as sites of popular education and political actions require more research, particularly looking at the extent to which teachers and students are collectively involved in transformative learning that goes beyond the idea of exam success.

Ironically, despite teachers' contributions to grassroots movements, their profession has rarely been honoured as transformative and their role as 'critical pedagogues' has been ignored (Aronowitz and Giroux, 1993). The growing influence of party politics on schools has resulted in teachers' solidarity in broader political struggles while fuelling a disconnect between their professional responsibility and children's learning. The poor-quality education in public schools, as indicated not only by continuous underperformance of students in national exams but also by the general failure of education to promote creativity, critical thinking and passion for knowledge and learning, is largely perceived to be the outcome of teachers' professional negligence. The revolutionary justification that systemic change in education is subject to broader social and political reforms and hence, the professional duty is subsidiary to the duty towards mass liberation from oppression, seems to have morally collapsed due to declining quality and widespread frustration at the state of public education. This indicates the enormity of the challenges associated with schools in terms of enabling young people to become active citizens who contribute meaningfully to their society.

Can Schools Be Responsible for Children's Safety during Ongoing Conflict?

The risk of children's abduction from school put enormous pressure on teachers who were unable to resist the Maoist intrusion. Schoolteachers in Udaypur indicated that the relationship between school and parents deteriorated as parents held teachers accountable for the security of their children during school hours. They claimed that schools were frequently attacked, and staff and students intimidated and victimized, during the violent conflict and it was virtually inconceivable to prevent intrusion of conflicting parties into the school while the state had completely failed to protect schools during the war. Elsewhere, parents in a private school in Kathmandu held contentious views about how their school dealt with the Maoist pressure of 'mandatory donations'. As mentioned above, the principal of this school lamented that some parents objected to providing financial support to the Maoists, while others blamed the school management for not complying with the Maoist demands, thereby inviting attacks on the school and endangering the lives of their children.

Students studying in a private school in Liwang, Rolpa, mentioned that their schooling experience during the conflict involved a great degree of anxiety and uncertainty about their educational future. Schoolchildren in all the selected schools claimed that they were often harassed and intimidated by the security forces on patrol or at the security checkpoints. One student in Rolpa described his experience as follows:

> During 2000–2001, I was a student in grade 6. Once, the police set up a security check post near our school. Every morning and afternoon when we crossed the checkpoint, they searched our bodies and treated us inhumanly. They used to grab the hair of teachers and students and point pistols at their heads. They [security forces] would come to our school almost every day and arrest anyone who they suspected of being a Maoist supporter or sympathizer. I have myself seen how they used to torture people. Many people were displaced due to repeated experience of arrests and torture by the security forces. (An eighteen-year-old female student in Rolpa)

In the post-war period, teachers reported a noticeable change in students' attitudes towards learning, future aspirations and in their general behaviour. They revealed that students were comparatively more hostile and showed behavioural problems, with a significant decline in their motivation to succeed in education. Most students at the secondary level showed a degree of schizophrenic symptoms

(A teacher in a focus group discussion in Kathmandu). The power relations between teachers and students have also shifted, allowing students more freedom and rights in the educational process. As indicated by teachers from a private school in Kathmandu during the interviews, this has affected students' ability to fully engage in the curriculum. Similar findings have been reported in Northern Uganda where students' behaviour in the post-conflict period was characterized as 'aggressive' and 'indisciplined' (Ezati, Ssempala and Ssenkusue, 2011).

To conclude, schools were the most productive sites for recruitment and mass mobilization for the Maoists while the security forces barely saw any difference between adult activists and children, who were equally tortured, maimed and killed due to their real or suspected involvement in the Maoist movement. Children were also affected when their families were caught in the conflict and displaced from their villages, while some children became victims in the clashes between Maoist rebels and government forces. Children's experiences of conflict overlap with those of their parents and are part of the overall impact on their families. These experiences also coincided with teachers' experiences of violence, as they all became the victims of school-based violence during the conflict.

The analysis of the interactions between education, children and conflict in Nepal shows that the links between armed rebellion and children's involvement are multidimensional and complex. While the general victimization of children during armed conflict does hold true in Nepal's Maoist rebellion, children and young people's involvement in conflict may not always have been forced by adults. In many instances, children make rational and well-informed decisions about participation in revolutions. This may be a somewhat uncomfortable notion from a Western liberal perspective: 'the concept of youth political participation remains controversial in many contemporary Western democracies' where children are 'regarded as incomplete and incompetent ("becomings" or "citizens in the making") who need protection and cannot be granted full rights and traditional participation options' (Toots, Worley and Skosireva, 2014: 54). While schools and education systems are fertile grounds of political socialization for young people, wider social issues, people's grievances and political tensions in the society also provide powerful informal education that shapes children's interactions with conflict and political upheavals. Children do not act alone. They organize and mobilize the support of their peers and comrades. Children's participation in the People's War has also demonstrated that 'children are acting with others, making and taking decisions and demonstrating commitments and responsibilities that at the very least confound a "care and control" model of childhood' (Wyness, 2006: 94). This means that young people can no longer be viewed as a passive and uniform category in the context of political participation; they do occupy increasingly diverse social positions and actively shape social arenas. ... Rather than interpreting increased youth activism as an abandonment of childhood and attempting to 'protect' children from political responsibilities, efforts should be made to encourage opportunities which allow children to embrace their rights as a distinctive category of citizens capable of taking action in matters that concern them. (Toots, Worley and Skosireva, 2014: 74)

Therefore, children are not just a 'becoming-ready' social constituency that needs to be protected by adults, they are also significant contributors in sociopolitical struggles that take place in their societies.

6

Education, National Identity and Post-Conflict Reforms

Now, I turn to the pertinent question of national identity, which has become a controversial political issue amid attempts for state restructuring and federalization of the historical monolithic Nepali state. Elaborating on theoretical concepts of 'identity' and social reproduction (Bourdieu, 1977), I highlight some of the key concerns relating to education and national identity in post-conflict Nepal. Specifically, I return to some of the earlier discussion about the role of education in the creation of national identity and highlight that historically disadvantaged communities in Nepal are increasingly reclaiming their ethnic and indigenous identities, which is paving the way for multiple national identities within one sovereign nation. The debates about post-conflict educational reconstruction, recognizing historical injustices and under-representation of ethnic and indigenous nationalities are presented. Some critical questions are raised around how educational reforms might support social and political structures that promote equality, social justice and peacebuilding.

Ethnic Diversity and Educational Development in Nepal

The evolving historical landscape of Nepal, reflected through its diverse ethnic and multicultural traditions, was perhaps first recognized by King Prithvi Narayan Shah (1723–75), who annexed between twenty-two and twenty-four different principalities and ethnic-based territories in his mission to create a strong unified nation. Following the national unification campaign, he proclaimed that *'Nepal char jat chhatis varna ko fulbari ho'* (Nepal is a garden of four castes and thirty-six sub-castes). The *Muluki Ain* (National Code) was formally introduced in 1854 to regulate caste relations as a legal system within Nepali society, until the caste system was abolished in 1963 by the *Naya Muluki Ain* (New National Code), which prohibited caste-based discrimination (Shields and Rappleye, 2008b: 266), although in reality social inequality persisted as hill high-caste groups continued to monopolize social and political institutions (Lawoti, 2005). Today, such diversity is manifested through multiple forms of ethnicity, caste/race, language, religion, society and culture. Sociological research in Western contexts has a long tradition of using 'race' as an analytical tool to study sociopolitical injustices and there are inherent tensions to the concept of 'race' and its interchangeable status with ethnicity. For example, Miles (1993) and Mason (2006) have argued independently that 'race' can be regarded as a naturalizing concept, which is socially, culturally and politically corrosive. In the case of Nepal, 'caste' and 'ethnicity' are significant explanatory factors for the manifestations of social exclusion, political monopoly and cultural repression. Even though the caste categories have long been recognized as the basis of unequal and exploitative social arrangements, attention to ethnicity began to grow only after the advent of democratic government in the 1990s when 'ethnicity' became a key identity marker and a source of political mobilization.

The high castes living in the hills (Brahmans, Chhetris) and the Newars have had connections to royalty and for centuries have enjoyed many state privileges, while the Dalits (treated as untouchable), indigenous nationalities known as Janajatis (e.g. Bhutia, Thakali, Magars, Limbus, Tharus, Dhimals, etc.) and Madhesis (ethnic groups dwelling in the Tarai/Madhes) have experienced deprivation and a lack of opportunity (Lawoti, 2005; Pandey, 2010; Pherali and NEMAF, 2021). However, the rupturing of the traditional power relations between various social groups during the armed conflict as well as the increasing tensions between such groups after the Comprehensive Peace Agreement have produced a partial redistribution of resources and access to power.

Nepal is home to over a hundred ethnic and more than seventy linguistic communities (Central Bureau of Statistics, 2003). Yet in the presence of such multilingual groups and castes, the state has promoted the Nepali language as the *lingua franca*: that which represents the prevailing orthodoxy or *doxa* (Bourdieu, 1977). However, the dominant view among ethnic and indigenous nationalities is that this is an act of 'symbolic violence' by the state, under the rule and influence of hill high-caste elite groups. For Bourdieu (1977), this is where particular forms of linguistic competence, realized through a national language, are strategically employed to dominate and suppress difference and diversity, and further obscure indigenous languages. As discussed in Chapter 2, the promulgation of *Rastrabhasha* (national language) has damagingly promoted a single identity, language and culture while ensuring the widespread dissemination of orthodox knowledge through a heavily prescribed curriculum. Without exception, all former regimes of Nepal – the Shah Kings (1768–1845), the Ranas (1846–1950), the Panchas (1960–90) and the parliamentary party leaders (1951–9 and 1990–2006) – have promoted 'a homogeneous, monolithic and unitary state by sanctioning and promoting only one language (Nepali), one caste group (Hill Brahman and Chhetri) and one religion (Hinduism)' (Hachhethu, Kumar and Subedi, 2008: 4). The politics of language has captured the central debate in Nepal's struggle for equity and recognition of cultural diversity. It was only the 1990 Constitution that officially recognized languages spoken as mother tongues by Nepal's diverse ethnic groups as 'languages of the nation' while still maintaining Nepali as the *rastrabhasha*. After the decade-long Maoist movement and subsequent ethnic uprisings in Madhes (2007–15), the Constitution of the Federal Democratic Republic of Nepal recognized all languages spoken in the country as national languages (Constitution of Nepal, 2015, Article 6). Educational structures including policies, bureaucracy and practice have historically played a complicit role in linguistic and cultural assimilation and still show an uneven distribution of socio-economic outcomes, perpetuating 'horizontal inequalities' in terms of caste, gender and ethnicity (Stewart, 2000; Tiwari, 2010).

Ethnic Discrimination in Social Domains

Scene 1:

A Pahadi hawker knocks on the gate of a house in Kathmandu city with strawberries in his traditional hill basket.

The landlady asks: *Dai kafal kasari ho?* [Elder brother, what rate are the strawberries?]

Pahadi hawker: *Bis ruppe mana ho bainee.* [Twenty rupees per *mana*,[1] younger sister.]

---

[1] Some of the ideas in this chapter were published previously in: Pherali, T., and Garratt, D. (2014). Post-Conflict Identity Crisis in Nepal: Implications for Educational Reforms, *International Journal of Educational Development*, 34: 42–50.

A traditional Nepali measurement of quantity.

The landlady:	*Bis ta mango bhayena ra dai? Milayera dinus na?* [Isn't twenty expensive, elder brother? Could you consider the price please?]

Scene 2:

	A Madhesi hawker shouts outside the gate – *Ye … Aalu, kauli, ramtoria, tamator …* [Potatoes, cauliflowers, ladyfingers, tomatoes …]
The same landlady asks:	*Ye madhise golbheda kasari ho?* [Hey Madhesi, how much are the tomatoes?]
Madhesi hawker:	*Hajur … kilo ko dus rupaiya parchha hajur* [My lady, ten rupees per kilo madam.]
The landlady:	*Kati mango, ali sasto de.* [That's expensive. Make it cheaper!]

The above two scenes can be read as textual and linguistic representations and political allegories of the attitudes of Kathmandu city dwellers towards hawkers in Nepal. They also depict the tensions between two prominent ethnic groups in contemporary Nepali society: *Pahadi* [Khas-Arya ethnic group] and *Madhesi*. Such prejudice is not uncommon among the many different castes and indigenous groups of Nepal. It is rather a typical reflection of culture, and of the attitude of socially and politically privileged classes (living in the hills) to people of the fertile southern plains (Tarai/Madhes). Against this backdrop, it is argued that it is the persistent negligence and symbolic violence (Bourdieu, 1977) of the state against the many marginalized castes and ethnic communities, which creates a justification for oppressed groups to rebel violently against Nepal's political system. The term symbolic violence is coined by Bourdieu to describe how particular forms of linguistic competence, in this case the process of learning Nepali, can become a signifier of domination over those for whom there appears no alternative choice. The dominant language is thus acquired as a form of misrecognition, a gentle violence that is unwittingly chosen as much as it is enforced. This has serious implications for notions of national identity and citizenship, as well as the critical role of education in producing social and political change in post-conflict peacebuilding. The analysis here primarily focuses on the context of Nepali society but also provides useful insights into similar scenarios in other regions where post-conflict educational reconstruction and peacebuilding face significant challenges: for example, those widely publicized by the Global Monitoring Report on the impact of armed conflicts on educational processes in conflict-affected societies (UNESCO, 2011).

The 'People's War' in Nepal served as a catalyst for an ethnic movement in the southern plains of Madhes that demanded equitable representation in the political realm and recalibration of national identity, recognizing cultural and linguistic characteristics of Madhesi and indigenous populations. In the midst of a rebellion against state nationalism and in response to a profound rupturing of Nepali tradition, there are new opportunities as well as serious implications for identity formation in the context of an evolving federal structure of the Nepali state. As the Constitution of Nepal, 2015, has mandated local governments to manage school education, it is important to reflect on how historically suppressed cultural, ethnic and linguistic identities are merged with new formations of national identity through educational change (e.g. curricular revisions, language of instruction and teacher development) at the local levels. The analysis reveals tensions between embedded notions of 'national unity', on the one hand and the political 'fragmentation' of the state, on the other, as new communities, identities and political affiliations continue to emerge and conflate in the post-conflict era. As the local authorities are beginning to take charge of education policymaking, these tensions may serve to undermine the significance of national identity unless there is a rigorous and critical debate to identify ways in which difference and diversity within 'Nepali' identity and citizenship may be usefully reconstructed through education.

Social Reproduction through Monopoly in Education

Society is often constrained by ideology (representing the interests of dominant groups) in ways that seek to fix (national) identity, and thereby suppress difference and diversity of particular indigenous marginalized communities. In response, a hermeneutic methodology is helpful to see how historical conflicts are recurring events located in particular ethnic and sociocultural structures and traditions (George, 2020; McCaffrey, Raffin-Bouchal and Moules, 2012). These identities can become locked in notions of subjectivity that serve to fix meaning while glossing over tensions that define our human condition. The value of a hermeneutic approach allows us to focus on issues of structure and agency, to consider both subjective and objective forces operating simultaneously, and to analyse conflict in terms of the historical context within which activists are effectively located.

Bourdieu's work (1977, 1986, 1990) is especially helpful in this regard, for all human and social action is culturally, ethnically and historically situated. This means we are all born into particular social and political settings, with individual and collective dispositions, influenced by prevailing structures and traditions. Action is constituted through a reciprocal (and reflexive) relationship between an individual's beliefs, thoughts and personal disposition – *habitus*, and relatively enduring social structures, defining a *field* of action, within which the opportunities and limitations of human agency are cast, but not interminably fixed. In the case of Nepal, this relates explicitly to the notion of social hierarchy, in particular social class identity and caste, which serve to define and mediate the uneven terrain of post-conflict political processes. In turn, *habitus*, 'which acts as a mediation between structure and practice' (Bourdieu, 1977: 487), serves to influence and structure (ideological) beliefs and political action, doing so discreetly across different castes and within the boundaries of different political and linguistic *fields*. Such *fields* define a terrain within which different and diverse ethnic groups with access to different levels of resources and *capital* (economic, educational, cultural and symbolic) struggle for power and the possibility of freedom.

The state-imposed homogenization project, while superficially appearing to achieve national unity, has been nevertheless hostile to communities whose social identities remain dormant behind the veil of the state. A key concept in this analysis is the notion of 'symbolic violence' (Bourdieu, 1977), which describes how particular forms of linguistic competence developed through a national language (Nepali) can become a persistent force in the reproduction of state-defined knowledge. This coexists alongside the notion of *habitus*, conceived as a fluid and enabling concept, which while recognizing the internal legitimacy of different ethnic groups, simultaneously allows such groups to challenge the *doxa* (or prevailing orthodoxy) and thus destabilizes the state. In this sense, the *field* of conflict changes over time, resulting in a partial redistribution of resources and access to important forms of *capital*: social and economic, symbolic and political. The following section will briefly discuss the *field* (of 'diversity'), before presenting the analysis around the interactions between education, conflict and identity.

Creating National Identity through Education

The emergence of a democratic political system in the 1950s and the subsequent inception of modern education during the Panchayat era were implicitly aimed at restoring traditional powers of the monarchy and the no-party democratic polity. As discussed extensively in Chapter 3, devotion to the monarchy, a commitment to Nepali as the *lingua franca* and loyalty to the Panchayat political system were promoted as key unifying factors of the nation which comprised significant sociocultural diversity. In Bourdieu's (1977) idiom, this can be expressed in terms of how different and unequal access to *capital* often correlates with uneven and inequitable relations of power. This suggests that more powerful groups can often gain access to influential social and political networks and thus determine what counts within particular socio-economic and educational *fields*. For example, only if the *field* changes, through conflict aimed at state-sponsored symbolic violence, would hitherto marginalized groups hope to acquire access to new forms of political power and resources (Bourdieu and Wacquant, 1992). As Lawoti (2007: 23) argues:

> The ruling group defined the rights and duties of citizens toward the state by conflating it with its own interests and adopting political institutions that concentrated power within the group. This disjunction between the state and society is the underlying cause for the eruption of many of the contentious activities in present day Nepal.

In educational terms, the project of creating a unified Nepali state was the top priority of the Panchayat system (1960–90), employed to produce a state-defined pedagogy. A policy of 'national schooling' was imposed through 'restrictive textbooks and curricula that aimed at reinforcing a one-party system' (Carney and Madsen, 2009: 175). The process of creating '*Rastriya Itihas*' (National History) led to the imposition of a national curriculum and further enculturation of a 'particular idea of nationhood' (Onta, 1996: 215), followed by the marginalization of indigenous culture(s) and language(s). As stated in the National Education System Plan (NESP), the goals of national education were:

> to strengthen devotion to crown, country, national unity and the Panchayat system, to develop uniform traditions in education by bringing together various patterns under a single national policy, to limit the tradition of regional languages, to encourage financial and social mobility, and to fulfil manpower requirements essential for national development. (HMG, 1971: 1)

This impacted on the learning abilities of children from minority castes/ ethnic communities and non-native Nepali speaking backgrounds (Ragsdale, 1989), leading to a situation in which 'most of the school dropouts belonged to these non-Nepali speaking communities' (Yadava,

2007: 14). Stash and Hannum (2001: 376) also show that irrespective of socio-economic status, caste is often a determinant of 'both selection into and attrition from primary school'. Educational expansion or competitive access to schools does not necessarily address the issue of inequality in terms of caste/ethnicity unless there are radical policy interventions allowing for positive discrimination in favour of historically underprivileged groups, to disrupt their cycle of socio-economic and cultural reproduction. Evidence from South Africa also indicates that a medium of instruction other than the child's mother tongue can sometimes hinder the realization of academic potential. For example, some Black children whose mother tongue is not English are restricted in terms of 'academic skills and intellectual growth' at both high school and university levels (Banda, 2000: 51), which suggests that 'the quality of education cannot be seen as an issue separate from the language of instruction' (Brock-Utne, 2012: 773).

Following the restoration of multiparty democracy in 1990, many underprivileged ethnic groups were still excluded by the state, in which the broad spectrum of political parties appeared more concerned with the struggle for power than addressing issues of poverty and social inequality. Even in 2001, a full decade after multiparty democracy was restored and equal rights affirmed in the new constitution (where educational 'development' began to intensify), literacy rates among Brahmans (upper caste) were seven times higher than among low-caste groups (Central Bureau of Statistics, 2003). Such inequality and social injustice reflects the uncompromising effect of state 'symbolic violence' against lower-caste groups and ethnic minorities, the outcome of which has stirred violent conflict.

While Maoists have long demanded that 'the right to education in the mother tongue up to higher levels should be guaranteed' (Maoist Statements and Documents, 2003), some initiatives have been taken by the Ministry of Education and donor agencies to develop materials in indigenous languages as part of the Basic Primary Education Programme II – 1999. These included 'the development of primers, textbooks, teacher guides, and curriculum materials in the languages of Limbu, Maithili, Bhojpuri, Awadhi, and Newari among others' (Shields and Rappleye, 2008a: 99). However, while such activity is undoubtedly positive, it is nevertheless inadequate and has largely been ineffective (Subedi, 2018) to address broader issues of ethnic discrimination, as well as the many linguistic barriers to teaching and learning of children from predominantly non-Nepali speaking backgrounds. As an articulate Madhesi youth suggests:

> Most Madhesi people would like to take up jobs in the technical fields such as engineering, medicine, technicians and so forth. If they ever became teachers, it would be Maths or Science teachers as these subjects would require a minimum use of Nepali language. Succeeding in the civil service for Madhesis is extremely challenging due to the language limitation. They would always fail due to the poor grammar in Nepali writing. (Madhesi male youth from Eastern Tarai)

The hint of resignation in this interview points to a notion of 'invisible violence' (Bourdieu, 1977), in which the self-subordination of Madhesi people reflects not only a form of tacit compliance in relation to the *doxa*, but also perhaps a discernible sense of agreement. However, the latter constitutes a form of 'misrecognition', whereby indigenous groups are constrained both by prevailing political orthodoxy (social structures) and the limitations of their agency and self-regulation, with the effect of reproducing the social order. As Gramsci (1971: 244) might say, this is where the 'ruling class not only maintains its dominance but manages to win consent from those over whom it rules'. Thus, the educational intervention to create a universally recognized Nepali identity can be interpreted as part of an elaborate apparatus of coercion: a state sponsored initiative to establish Nepali as the *lingua franca* and thereby secure compliance through a form of deception and/or widespread 'misrecognition'. However, post-war political debates have emerged in favour of emphasizing the linguistic and cultural restoration of ethnic and indigenous communities through bilingual educational policies in federal states. To oppose a history of linguistic coercion and enculturation forced upon them, ethnic minorities and indigenous nationalities have actively sought for the revival of their own native languages in the post-war political transition. A youth peace activist in Janakpur reported:

> There has been a movement for the revival of Maithili language in Janakpur. All FM stations in Mithila now broadcast programmes in both Nepali and Maithili. People in Janakpur do not want Hindi (often argued by Madhesi leaders as being the lingua franca in the Tarai/Madhes), yet another foreign language to dominate our native Maithili, nor will they accept the continuing dominance of Nepali language either. (A Madhesi male youth in Janakpur)

Further examples of exclusion include the appropriation of civil service examinations and teacher selection exams, which are presented in Nepali (Jamil and Baniamin, 2020), and which, of course, inevitably disadvantage non-Nepali speaking Nepalese citizens, who are left with no alternative but to opt for their non-native language as a means of achieving upward social mobility.

Since education in the Nepali language makes it hard for non-Nepali speaking students to succeed in their school examinations (Bennett et al., 2006), many of them would not even meet the minimum qualifications to apply for Civil Service jobs (Dong, 2016; Jamil and Baniamin, 2020; Sunam and Shrestha, 2019). As Shrestha (2007: 201) notes, 'the ruling minority has been imposing its language, religion and culture upon all other Nepalese groups on the pretext of "national unity" or "Nepali nationalism".' As such, the policy to adopt Nepali as the only official language, across all spheres of life, has come at the cost of cleansing particular ethnic groups of their indigenous languages and often precious cultural identities. The practice of state-imposed cultural assimilation is illuminated through the following extract, which highlights the exclusion of Madhesi people who have been systematically disenfranchised by the state:

> Talking about other weaknesses, education has not been an easy access to all. There has been an opportunity to gain education for higher class [generally hill based high caste elites such as Brahmans and Chhetris and high caste Madhesis], whereas the low class [generally neglected groups such as Dalits, indigenous nationalities and low caste Madhesis] has been deprived of this opportunity. (Brahmin male teacher from a public school in Dang)

Promisingly, the Constitution of Nepal 2015 has made provisions of reservation for women, Dalits and marginalized caste and ethnic groups in the civil service (Constitution of Nepal, 2015). This is a post-conflict response to long-standing grievances and misrecognition of diversity felt by ethnic communities. In this process, structural reforms in education are vital to uphold principles of inclusion while ensuring quality and standards in public service. Even though affirmative action policies are crucial to 'rectify contemporary processes of social exclusion and marginalization', recent studies show that there are concerns about the opportunities created by new civil service reservation policies being monopolized by elite members of the ethnic minorities, thereby failing to benefit the most under-represented (Shrestha and Paudel, 2019: 113; Sunam and Shrestha, 2019: 283). Another issue that Dong (2016) raises is that historically under-represented groups should also be enabled and promoted through fair and inclusive promotion policies to hold senior positions as a sign of real inclusion, rather than simply recruiting them in junior posts to increase representation. The hollowness of the policy reforms also stems from the deeply rooted culture of *Afno Manchhe* (favour towards one's own people) within the institutions that are dominated by high-caste groups, which continue to discriminate 'against people based on their family, relatives, caste, and social relationships' (Jamil and Baniamin, 2020: 154). Hence, the difficulties around redressing structural inequalities relate to the need for technical, institutional and social change.

The 'People's War' as a Response to Ethnic Discrimination

Enhanced democratic freedom during the 1990s allowed ethnic and diverse cultural groups to participate in multiparty politics and also to reflect on their ascribed social and political status, linked with their ethnic and caste-based identities. This period thus saw the establishment or expansion of ethnicity-based parties such as the Nepal Sadbhawana Party and Nepal Janajati Party, which started to challenge the oppression and long-standing monopoly of a single language, culture and policy of state-defined nationalism. The increasing migration of people from the hills to the Tarai, and their political power and control over land became a critical issue within the realm of Tarai-based regional politics. The new-found political freedom in the 1990s created an opportunity to examine 'inter-ethnic relations' more critically: relations which were hitherto 'stratified' and thus 'fragmented' (Cohen, 1978). Hence, this period became a time for 'ethnic building' as opposed to 'nation building' (Gellner, 2007), providing a political logic for the Maoists to mobilize people at the margins. In other words, the 'People's War' capitalized on these tensions to orchestrate a political action and discourse of 'liberation'. Sudheer Sharma, a well-known journalist in Nepal, notes:

> The Maoists systematically used ethnic groups that were largely ignored by the ruling elites by offering them a share of governance in areas they controlled during the insurgency. In exchange, the ethnic groups provided the rebels with manpower to fight government forces. (Sharma, 2007, para 3)

This concurs with Gramsci's (1971) notion of articulation, in which the dominant Maoists were able tactically to concede a share of power and governance (to subordinate ethnic groups) in order to preserve their own hegemony. The Maoist 'revolutionary liberation fronts' such as Tharuwan Mukti Morch, Madhesi Mukti Morcha, Newa Mukti Morcha and Limbuwan Mukti Morcha were supported by different ethnic groups and are thus represented by people from different ethnic regions and across the social strata. A school principal in Kathmandu reported:

> If you view the Nepalese context it is not that all who went into conflict are ignorant people. Many intellectual and conscious people have also plunged into conflict. Due to the reason that there are social, political and cultural oppressions

prevailing in our society, even the educated people have taken part in the conflict with an objective to end this, or to liberate people from these oppressions or to gain freedom. (Private school principal from Kathmandu)

While it was noted elsewhere that the Maoist rebellion was largely envisioned and proclaimed by the educated elite (e.g. Brahmans and Chhetris) (Pherali, 2011), the majority of Maoist activists and People's Liberation Army cadres are young people from 'indigenous nationalities', downtrodden castes and unjustly marginalized ethnic groups (Lawoti, 2005). A school principal who represented an indigenous Magar community in Rolpa explained that Magars in his district had always been oppressed by the Brahman-dominated state structure, and access to education and other opportunities for people in his community has always been comparatively lower than for those in other neighbouring districts of his community (Interview with a school principal in Rolpa).

This reinforces the point that for a long time, regions inhabited by indigenous populations have been chronically neglected both educationally and developmentally. More significantly, they were also simultaneously controlled, indoctrinated and all but homogenized through the 'triumvirate' of Nepalese culture (language, religion and monarchy), where 'national culture was both elaborated in, and propagated through print, radio and visual media as well as educational resource materials' (Onta, 1996: 214). While the progress made in the past few decades in access to primary education can be regarded as a positive step towards developing basic levels of literacy across all sections of Nepali society, many learning materials tended to focus on creating a loyal and obedient citizenry, as well as preserving the hegemony of 'one nation' through the concept of state-defined politics.

Moreover, ethnic divisions and hierarchies displayed through public images in textbooks have promoted an 'evolutionary understanding of social stages': moving from deprived rural lifestyles to more affluent and advanced urban cultures (Pigg, 1992: 501). Centrally produced school textbooks serve to propagate cultural homogeneity linguistically, through a process of 'indoctrination', values and cultural signifiers sponsored by the dominant regime. Pigg (1992) argues that such schoolbooks not only 'propagate' and 'legitimate' a theory of social stratification but implicitly ascribe values that locate the Nepali language and culture at the heart of education through socialization. The idea of *bikas* (development) and its representation in the formal curriculum – (by envisioning a move from rural life to urban 'modernity', agriculture to office work and situations of poverty to more sanitized urban settings) – creates an aspirational pressure, not only in terms of social and economic mobility but also by affirming a perceived 'high life' to which everyone should sensibly aspire. The promise of social mobility thus inculcates loyalty to a system that claims to care deeply about its people and at the same time negates entirely any critical debate about social inequality, stratification, deprivation and social exclusion, which are seen as culturally predetermined and hence almost inevitable (Bista, 1991). Even following the Panchayat system, no serious efforts were made to correct the biasing and exclusionary nature of education (except for removing references in school textbooks to the previous regime) in the process of creating a single national identity.

Post-Conflict Identity Crisis

The post-accord political transition saw an explosion in demand for more equitable social and political representation from various castes and ethnic and political groups. As Pandey (2010: 40) argues, 'the sudden onslaught of the Maoist rebellion in 1996 contributed directly to a series of upheavals leading many Nepalese to redefine the structures of common difference and to a fracturing of national identity'. The 21-day Madhes uprising in January–February 2007 radicalized the agenda to establish a new ethnic and regional autonomy, forcing the transitional government to concede to the demand of federalism and ethnic-based representation in the elections of the Constituent Assembly (CA). This agreement enabled the United Democratic Madhesi Front to win eighty-two seats in the CA, thereby emerging as the third largest party with a crucial role in the formation of coalition governments during the transition. Their political dominance lies in the Tarai, southern plains of Nepal, populated by Madhesi (though some ethnic groups within this category refuse to be labelled as Madhesi) and Tharu ethnic groups, most of whom speak Maithali, Bhojpuri, Awadhi, Tharu or Hindi as their mother tongue. However, Hindi, one of the official languages of India and dominant language in its northern states, is the *lingua franca* in the Tarai and the front has demanded it should be the official national language of the Tarai. This issue has become contentious and occasionally triggers violence on the grounds of imposed nationalism.[2]

---

[2] Parmanand Jha, vice president of Nepal (2008–15), who represented Madhesi ethnic groups, took the oath of office in Hindi on 23 July 2008. This incident sparked civil protest followed by a legal battle in the Supreme Court that declared Jha's oath null and void, subsequently suspending him from the post. He was reinstated after he took the oath of the office a second time on 7 February 2010 in Nepali and Maithali, his mother tongue.

A major political change in the post-accord democratization of Nepal has been the unsettling of high-caste groups, leading to improved ethno-regional and caste-based representation in the CA and then in legislatives of federal, provincial and local government bodies. However, such change is intertwined with the issue of national identity, the antecedents of which are problematic and often regarded as untrustworthy among proponents of national integration. Accordingly, the historical formation of Nepali identity has recently become fragmented to the point where the struggle to establish distinct national identities has gained some considerable momentum. The demand of *Ek Madhes Ek Pradesh* (the entire southern plains as one federal Madhes state) by the United Democratic Madhesi Front, who have redefined the identity of people living in the Tarai as distinct from those who 'live outside of it', served to exacerbate 'ethnic division and violence at the grassroots level' (Miklian, 2008: 2). During the first period of the Madhes movement, there were widespread incidents of expulsion of Pahadi people from the Madhes (Haviland, 2007), and the ethnic riots in Kapilvastu (as discussed in Chapter 5) indicate the fragility of interethnic relationships in Madhes that, if triggered by incidents in future, can easily turn into identity-based ethnic violence. For example, a Madhesi youth activist holding a prestigious post in a Tarai-based political party argues that while the state has tried to intercede with indigenous factions and identities, it has made no real attempt to integrate the people of the Tarai, who were left to live and survive in a colonized state within their own nation:

> The notion of Nepali identity was promoted in line with the Pahadi ethnic groups. The Madhesi people were treated as second-class citizens and their languages and culture were oppressed by the state. Pahadi people ridiculed the people who preferred to wear Madhesi cultural dress in the capital. (A male Madhesi youth from Eastern Tarai)

While this perception might hold some truth it does not justify the political misconception that Tarai/Madhes is a homogenous territory in terms of language, culture and identity. The four key indigenous languages in Tarai (Maithili, Bhojpuri, Abadhi and Tharu) and their distinctive cultural identities may not be represented in one linguistic or cultural identity whatever it might be. Education is related to an individual's culture and identity and must therefore be provided in the mother tongue, as 'language is not just a medium but the cultural knowledge' (Interview with a lecturer in Janakpur). A different academic in Janakpur disagrees with the totalizing construction of Madhesi identity to encapsulate the nuances and diversity of the Tarai:

> We are not Madhesi. We are Maithili. Mithila does not exist in the political map but it does in people's mindset living here. We are proud of being Maithili

rather than Nepali. Our language, culture, art etc. were suppressed historically, which we would like to regain through federalism and believe that this would strengthen Nepali nationality. (Maithili-speaking lecturer in Janakpur)

Elsewhere, a youth activist affirmed: 'I am Madhesi first and then a Nepali' (A male youth in Kapilvastu).

This type of sentiment, in which ethnic identity is put before national identity, is not uncommon among those who represent marginalized groups. Similar insights on redefining the process of Nepali identity have been reported by Hachhethu, Kumar and Subedi (2008: 93–4) suggesting that ethnic identity and national identity are not incompatible: people can be 'proud of both'. The notion of pluralistic nationalism, creating a space for indigenous and ethnic identities to flourish, has been viewed suspiciously in relation to national integration and has therefore become an issue of major contention among political parties. The challenges for uniting the country 'socioculturally and emotionally' to prevent disintegration (Lawoti, 2005: 159) and the debate about the modality of federalism were further compounded by the lack of mutual trust among the political parties, along with an emerging regionalization of politics which potentially threatens disintegration. One Nepali scholar argues as follows:

> Federalism on the basis of identities such as ethnicity or language would be a peril rather than promise in a developing a country like Nepal. It may result not only in caste based politics like in Uttar Pradesh and Bihar [India], but more so invite historical accidents if one or the other federal unit decides to secede from the reset of the country. (Pandey, 2010: 51)

This controversial issue dominated debates within academia and also among the political parties before the declaration of the constitution in 2015. However, the political schooling of the Maoists and the Madhes Movement escalated the ideology of regional divisions and ethnic identities, which in turn stirred the ethnic sentiments of young people active in the war and those who were part of the ethnic movement in Madhes. The tensions around the nature of federalism and state restructuring have been constitutionally resolved even though some disagreements and dissatisfaction exist in some political factions. The provision of seven provinces in the federal constitution represents a compromised hybridity of political positions of different political forces and addresses the questions of geographical and ethnic balance in the territorial demarcation only to a limited extent. However, it is too early to gauge the success of federalism as a political project as well as a means to redress grievances of marginalized ethnic communities.

Educational policies have rarely dealt with the issue of identity formation. In the previous School Sector Reform Plan (SSRP), the government set out to provide multilingual education in 7,500 schools by 2015 (MoE, 2009: 26) and the Ministry of Education (MoE) has a policy to support mother-tongue based multilingual education up to grade 3 (MoE, 2016: 26), which may be regarded as an initiative to address the needs of children from non-Nepali-speaking communities, and an effort to nurture their linguistic identity. However, there is a lack of capacity and resources within community schools in terms of qualified teachers and teaching and learning materials to deliver lessons in local languages (MoE, 2016). As parents are increasingly demanding education in a language that is valued in the national and global economic markets rather than in the children's mother tongue, community schools are keener to adopt English as the medium of instruction (Subedi, 2018). The Maoist rebellion and the Madhes Movement have fundamentally altered the social fabric of Nepali society, while formal education and curricula have remained largely the same. Educational debates within and outside the classroom have been slow to redefine the character of national identity in the new sociopolitical context. Thus, in contrast to the historical notion of Nepali identity, several fragmented cultures and identities along regional and ethnic lines seem to have emerged, stressing the need for redefining national identity and the role of formal education in this process. Failing to do this urgently can potentially lead to a crisis in the formation of national identity (Figure 6.1).

Implications for Educational Reconstruction

The decade-long armed conflict and the ethnic uprising in Madhes have unsettled the monolithic view of national identity, and new structures of governance and policy formations have now been established under the new federal constitution. Despite the inertia within the strong centralized bureaucracy, the bottom-up pressures for recognition of diversity and devolution of power are growing under federalization. However, debates about conflict-sensitive education policies are somewhat buried in the race for increasing school enrolments and improvement in exam results to show the measure of quality education. Local authorities broadly lack appreciation for education's role in conflict mitigation, post-war reconciliation and peacebuilding, and this is partly because of the delay in delivering the Comprehensive Peace Accord's (CPA)'s promise on truth and reconciliation. Research shows that the Truth and Reconciliation Commissions in post-conflict nations (e.g. Timor-Leste, Peru and Sierra Leone) are persisting

Figure 6.1 A primary school in Sankhuwasabha.

with recommendations for the reconstruction and reform of national education (Paulson, 2006). This creates an opportunity for post-conflict governments to implement representative measures in light of the testimony from victims and perpetrators of violence while also correcting education's role in fuelling violent conflict (Bush and Saltarelli, 2000; Davies, 2005; Novelli and Lopes Cardozo, 2008). In Nepal's case, it is difficult to address the impact of violence on educational stakeholders, especially teachers and young people who rarely have their testimony heard. The victims of violence, including orphans, widows, families of those 'lost' or disappeared and many war survivors, are still awaiting justice. The continued political instability, factionalism within political parties and massive impact of Covid-19 makes the task of envisioning a new education system increasingly onerous and the process of educational reconstruction largely remote.

In a crucial report some twenty years ago, Neupane (2000) noted that, on an average, some 91 per cent of all leadership positions in professional bodies are occupied by high-caste groups (Brahman, Chhetri and Newar constituting 37% of the total population). In contrast, the Dalit (approximately 15% of population), indigenous nationalities (approximately 22% excluding indigenous nationalities dwelling in Tarai) and Madhesi (approximately 32% including Madhesi Dalit and

Tarai indigenous nationalities) have only 0.3, 7 and 11 per cent representation, respectively, in twelve influential sectors, including the executive branch, parliament, judiciary, public administration, security forces, politics and academe (Neupane, 2000). In 2007, an inclusion policy was adopted by the National Civil Service (NCS) to make the system demographically representative by ensuring the participation of women, ethnic communities, Dalits and Madhesis (Shrestha and Paudel, 2019). However, women still represent around 18 per cent of the civil service workforce (Paudel, 2018), and the special and gazette class positions in the civil service are still overwhelmingly monopolized by hill high-caste males and Newars. Table 6.1 shows the distribution of caste/ethnic groups in special and gazetted positions in the NCS:

Young people representing sociopolitically excluded communities lack the 'social capital' (Bourdieu, 1986) needed to participate in key realms of social and political structures. A young graduate from a Tharu ethnic group lamented how, despite obtaining relevant qualifications, he would find it impossible to penetrate the prevailing system of patronage:

> I hold a degree in education and have obtained a teaching license and I am probably the only graduate from my community but it has become impossible to find a job at school. It is so frustrating as I have wasted my time by going to university. Even with a decent university degree, I have had to do the same manual work as others who dropped out of school. Had I been from a privileged social or ethnic background, I would have secured a teaching job so easily. As I do not have political connections and influential social network, I am always ignored by the system. (A Tharu male from Kapilvastu)

Table 6.1 Percentage of Caste/Ethnicity Group Representation in Special and Gazette Class[a]

SN	Caste/Ethnicity	Population (%)	Representation (%)
1.	Brahmans	12.74	72.00
2.	Chhetri	15.80	15.89
3.	Newar Janajati	5.48	7.14
4.	Non-Newar Janajatis	30.83	1.64
5.	Madhesis	12.32	1.17
6.	Dalits	14.99	0.67
7.	Muslims	4.27	0.10
8.	Others	3.57	1.39
Total		100	100

a. Ministry of General Administration: Department of Civil Personnel Records, 2010.
Source: Dong (2016: 125)

This shows that patronage works against social mobility for historically disadvantaged ethnic groups. Hence, for these groups, educational attainment, at least in their perception, does not always offer a meaningful reward. In such a context, as Gramsci (1971: 43) argues 'if our aim is to produce a new stratum of intellectuals ... from a social group which has not traditionally developed the appropriate attitudes, then we have unprecedented difficulties to overcome'.

Accordingly, while the post-conflict scenario in Nepal appears to have a promising way forward through federalism to allow ethnic and indigenous populations to regain their cultural and national identities and further enhance the role of education in the process of achieving long-term peace and social cohesion, such radical political change is less than straightforward, especially in a context of extensive social exclusion. The tense geopolitical situation in Nepal, with a legacy of caste-based ethnic discrimination, threatens the process of determining a new politics for social change and thus any hope of a reshaped and revitalized social and political infrastructure. Educational change also depends on how successfully federalism functions and whether the promises made in the constitution are delivered. As teachers in Kathmandu explained:

> Free basic education should be provided by devolved governments in 'New Nepal' and the curriculum and medium of instruction must be decided in a way that reflects the economic needs of each province. (Focus group discussion with teachers in a public school in Kathmandu)

Here, teachers believe that education should be relevant to local economies – that it should be managed by provincial/local authorities so that it serves the needs of people who represent diverse cultures, histories and identities and live in diverse geographical regions. There is also a real opportunity to address contentious elements in the education system that have created and fuelled conditions of conflict. In a nutshell, decisions about education (e.g. curriculum, teacher recruitment, language of instruction) should be taken sensitively so that education does not reproduce social divisions but creates a conducive environment for peace, community cohesion and social justice.

Moving Forward

It is evident that all that has been done to produce a single 'national identity', through a unified culture, single language and integrated system of politics has, in Nepal's case, clearly not worked. Despite rapid expansion over the past decades and increased access to education throughout the country, Nepal's education system has failed to address persistent 'horizontal inequalities' (Stewart, 2008) and thus nurture social cohesion. The legacy of the armed conflict and Madhes uprisings has also demonstrated that political belief in the value of national identity as a form of cultural assimilation is nothing but a flawed concept. In seeking to impose indiscriminate regime change in the context of an increasingly heterogeneous empirical reality, such centralized policy does little to enhance the prospect of social and political stability. The coexistence of different ethnic identities alongside a unified concept of Nepali identity is not without opposition, for this paradoxical scenario highlights the extent of the crisis of identity as Nepal has transitioned to a new era of stability, development and prosperity. It further poses critical questions around how Nepal's education system responds to the political and economic vision within the federalized governance structures: What does the claim for ethnic identity within the context of local autonomy serve to produce? How would the ethnic make-up of individual, local and provincial governments ensure inclusion and begin to address widespread poverty? How is the process of national integration to be addressed and national unity promoted? Finally, how is the idea of national identity and integration embedded within formal education?

These questions have complex and potentially controversial answers. Recognition of ethnic identity can revitalize the self-esteem of ethnically marginalized groups and further encourage proactivity within provinces. However, it needs to be realized that ethnic liberation is only a means and not the ultimate goal. So, while improved freedom can pave the way for more inclusive democracy and equitable economic growth, it remains the case that politicians and ordinary people have a major challenge to avoid potential tensions on matters of ethnic and cultural identity within their provinces and local authorities, especially because many of the local constituencies are ethnically heterogenous. Education policymaking, in this sense, will inevitably become a process of intense negotiation and compromise. In this situation, rather than being nostalgic (some might say obstinate) about traditional notions of national identity, new political realities need to be embraced to reconstruct and redefine the national identity in the emerging cosmopolitan landscape. As we are reminded in terms of citizenship theory, education and practice (Osler and Starkey, 2005), matters of identity and citizenship constitute more than a legal status. They are a form of social practice and so confer a sense of belonging that is respectful of difference and diversity, as well as a more equitable distribution of power and resources. Indeed, these are likely to be the key determinants of national integration rather than traditional notions, symbols and signifiers such as 'brave Nepali', 'land of Buddha', 'country with Mount Everest' or Nepal's 'natural beauty'.

Hence, the main issue here is not the state's dismissal of indigenous identities in a bid to homogenize national characteristics; rather, it is the systematic exclusion of various groups and their participation in crucial meaningful activities involving politics, bureaucracy and the institutions of national security on the basis of caste, gender and ethnicity. The examples of two distinctive responses to the two hawkers in Kathmandu cited at the beginning of this chapter are not merely derogatory and divisive but perhaps further symbolic of the hierarchical sociopolitical realities of the two distinct ethnic cultures. Hence, the present crisis of identity is not limited simply to the quest for victory over prevailing Pahadi hegemony. It is more a struggle for an inclusive democracy and just society, one that provides more equitable opportunities for diverse ethnicities, castes, gender relations and indigenous nationalities. The very concept of national identity is hence defined within the realm and parameters of social justice and not in the web of political myth-making, the volatility and vagaries of which can often overlook fundamental problems in people's lives. This is the reality of peacebuilding, citizenship and contemporary educational reform in Nepal.

Yet, the scale of the task is considerable as much of the regional politics is fast shrinking back to the old, centralized and corrupt culture rather than capitalizing on and institutionalizing the opportunities created by recent political achievements. It is important to recognize also that evidence from international contexts concerning the presumed benefits of multilingual education cannot be viewed as a panacea for 'tensions and contradictions in translating official multilingual policy into actual classroom linguistic practice' (Hornberger and Vaish, 2009: 309). In the present context of globalization where the English medium predominates, the prospect of nurturing indigenous ethnic identities through the mother tongue has become a much less attractive proposition for parents (Banda, 2000). Nevertheless, it is important to escape the hegemonic grip of any foreign language, whether it be English or Nepali, in order to seek to enable the effective learning of all children regardless of background. Drawing on her extensive research in Africa, Brock-Utne (2012: 787) concludes as follows: 'Our greatest challenge as educators working in Africa is ... the common belief among many lay people that the best way to learn a foreign language is to have the language as a medium of instruction. This is not true, not in a situation where you hardly ever hear the language outside of formal schooling.'

This issue is of primary importance and requires extensive debate among politicians, policymakers and practitioners who have a colossal task of restructuring the education system under the new constitutional provision. While only radical change can address such issues as those detailed throughout this chapter, the scale of educational reform would inevitably pose substantial technical challenges, including managing the transformation of teacher education programmes, improving the autonomy of federal states and undertaking the task of extensive curricular reforms. In actuality, this is likely to happen only through the political will for positive social transformation and hence the resolution to develop conflict-sensitive educational reforms. Although the decade-long armed conflict has had a devastating impact on teachers, parents and children in Nepal (Chapters 4 and 5), it has also offered enormous opportunities, especially for meaningful reconstruction of the education system. Most importantly, the emerging new education system under federalism has provided ample opportunity to incorporate notions of inclusion and diversity (plural national and ethnic identities) within the concept of a 'new Nepal'. These are the real aspirations generated by the recent 'People's War' and its subsequent movements during the peacebuilding process; whether they will be realized remains to be seen.

7

Education for Peace and Development

In this chapter, I attempt to synthesize discussions in earlier chapters to specifically highlight the peacebuilding role of education in post-conflict Nepal. The arguments will draw on concepts of peace and social justice to elaborate on how to address the grievances of diverse disenfranchised communities and reduce deeply rooted conflict drivers both within and outside the education system. In this process, I begin with a brief overview of relevant theoretical concepts and frameworks that have emerged in the growing field of education and conflict and then critically explore possibilities for educational reforms in the context of Nepal, drawing upon these global theoretical and conceptual debates.

Locating Education in Debates about Social Transformation

The idea that education can serve peace and social transformation stems from education's potential to address root causes of sociopolitical tensions and violent conflicts as well as to provide necessary knowledge and skills to deal with potential differences in a non-adversarial manner. Firstly, a well-established argument around the role of education in conflict mitigation emanates from the influential works on human capital theory – that education provides economic benefits to individuals and societies through employment skills, innovations and entrepreneurship (Becker, 1975; Psacharopoulos and Patrinos, 2018; Schultz, 1961). The human capital theory and the evidence on high rates of returns to investment in education suggest that increased economic outcomes through education increase opportunity costs for individuals to participate in armed conflicts. Hence, access to universal quality education is a policy prescription for peace and stability (Rappleye, 2011).

Another argument around education for peace is concerned with the role of education, when it is designed and delivered sensitively, in promoting human rights, gender equality and civil liberties. Education also improves people's health outcomes, and equitable access to learning can reduce horizontal inequalities across gender, castes and ethnicities (Stewart, 2008) and enhances individual capabilities to achieve what they value in their lives (Sen, 1999).

Thirdly, since the 1990s, there has been a growing resistance to externally driven development models and epistemological paradigms that undermine and colonize indigenous knowledge and cultural ways of life. Here, the benevolent or altruistic view of development is questioned and it is rather viewed as a tool to promote Western hegemony (Escobar, 1995), while educational provisions underpinning the Western logic of development are perceived to be repressive of local, cultural and religious values and therefore rejected (Peters, 2014). As Shiva (1997) argues, 'reductionist and universalizing tendencies' of modern science that development hinges on are a source of violence to women and nature. The state is becoming weak amidst dominance of neoliberal capitalism and homogenizing technological expansion, and is failing to embody civil society voices and protect the poor and the weak and the oppressed. As a result, 'the assertion of cultures, ethnicity, nationalities, pluralism with a vengeance' is growing (Kothari, 1997: 149). The rejection of neoliberal development paradigms is the central goal of many social movements in conflict-affected contexts, where activists and masses are engaged in new methods of learning and peacebuilding (Novelli et al., 2021).

Finally, Brazilian educator, Paulo Freire, provides a powerful philosophy and method of education through which it can serve for critical consciousness, a process called 'conscientization', rupturing the domesticating tendency of the 'banking model' of education that treats learners as passive recipients of codified knowledge chosen by those who control power in society (Freire, 1974, 2014; Magee and Pherali, 2019). The critique of the 'reproductive nature' of education (Bourdieu, 1984) points out that education is complicit in perpetuating unjust political and economic relationships, fuelling the causes of tensions and violent conflicts, whereas critical education enables learners to take control of their learning and exercise their agency to redress inequalities. Political education campaigns during the Maoist movement and Madhes uprising in Nepal, often termed 'indoctrination' by liberal proponents, provided the movement participants with knowledge and tools to critique and overcome injustices in education and society through resistance. This process can be argued as a struggle for peace with justice. From a social justice perspective, education for critical consciousness serves as a vehicle for grassroots empowerment and political activism and builds strong foundations for participatory democracy, sustainable development, capacity for conflict resolution and social transformation.

The Peace Theory and Education

The UN approach to peacebuilding has historically been problematic as it emphasizes peace as the absence of violence, labelled 'negative peace' decades ago by Johan Galtung as a social condition characterized by 'the absence of violence or war', whereas 'positive peace' is characterized by absence of structural violence and 'integration of human society' (Galtung, 1964: 2). Galtung's theoretical analysis of peace suggests that the prevalence of structural violence is the biggest threat to 'positive peace', so he urges that it is important to understand violence in the structure of society that predicates direct or personal violence carried out by an actor. For example, in order to understand the reasons behind a higher level of participation of untouchable castes and indigenous ethnic groups in the 'People's War' in Nepal, it is crucial to understand the social structures of the caste system and monopoly of the hill high-caste groups in social and political domains. The structural violence caused by the state (by neglecting unjust socio-economic conditions) and social structures (e.g. discriminatory cultural practices, unequal access to resources, unequal political participation, varied access to cultural capital and caste-based and gender hierarchies) systematically discriminate against these marginalized groups, making it difficult to gain upward social mobility. As a result, this frustration may be manifested through resistance and violence. This understanding of violence calls for an extended definition of peace, where peace is not merely the absence of direct violence but also the absence of structural violence (Grewal, 2003). Figure 7.1 illustrates Galtung's (1969, 1971) typology of conflict and peace.

The above conceptual model of peace implicitly speaks to what education can do to promote positive peace. Absence of direct violence is a starting point for peacebuilding rather than the end point. Education systems are situated within the social and political culture of a society and can harbour structural inequalities within the system. Schools are 'dialectically interwoven so that economic power and control is interconnected with cultural power and control' (Apple, 2004: 61). He elaborates that

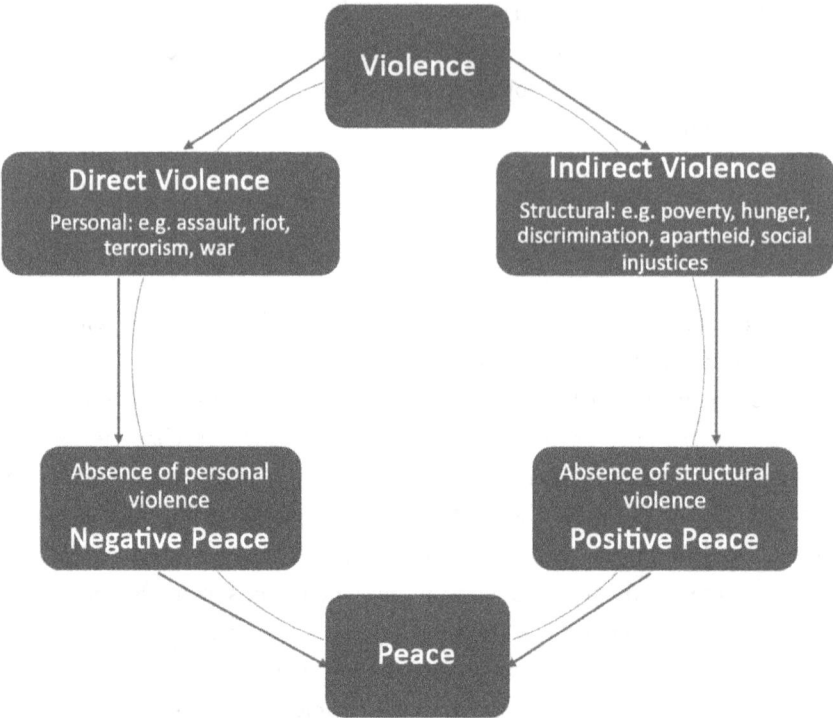

Figure 7.1 The extended concepts of violence and peace.
Source: Galtung (1969: 183).

> schools are 'caught up' in a nexus of other institutions – political, economic and cultural – that are basically unequal. That is, schools exist through their relations to other more powerful institutions, institutions that are combined in such a way as to generate structural inequalities of power and access to resources. (Apple, 2004: 61)

For Apple, inequalities along economic, political and cultural lines are partly reproduced and preserved by schools through their 'curricular, pedagogical and evaluative activities' (Apple, 2004: 61). As a result, formal education contributes to the reproduction of social divisions and existing economic disparities through disproportionate educational achievement across different groups. This process becomes even more problematic in contexts of ethnically divided societies such as Nepal where privileged caste groups have historically monopolized the purpose, processes and goals of education. To support peacebuilding, education systems must prioritize equity, inclusion and diversity in policies and practice so that the outcomes serve 'positive peace'.

Peacebuilding through education involves the ways education systems promote political, social and economic transformations. Since the term 'peacebuilding' was introduced by the UN Secretary General in *An Agenda for Peace*, the UN peacebuilding approach has focused on prevention or management of conflict rather than social transformation (UN, 1992). The earlier UN report rendered 'peacebuilding' as 'preventative diplomacy' whose aim was to 'identify and support structures which will tend to strengthen and solidify peace in order to avoid a relapse into conflict' (UN, 1992: 5). Since the establishment of the Peacebuilding Commission, the Peacebuilding Support Office and the Peacebuilding Fund (PBF) in 2006, peacebuilding has become a key element in the UN agenda that aims to utilize coordinated interventions of the UN as well as the international community in various domains in conflict-affected countries. The PBF received US$ 360 million to support more than 150 projects in eighteen countries which primarily focus on preventative measures such as security sector reform, disarmament, demobilization and reintegration or post-conflict national reconciliation, good governance, rehabilitation of ex-combatants and youth employment programmes (UN, 2010a). These areas of intervention broadly reflect the goal of stabilization or pacification, rather than addressing structural causes around inequalities and injustices that fuel violent conflicts. The UN Secretary-General's Policy Committee redefined 'peacebuilding' in May 2007 to incorporate the goal of social transformation, albeit implicitly, in the UN peace architecture:

> Peacebuilding involves a range of measures targeted to reduce the risk of lapsing or relapsing into conflict by strengthening national capacities at all levels for conflict management, and to lay the foundations for sustainable peace and development. Peacebuilding strategies must be coherent and tailored to the specific needs of the country concerned, based on national ownership, and should comprise a carefully prioritized, sequenced, and therefore relatively narrow set of activities aimed at achieving the above objectives. (UN, 2010a: 5)

The UN approach to peacebuilding is largely predicated on the liberal model of peacebuilding which has been widely criticized as 'top-down, formulaic and ethnocentric' (Haider, 2014: 95). Liberal peacebuilding assumes that

> the promotion of a liberal democracy and market-oriented economy in post-conflict countries will create the conditions for lasting peace. Democratization, under this model, is considered essential for creating the space for non-violent conflict management and resolution, and market economics is seen as the best method of promoting economic growth. (Haider, 2014: 95)

Liberal peacebuilding is based on the notion that violent conflicts are 'internal problems that require external solutions to drive peace' by pressurizing national actors to follow the liberal orthodoxy (Goodhand and Walton, 2009: 306; Paris, 2004). Those who refuse to follow this model of conflict transformation are labelled 'spoilers' (Newman and Richmond, 2006). The emphasis is on stability and illiberal forms of rule, paradoxically linked with the basic tenet of liberalism which gives primacy to individualism rather than collective good (Goodhand and Walton, 2009: 306). Liberalism assumes that individuals are rational decision-makers – and that, by making such choices, they are more likely to choose to contribute to society in ways most suited to their abilities. Hence, liberal peacebuilding imposes a particular type of political and economic ideology that denies collective response to the problems of inequalities and social exclusion. The liberal peacebuilding model fails to address identity-based interethnic tensions and distrust between different actors of violent conflict. Political and economic liberalization exacerbates the unequal power relations between the privileged and historically excluded groups by promoting market-based policies, consequently reducing much needed investments in schools, local enterprises and health systems in most deprived areas. Such approaches to development are likely to intensify inequalities and marginalization of the poor.

Given that educational reforms in post-war societies are driven by 'liberal peacebuilding' goals, much of the educational reconstruction fails to transform the system into one that supports sustainable peacebuilding (Novelli and Higgins, 2017). This is exactly the problem Nepal faces today, and the task of educational rebuilding in line with new transformative visions, as set out by the federal constitution, is prevented by the same old monolithic cultural hegemony that engendered conflict drivers.

However, transformative peacebuilding theories emphasize the importance of change on multiple levels and tracks, with the ultimate goal of 'increasing justice, reducing violence, and restoring broken relationships' (Lederach, 1995: 23). At the heart of this approach is reconciliation, revealing truth, transitional justice and systemic change in power relationships. The role of external peacebuilders is limited to supporting internal actors in their peace efforts. Their engagement should prioritize the long-term vision of conflict transformation and must not exacerbate the fragility of peace negotiations. A transformative approach to peacebuilding involves negotiations and resolution of disagreements at international, regional, national and local levels to address the short-term goals of justice and reconciliation while the long-term visions of structural reforms are set in motion. Reopening schools, reinstating teachers, provision of school meals and providing security to communities might be crucial to provide a sense of normality in the immediate term. Transformative reforms such as the following could begin fairly swiftly: curriculum reforms to improve inclusion; teacher recruitment, continuing professional development and redeployment; introduction of new education policies that address historical grievances of certain communities; establishing new schools in areas where access to education has been historically neglected; and provision of scholarships for girls, the poor and children with disabilities. Peacebuilding should be concerned with the process of transforming negative relations into positive, behavioural, attitudinal and structural change (Lederach, 1995), in which education can serve both as a domain of change and a vehicle for social transformation.

Promoting Peace Within and through Education

Despite facing attacks from both Maoists and security forces, schools and the education community displayed enormous resilience during the armed conflict. Schools and non-governmental organizations created pressures and relentlessly called upon conflicting parties to treat schools as zones of peace (SZOP); to respect the rights of children to attend schools and to refrain from using children in conflict. The SZOP campaign was endorsed by the state and international community and created moral as well as legal pressures on the warring parties to keep their activities outside the educational institutions. The SZOP formed part of the UNICEF country programme and its peacebuilding framework 'to promote a culture of peace, tolerance and respect for different ethnic groups, opinions and values, as well as a culture of civic responsibility among children and young people' (UNICEF, 2010b: 1). The overarching goals of the SZOP were to:

- reduce school closures as a result of political activities;
- reduce presence of armed forces in and around schools;
- reduce misuse of school grounds and buildings;
- support political parties to honour commitments with regards to school functioning;
- improve governance by SMC/PTA systems and local ownership of schools;
- improve school functioning and resolution of internal conflicts; and increase inclusiveness at the school level. (UNICEF, 2010b: 2)

Even though the impact of the SZOP campaign on maintenance of peace within school zones has not been properly researched and many of the claims about the programme's success are reported by the agencies and actors who were directly involved in designing and delivering it, the programme has been widely applauded by the education community in Nepal and globally, and several educational initiatives led by UNICEF in other conflict-affected countries have been inspired by the methodology of SZOP (Vaux, 2011). There is, however, danger in generalizing the SZOP initiative without contextualizing its success in the unique nature of Nepal's Maoist rebellion.

A striking feature of Nepal's armed conflict was that both conflicting parties were seeking international support for their armed campaign. The state was in an advantageous position after the 9/11 Al-Qaida attack on the United States. The Western nations led by the United States formed a coalition against global terrorism and the Maoists were also labelled 'terrorists' by the United States. This helped the state to gain international financial support to fight the insurgency. However, the Maoists were firmly asserting their position as a political movement that aimed to overthrow the feudal monarchy and liberate the masses from the centuries-old social, political and economic oppression. Hence, it was vital for them to gain international recognition as a political struggle. Thus, Shah (2004: 224) quoted an editorial in the *Times of India* that criticized the then US secretary of state Colin Powell for offering military support to the Nepal government: 'Unlike the Taliban and many outfits inspired by Osama bin Laden, the Maoists of Nepal, for all their violence, represent a progressive protest movement which is neither anti-modern nor exclusivist in ethnic and religious terms.' This indicates that in contexts where militant groups are at war against liberal ideology, which the Western countries and international organizations represent, such as in the case of Afghanistan where girls are denied education or Nigeria where Boko Haram militants have waged a war against the Western model of education, SZOP campaigns might make little or no impact. However, in Nepal, civil society and schools launched effective campaigns against violence against children and schools.

Teachers in some schools claimed that schools had made a significant contribution to building peace during the emergency. They reported that schools collaborated with NGOs and community-based organizations to engage with both security forces and Maoists to respect children's rights to safety and education. A teacher from Sankhuwasabha noted:

> The education sector has played a major role in reducing the conflict. In the context of our district, the education sector including schools, teachers, guardians, students and their respective organizations raised their voice to keep schools away from tensions and declared educational sites as the peace zones even during the frightening times between 2058 [2001] to 2063 [2006] ... they didn't hesitate to make appeals and hold sit-ins, rallies. And students' organizations too were involved in demanding that education sector not be ruined. In many places there were sporadic strikes and in some places the schools might have remained closed for a long time, but it did not exceed more than seven or ten days. When they were closed for a few days, the guardians were involved in keeping both Maoists who were aiming to intensify the conflict, and army who were trying to suppress it, in balance. Hence, those involved in the education sector played a role in warning both sides. (A teacher from a public school in Sankhuwasabha)

Even though the education community lived in fear, they did not always remain docile or passive about the forced closure of schools. Particularly, children were organizing in local child clubs, peace rallies and 'raising awareness of peace, promoting the social values needed for peace, strengthening (and in some cases rebuilding) social relationships, and in some contexts demonstrating peaceful ways of resolving conflicts with families, schools and communities' (Feinstein, Giertsen and O'Kane, 2010: 56). These activities were significant in promoting peace not only within educational spheres but also making contributions to wider communities that were struggling for peace during the armed conflict. Child clubs became crucial organizing spaces for peace where young people were:

- promoting understanding and respect for 'Children as Zones of Peace' and 'Schools as Zones of Peace' – including negotiations with Maoist and government army officials not to interrupt children's lives or education;
- advocating for peace through the organization of peace campaigns, rallies and workshops at local, district and national levels;
- raising their voice against violations of children's rights, including early marriage, discrimination, abuse and violence;
- engaging in the constitutional election process through the development of a twelve-point Declaration by children's representatives from across the country which has been presented to concerned political parties and agencies. (Feinstein, Giertsen and O'Kane, 2010: 56)

The above campaign agendas represent the strength of civil society spaces that young people in Nepal were creating when the state and Maoists were engaged in conflict and schools and communities were deprived of their right to live peacefully. Some teachers were also actively involved in local level negotiations with conflict actors to keep their schools safe from violence. A former school head teacher in Sankhuwasabha reported:

> When I was in a school in Bahrabise, there was a fight between the two sides. The army threw bombs inside the school ground and the Maoists laid mines inside the school premises. They kept signposts with 'Danger' printed on them. Even during such times of risks, we managed to hold meetings with both the sides and urged them to remove explosives and spare school premises from becoming a battle ground. Finally, they listened to us and removed the landmines. (Former school head teacher from Sankhuwasabha)

Some teachers in the Eastern districts reported that the SZOP campaign and schools' efforts achieved some positive outcomes in relation to maintaining peace within the educational settings. For example, it was reported that as a response to the pressure created through these campaigns, 'political armed groups and police have moved camps out of schools; armed groups are cautious and do not enter schools with arms as they have done in the past; many schools have been successful in reducing inappropriate use of school property for [private] agricultural activities, animal slaughter, weddings and political programs' (UNICEF, 2010b: 2). Teachers in Doti and Rolpa reported that the SZOP campaign was predominantly urban-based and did not reach remote districts, most of which were controlled by the Maoists. Many participants lamented that the state of fear was so intense that not everyone would feel confident to challenge armed actors who were engaged in a war. This was also difficult because of the Maoist narrative of 'people's war' that had no boundaries in terms of mobilization and political action: teachers and students were also required to play their part in the resistance, and schools were deemed an inseparable constituency of the rebellion.

As the private schools were disproportionately targeted for violent attacks by the Maoists (Caddell, 2006), the umbrella associations of these schools also campaigned for peace. However, a teacher from a private school in Kathmandu mentioned that 'even though school owners or principals did engage in dialogue with the political leaders and the Ministry of Education, requesting them to make schools conflict-free zones, the outcome was not that significant'. He further revealed that it was due to 'fear' that schools were unable to create pressure and there were no consequences for the conflicting parties for their violent actions. He lamented that 'when the struggle was at its peak, everything was moving out of control, so speaking against the movement meant that you became a target' (A teacher from a private school in Kathmandu).

Matsumoto (2011) argues that education, as an independent institution, cannot be assigned the full responsibility to build peace while existing socio-economic conditions fuel inequalities and injustices. The analysis of post-conflict peacebuilding in Sierra Leone demonstrates that educational reforms tend to continue more of the same practice as that of pre-conflict times, potentially undermining the nexus between education and conflict (Matsumoto, 2011; Novelli and Higgins, 2017). Societal problems such as cultural and ethnic dominance, discrimination against women, monopoly of state power by certain privileged groups, regional and ethnic exclusion and unequal distribution of land and resources serve as the key barriers to sustainable peace. Thus, Novelli and Higgins (2017: 42) argue that in Sierra Leone

> the international community has contributed to the restoration to power of the old order – albeit in a slightly more democratic form – and side-stepped the need for more widespread social transformation. This reflects a narrow conceptualization of peacebuilding that appears dominant within international policy debates on post-conflict intervention, which reduces the term to a mode of stabilization and avoids notions of transformation. As a result of the prioritization of security, democracy and markets, education appears as a marginal component in the overall picture of reconstruction, which is lamentable as education appears to be both at the heart of the core problems of SL society and one of its potential solutions.

Education is seen as the 'fourth pillar' of 'humanitarian response' during emergencies and can play a crucial role in protecting children from violence (Nicolai and Triplehorn, 2003), providing a sense of stability even during violent conflict. Given the positive role of education in minimizing ethnic and racial tensions through equity and inclusion in access (Bush and Saltarelli, 2000), the educational response to conflict mitigation should not wait until the war ends. These inclusive educational approaches can help communities 'to develop inclusive ethos' and enhance their agency to deal with the effects of ongoing violence by providing 'knowledge and means to defend their interests as well as revitalizing and strengthening their own cultures' (Bush and Saltarelli, 2000: 18).

Initiatives around Peace Education and Curricular Reforms

In the aftermath of the conflict, there have been some notable attempts to embed elements of peace education in Nepal's school curricula. Most of these initiatives were supported by international development agencies as part of their aim to overcome the historical problem of cultural assimilation through education (Smith, 2015). Following the Comprehensive Peace Accord (CPA) that made commitments to end ethnic, caste-based, regional and gender-related injustices (CPA, 2006), new opportunities emerged for curricular reforms to support sustainable peace. In 2007, the Government of Nepal formulated a new national curriculum framework (NCF) that would promote conflict-sensitive education by recognizing cultural, regional and religious diversity; promoting gender equality and human rights; and commitment to peace and justice (MoE, 2007). The NCF recognized the importance of equality and justice and incorporated goals around peace, conflict resolution and multiculturalism, which included to:

- Help prepare citizens with good conduct and morals for a healthy social and collective lifestyle by promoting supreme human values inherent in each individual, national culture and dignity, social values, beliefs and experience.
- Consolidate social integrity through socializing individuals.
- Be insightful to social equality and justice and develop conduct accordingly to help create inclusive society.
- Foster the feelings of peace, friendship, goodwill, tolerance and fraternity in local, national and international context and adopt one's conduct accordingly; and prepare citizens capable enough to resolve any kind of conflict.
- Prepare citizens respectful to nation, nationality, democracy, judicious, creative, self-honored, respecting others and feel proud of being Nepali.
- Help prepare citizens committed to conserve and promote Nepali art, aesthetic values, ideals and other specialties. (MoE, 2007: 31–2)

Dhungana (2021: 11) notes that this new curricular framework 'opened the scope to revisit the monocultural education system which was based on the belief that the cultural diversity is a major risk to Nepalese unity, integrity, and sovereignty'. In line with these goals, the Curriculum Development Centre of the MoE collaborated with Save the Children, UNESCO and UNICEF to integrate Peace, Human Rights and Civic Education (PHRCE) into the social studies curriculum. The aim was to 'create a culture of peace and an understanding of human rights and civic literacy' in the education system to:

- prepare students with the skills, attitudes, values, and knowledge necessary to understand and assert their rights within the framework of the rule of law;

- develop the values of tolerance and commitment to peace and justice; and
- build critical thinking, problem solving and conflict resolution skills to function as citizens in a post conflict environment'. (Smith, 2015: 7)

Dhungana (2021) provides an extensive analysis of the inclusion of PHRCE in the social studies curriculum in school education. As a development practitioner who had been involved in this multi-stakeholder educational initiative, he provides insights into the process and scale of success in embedding PHRCE in the national curriculum. After the completion of the review and reform process, he highlights that 15 per cent of the content in social studies for grades 6–10 is relevant to promoting multicultural education, including for peace. Similarly, more than half of the learning objectives in grades 6–8 and 20 per cent in grades 4–5 cover values of peace, human rights and multicultural education (Dhungana, 2021). The goals of peace with justice have now been enshrined in the Constitution of Nepal 2015 that guarantees the rights of children to learn in their mother tongue and develop their cultural identity with dignity through education. Nevertheless, effective implementation of policies and pedagogical transformation through effective teacher professional development is a real challenge to achieve the goals of these curricular revisions. As Dhungana (2021: 18) concludes:

> Such redressal process is effective when the macro-education policies provide necessary space to initiate new education initiatives, and the multiple stakeholders with relevant mandate and competencies are engaged for a sustained period, and teachers and stakeholders work together nurturing the value of 'celebrating diversity' through education.

Bajaj and Hantzopoulos (2016) note that peace education is also a field of practice in which educators and learners are engaged in developing tools to dismantle all forms of violence as well as to create structures and mechanisms to build and sustain a just and equitable peace. The curricular revisions in post-war Nepal evidence a significant achievement around incorporation of new peace dimensions that speak to the demands of cultural minorities that have been suppressed by the monolithic version of education in the past. However, the outcomes of peace education rely on 'knowledge about requirements of, the obstacles to, and possibilities for achieving and maintaining peace; training in skills for interpreting the knowledge; and the development of reflective and participatory capacities for applying the knowledge to overcome problems and achieve possibilities' (Reardon, 2000: 399). Hence, peace education programmes would work when the curricular reforms including peace education dimensions are accompanied by radical shifts in educational structures, pedagogical practices and relationships between educators and learners (Bajaj, 2019: 66). In this process, teachers have an enormous responsibility of critical self-reflection to challenge their own beliefs and ideological positions. For example, the teaching workforce in Nepal has been historically dominated by hill high-caste males who have been part of the assimilationist cultural hegemony and monolithic national ideology (Pherali, 2011). To rupture this deeply rooted teacher psychology and enable them to celebrate pluriversality in educational practice, a more comprehensive policy drive and structural reforms within the system may be necessary.

Another issue related to the peace education initiative in Nepal is concerned with the nature of education policymaking. As Nepal is reliant on aid, educational reforms are often driven by international actors who draw on global frameworks of education and peacebuilding (Bhatta, 2011), which do not always accord with local practices and political economy of education (Pherali, Smith and Vaux, 2011). It is often the case that such a reform process is top-down, centralized and prescriptive – that the intentions of rapidly formulated policies and curricular change are not always understood and owned by those who have the responsibility to implement them. The revisions of curricular contents and educational goals at the macro level do not always translate into practice.

The real challenge in Nepal is to translate the idea of critical peace education into practice. Critical peace educators, as Bajaj (2019: 67) argues, 'pay attention to how unequal social relations and issues of power must inform both peace education and corresponding social action'. She further notes that the key to critical peace education in conflict settings is: how to rupture the potential role of education in social reproduction and transform practices to ones that promote transformation. In this new pedagogy of change, educators should pay 'close attention to local realities and local conceptions of peace, amplifying marginalized voices through community-based research, narratives, oral histories and locally-generated curricula' (Bajaj, 2019: 67).

The Social Justice Approach to Education for Peacebuilding

The 4Rs framework of education and peacebuilding (Novelli, Lopes Cardozo and Smith, 2017, 2019) conceptually distinguishes 'peacebuilding education' from 'peace education'. Paying attention to *redistribution, recognition, representation and reconciliation*, peacebuilding education goes beyond 'educationism', the research and practice in education that primarily concentrates on what happens within the education system. It contends that education is an integral part of the broader political economy constituting the relationships between power (e.g. who decides the curriculum and who sets the policies), resources (e.g. how educational funds are allocated and to which communities, regions and social groups) and markets (e.g. how local, national and global markets influence priorities in education). In this sense, peace orientation in the curriculum and instruction is important to equip learners with knowledge, skills and commitment to a culture of peace but is insufficient to transform the education system that may be inherently exclusionary. In other words, peace education is an important dimension of peacebuilding education. The 4Rs framework speaks assertively for the socially transformative role of education, and reforms in education are aimed at not only redressing unfair educational practices within educational institutions but also transforming economic, political and social conditions that are fundamentally unequal, unjust and discriminate against 'low power' groups in society. Interventions should prioritize equitable access to educational services and resource allocation; participatory approach to educational decision-making; recognition of cultural diversity; and the role of education in reconciliation (Novelli, Lopes Cardozo and Smith, 2017). These reform processes underpin the principles of social justice (Fraser, 2005) to significantly improve educational access and outcomes in education for marginalized communities such as Dalits, Madhesis, girls and indigenous nationalities. Fraser (2005, 73–6) points out that 'parity of participation' is a key element of social justice which, in educational terms, means that education is *available* for free and supported by necessary infrastructure; *accessible* to all including the most marginalized; *acceptable* in terms of its content, cultural appropriateness and fairness; and *adaptable* to meet the needs of children who live in challenging environments (Education Cannot Wait, 2018: 13; Tomaševski, 2001).

The post-1990s people's struggles and political turbulence culminated in the promulgation of a new constitution in 2015, which redefines the Nepali nation to reflect its rich diversity and gives provincial and local governments substantial powers to manage education (Constitution of Nepal, 2015). The constitution in the preliminary states:

> Having multi-ethnic, multi-lingual, multi-religious, multi-cultural characteristics with common aspirations of people living in diverse geographical regions, and being committed to and united by a bond of allegiance to national independence, territorial integrity, national interest and prosperity of Nepal,

Figure 7.2 Mahendra HS School, Sankhuwasabha.

all the Nepali people collectively constitute the nation. (Constitution of Nepal, 2015)

In a broad sense, at the core of the nation is the recognition of what has been historically overlooked in the process of nation-building. The principles of diversity and the pluriverse guide policies and laws as a means to build peace with justice and sustainable prosperity. Education, as a key foundation of nation-building and development, is also required to underpin these important national characteristics.

Redistribution of Education and Limitation of Decentralization

In post-conflict educational reconstruction, local authorities should formulate policies to ensure equitable access to safe and secure educational opportunities and resources for children from Dalit communities, girls, children with disabilities and those who represent children from families in economic hardship. The Ministry of Education needs to adapt its education information system to identify horizontal inequalities across castes, gender, religions and ethnicities (Tiwari, 2010) and invest in education of those who have been historically marginalized. School education funds are largely consumed by teacher salaries, and investment for school improvement and improved learning outcomes is weak, so 'instead of blanket policy of resource distribution like in scholarship and other grants to schools, there should be a bracket approach focusing on targeted groups and their needs to get access in education' (Sharma, Dangal and Pande, 2015: 20).

Although there has been a marked increase in the enrolment of girls in government schools, parents prefer to invest in boys when it comes to paying for private education, which Stash and Hannum (2001: 355–6) term 'rational cost-benefit analysis'. Stash and Hannum (2001: 356) further note:

> If parents feel that their daughters will be unable to capitalize on education in the labor market, they will be more likely to depend on sons for support in old age. When household resources are tight, investments in long-term contributors to the household economy (i.e., sons) are more easily justified than investments in short-term ones (i.e., daughters).

The lack of social priority on girls' education, particularly among poor communities in the Madhes region, means that girls enrolled in government schools have higher dropout rates than boys. This problem further reflects ongoing deficiencies such as lack of female teachers and discriminatory social practices that require daughters to perform household chores at the expense of success in education. However, there has been a consistent drive for educational expansion and school enrolment in recent years. Sharma and Donini (2010: 21) note that education was 'seen as the most important factor in bringing about transformation in Nepali society'. For example, Province 2 has a flagship programme led by the chief minister: *beti padhao, beti bachao* (educate the girls, save the girls). What has been less promising in policies and development efforts is affirmative action and systemic change to redress obstructive structural conditions faced by underprivileged groups. Nevertheless, growing literacy rates, political movements and civil society activism around education have helped these groups to build up their confidence to express their rights and demand increased educational services (Sharma and Donini, 2010).

Since the 1990s, management of Nepal's state schools has been transferred to school-based committees with the view of enhancing participation of stakeholders at local levels. This form of educational governance mainly involves 'the transfer of decision-making authority, responsibility and tasks from higher to lower organizational levels or between organizations' (Hanson, 1998: 112).

McGinn and Welsh (1999: 17) also note that decentralization involves 'shifts in the location of those who govern' and transfer of authority from central locations to those who are on another level, such as local government bodies and schools. The rationale for education decentralization is often argued as being 'to increase both the productivity and efficiency of educational delivery systems, based on a presumption that local actors are better equipped to make appropriate decisions for their local context and better able to hold local actors accountable' (Edwards, 2011: 69). Educational reforms towards decentralization are inspired by external actors and their ideological motivation, which have failed to produce outcomes around equity, quality and inclusion (Carnoy, 1999; Pherali, 2012; Poppema, 2009).

Education decentralization is often driven by the motives of central governments or international agencies and based on the general assumption that the same policy aims and objectives are shared by the stakeholders at community levels (McGinn and Welsh, 1999). It is based on the idea that effective monitoring and local level accountability enhances equity in access and efficiency in the delivery of education. Carney, Bista and Agergaard (2007: 614) argue that 'most decentralization initiatives have struggled to realize their goals' as there is often a lack of understanding about the policy aims and objectives among the local level stakeholders. The independent evaluation group's report on the Community School Support Programme (CSSP) in Nepal has also pointed out the lack of clarity in roles and responsibilities of the SMCs and absence of effective mechanisms for their capacity building (World Bank, 2010). Edwards (2011) uses the terms 'policy disconnect' and 'capture' to problematize the education decentralization process in which the policy aimed at mobilizing parents and communities fails to reach its intended stakeholders, or the authority devolved to the local level is captured by unintended agents who monopolize the policy reforms to work in their favour. There is also a risk of devolution of educational authority being strategically used to provide the false hope of autonomy and reduce the chances of outbreak of violent conflicts (Cronwall and Brock, 2005), while still maintaining control over structural aspects of education (e.g. national curriculum, language of instruction, teacher recruitment policy and assessment, economic processes). This phenomenon further exploits the poorest by making them contribute to the fundamental duty of the state – providing basic education to its citizens (Poppema, 2009).

These manifestations of educational decentralization can be collapsed into three main concerns that often act against the interests of the poorest in society. This discussion is pertinent in Nepal's case because the legacies of educational decentralization are likely to underpin the culture of educational governance within local authorities. Firstly, such policies facilitate cost sharing of the provision of education with local communities that are already under-resourced. Even when local authorities are in charge of education and managing the entire education funding, there is no guarantee that parents would not be expected to cover certain costs of school education. Secondly, decentralization policies promote the culture of privatization, competition and market-driven economy that further marginalize those in the bottom pile of society. Finally, they falsely presume that transfer of school management to the local community can instantly result in school effectiveness and improvement in the quality of education. However, evidence from the political economy analysis of education in Nepal indicates that school-based management is often monopolized by social elites who abuse the authority for their own political and economic benefits (Pherali, Smith and Vaux, 2011). In this sense, social accountability and integrity in school governance are going to be the key issues.

The federal constitution of Nepal has made special provisions to empower Dalits and women through education and proportional representation in the state apparatus. Particularly, with regard to education, Article 40 (Clause 2) states:

> Provisions of free education with scholarships shall be made for Dalit students from the primary to higher level of education as provided for in law. Special provision shall be made in law for Dalits to pursue higher education in technical and professional subjects. (Constitution of Nepal, 2015)

Similarly, Article 38 (Clause 5) states:

> Women shall have the right to obtain special opportunity in education, health, employment and social security, on the basis of positive discrimination. (Constitution of Nepal, 2015)

These are significant provisions in the constitution that reflect the state's commitments to redistributive policies and endeavour to address historical grievances of these social groups. More research is needed to understand how local authorities are making progress in the spirit of the constitutional provisions.

Politics of Identity and Recognition in Education

Nepal's social segregation and the domination of a few hill high-caste groups in key realms of society has been the most fundamental cause of the Maoist insurgency (Kumar, 2003; Pherali, 2011; Shields and Rappleye, 2008a;). More specifically, the three decades of the Panchayat system promoted a national homogenizing project in line with the characteristics of the groups that enjoyed political and social power, which fuelled the grievances of other ethnic groups and indigenous nationalities. In this regard, education was complicit in both cultural assimilation of ethnic and cultural diversity and neglect of those who were struggling to benefit from it because of various structural causes. Consequently, education was contributing to production of discontent and frustration among those whose cultural identities, languages and ways of life were neglected in education policies, medium of instruction and the national curriculum. As discussed in Chapters 3 and 6, education failed to uphold the principle of recognition and became part of the hegemonic process of cultural misrecognition and social neglect.

Since the establishment of a liberal state and expansion of the role of civil societies in Nepal's social development, international development partners have been particularly concerned about the lack of 'social inclusion' in relation to Dalits, women, indigenous and ethnic groups (Bennett, 2005; Jones, 2010: 3; Lawoti, 2005) as part of their commitment to peace and development. Bennett (2005: 8–9) notes:

> Social inclusion requires *a shift from an institutional environment, which gives some individuals and groups more opportunity to realize their agency than others to one where the political system and the rule of law support equal agency for all* [sic].

This idea of 'shift' in enabling 'equal agency for all' is significant for the role of education in peacebuilding in post-conflict Nepal. As the 4Rs framework points out, the education system needs to 'acknowledge and support diverse perspectives, identities, communities and individuals' to provide a sense of justice through an inclusive approach to the language of instruction, celebration of diversity through the school curriculum, recognition of learners' ethnic and religious identity in teaching practices and inclusion of multiple historical narratives, citizenship and civic responsibilities (Novelli, Lopes Cardozo and Smith, 2017). These new practices in education could help mitigate grievances of social groups that have been drawn into conflict and violence through the Maoist ranks (Lawoti, 2005; Leve, 2007). In the last two decades, there have indeed been improvements in social inclusion, especially in the school enrolment of Dalits and girls (Sharma and Donini, 2010). The Maoist movement has significantly ruptured deeply rooted discriminatory social practices and built confidence

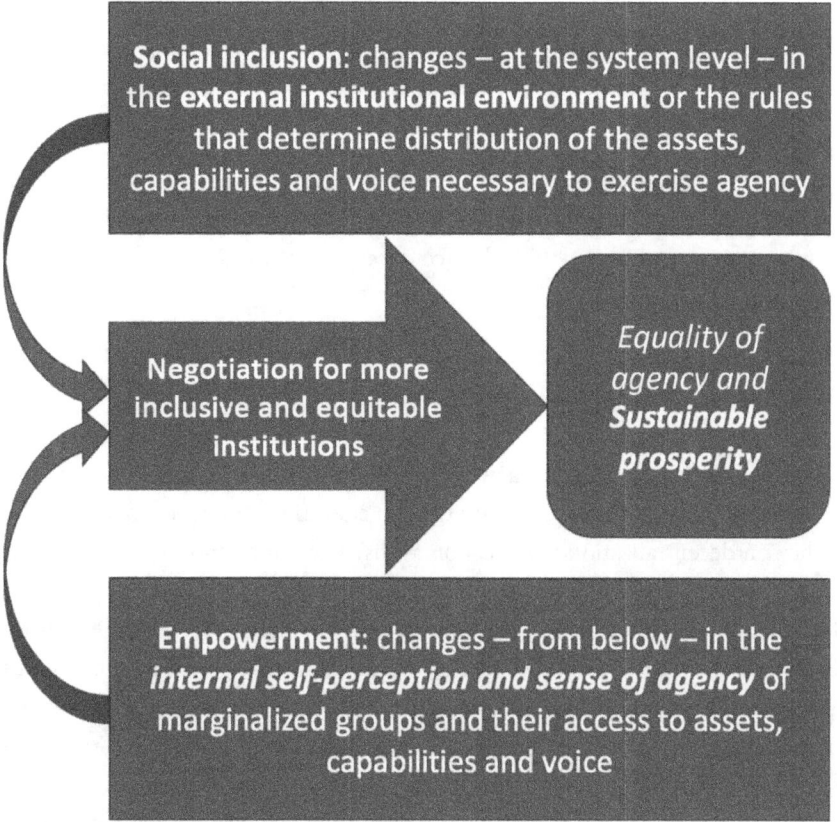

Figure 7.3 The complementary roles of empowerment and social inclusion.
Source: Bennett (2005: 10).

among Dalit communities to resist any maltreatment by upper-caste people. The formation of political 'coalitions' between the revolutionary agenda of the Maoists and the historical grievances of the Dalits brought them together to share their 'common change objectives' (Bennett, 2005: 9) (see Figure 7.3). However, in rural areas, particularly in Madhes, caste-based discrimination is still overt.

Improved recognition such as education in the mother tongue, inclusion of Madhesi, indigenous and diverse ethnic cultures in the curriculum and equitable representation of these communities in the teaching workforce and civil service can help better connect minority communities with the state and enhance their access to economic opportunities and political representation. Article 31 (Clause 5) of the constitution guarantees right to education in the mother tongue:

> Every Nepali community living in Nepal shall have the right to acquire education in its mother tongue up to the secondary level, and the right to open and run schools and educational institutions as provided for by law. (Constitution of Nepal, 2015)

Educational processes that are inclusive of diverse identities can bring divided communities together to develop a collective sense of national identity, empowerment and agency to influence development processes that ameliorate risks of conflict.

Inclusive Representation in Education

The third R in the 4Rs framework highlights the significance of equitable representation of diverse communities in educational decision-making. The policy on decentralization of education as discussed in the previous section was aimed 'to involve guardians, local elected bod(ies) and people in the programme formulation, implementation, monitoring and evaluation' (HMG, 1998: 620). Even during the armed conflict when the schools were engulfed by the 'People's War', transfer of state schools to communities became a popular phenomenon. The education section of the National Planning Commission's Five-Year Plan (1997–2002) also articulated that the educational decentralization policy would 'increase the active local participation in management and operation of education institutes, and improve their capability' (HMG, 1998: 618). However, the processes of educational decentralization in Nepal have been less effective in enabling representation of minority voices in school management committees (Pherali, 2012). School management committees are heavily politicized and serve as sources of power for local leaders to carry out party-based political activities, while the representation of women has been tokenistic rather than inclusive of their voices.

The 'representation' dimension of the 4Rs framework refers to the need for ensuring fair and transparent representation and responsibility for educational decision-making (Novelli, Lopes Cardozo and Smith, 2019). In the policymaking process, local education stakeholders have rarely been represented. Policies are usually formulated in collaboration between international development agencies and political elites, primarily the same hill high-caste civil servants in the Ministry of Education and its various departments (Bhatta, 2011; Regmi, 2021). The outcomes of such processes do not go far in meeting the demands of the grassroots struggles led by ethnic groups and indigenous nationalities. Even though the election of local bodies and devolution of powers provide some hope for inclusive representation of minority communities, the legacies of centralization and long-standing repression of minority cultures and languages make it difficult for many of these policies to produce intended outcomes. For example, schools at the local level lack the necessary autonomy, capacity and motivation to design and implement a local curriculum with education in the mother tongue, given the domination of the national curriculum framework, growing competition from private schools that provide education in English and conventional use of Nepali as the medium of instruction (Subedi, 2018). The lack of diversity in the teaching workforce and inequity in civil service and decision-making positions (Dong, 2016) leads to insufficient prioritization of radical shifts in policy reforms.

The idea that local authorities and communities would be committed to progressive education policies is also problematic. Carney, Bista and Agergaard (2007) note that there is a definitional problem with the construct of 'community', which is characterized by concepts of fellowship, harmony and social cohesion. This notion neglects the community realities where 'inequalities, oppressive social hierarchies and discrimination' are pervasive (Carney, Bista and Agergaard, 2007: 616). Local communities are visibly heterogeneous in their composition and intergroup relations, and their differences are seen in different degrees of influence on educational decision-making. Hence, local autonomy in educational governance, as mandated by the Constitution of Nepal 2015, needs to be cautiously viewed in relation to the needs around structural reforms. Despite the successful state restructuring to a federal system, development processes are heavily dominated by a national and global neoliberal agenda that constantly pressurizes state institutions to reduce public spending on education through increased community ownership of schools and privatization (Carnoy, 1999; Pherali, 2012; Regmi, 2021). More importantly, neoliberalism ignores the welfare and empowerment of marginalized groups (Cuellar-Marchelli, 2003; Geo-Jaja, 2004; Wankhede and Sengupta, 2005). At the local level where strong patronage systems prevail, fair representation of ethnicities, castes and gender and equitable resource allocation require strong commitments by elected leadership and civil society organizations.

Promoting Reconciliation through Education

The two decades of political turmoil involving armed conflict, a tumultuous peace process and Madhes resistance have destabilized conventional ideas underpinning Nepali nationhood. While the old foundational ideas have been ruptured and new relationships between ethnic groups and the state are yet to be practically built up, education has the enormous task of laying out foundations of national reconciliation. In this regard, the education system needs to offer a new discourse of nation-building that resonates with the strong emotions of ethnic, religious and regional identities and feelings of injustice felt by different groups following the conflict, while promoting a sense of representative national identity that expresses loyalty to national independence, territorial integrity and prosperity of the whole nation.

The history of the Maoist rebellion is still an enormously divisive factor amongst Nepalis. The death of over 17,800 people[1] in the armed conflict is still a fresh memory and the victims of violence and families of those who lost their lives harbour deep pain and emotions. Clause 5.2.5 of the CPA states:

> Both sides agree to set up a High-level Truth and Reconciliation Commission as per the mutual consensus in order to probe about those involved in serious violation of human rights and crime against humanity in course of the armed conflict and develop an atmosphere for reconciliation in the society. (GoN, 2006)

Yet, no governments in the last fifteen years have seriously attempted to complete the important task of truth and reconciliation, and it took almost a decade to establish the commission since the signing of the CPA (Jeffery, 2021). The failure of the Truth and Reconciliation Commission (TRC) in Nepal is probably unsurprising owing to the nature of political compromise made between the government and the Maoists to end the conflict. Jeffery (2021: 318) argues that the unstable post-accord 'legislative process, lack of commitment to human rights, and weak respect for the rule of law – has made it nearly impossible for the TRC to make any meaningful contribution to truth, justice, or democracy'. She concludes that TRCs can be manipulated in favour of authoritarian ideals when the political leaderships are not democratic and 'without other measures in place to establish, uphold, and defend democratic values and ensure accountability for human rights violations, the expectation that truth commissions will not only function effectively to uncover the truth and facilitate reconciliation but also contribute to democratization may well be unrealistic' (Jeffery, 2021: 334). Because of the significant delay and perhaps, the loss of hope that the TRC would ever deliver its mandate meaningfully, the victims of armed conflict have

---

[1] As reported by the Ministry of Peace and Reconstruction, Relief and Reconstruction Unit in June 2012 https://reliefweb.int/report/nepal/17800-people-died-during-conflict-period-says-ministry-peace.

been denied justice and no reparation has been provided to those who suffered from the grave violations of the human rights.

Research into truth and reconciliation in other conflict-affected contexts reveals that education is marginally represented in TRCs and peace agreements (Harbom, Högbladh and Wallensteen, 2006). Even though truth commissions are increasingly making reference to the role of education, their focus has been on 'forward looking' dimensions of education, including decontextualized notions of peace education and human rights, rather than engaging in the process of 'backward looking' to remedy systemic problems inherent in the education systems (Paulson and Bellino, 2017). The CPA in Nepal also acknowledges education only in terms of right to education for children by putting an end immediately to occupying educational institutions, abducting teachers and students or establishing barracks within school premises that would disrupt educational activities. Education is less recognized as a domain that requires structural reforms to promote peace and reconciliation. Smith (2010: 14) also argues that education has 'a key role in dealing with the past (truth telling and understanding what happened); the present (addressing current needs, recovery from the legacies of conflict, educational opportunities that have been missed); and the future (contributing to reconciliation and sustainable, peaceful development)'. He points out that education can support post-conflict reconciliation in helping to:

> **Raise awareness.** By disseminating findings of a TRC to the public to garner support as well as including the information in the formal curriculum.
> **Promote understanding.** Education can provide a critical understanding of the history of conflict and current issues that disrupt peace.
> **Contribute to reform.** Given the plethora of evidence around the role of education in hardening inequalities and injustices, reforms within education systems can promote post-conflict reconciliation.
> **Aid social reintegration.** Schools can serve as spaces of social reintegration by bringing communities from across dividing lines together and creating opportunities for dialogue for educational change and more practically, by bringing out-of-school children, orphaned children, former child soldiers and children with disabilities into the education system.
> **Contribute to child protection.** Schools provide a sense of normalcy in the aftermath of conflict and provide important life skills, information about safety from landmines and potential manipulation by armed groups.

Support economic regeneration. Educational investment after the conflict provides a sense of hope for economic benefits through development of employment skills. Support to education can serve as a 'peace dividend' and revive economic activities that may have been adversely affected by the violent conflict. (Smith, 2010: 13)

Despite the above benefits of education in post-conflict reconciliation, Smith (2010) also highlights that there are complex conceptual and epistemological dilemmas about the idea of 'reconciliation', which makes it difficult to implement fully through teaching and learning at schools. The basic contention of 'truth' is concerned with the epistemological positions around 'objectivity' and 'relativity' in establishing the 'truth', which leads to tensions around what should be included in the curriculum and how it should be taught. Reconciliation is also contested as it elicits controversial issues which may involve fundamental disagreements between the political groups that have been involved in conflict. In Nepal, the question of the rationale for an armed rebellion and the colossal loss in terms of human lives, sufferings of thousands of people and destruction of infrastructure is a hugely divisive issue. Teachers, parents and other educational stakeholders have contradictory views and strong emotions about the violent past. These could potentially be addressed through sensitively designed, inclusive and well-supported educational programmes that promote social and psychological healing processes through remembrance and commemoration, debates about forgiveness, expressions of regret, apology and symbolic events, which need to be embedded into the education system and conflict transformation mechanisms of the state (Smith, 2010). The constitution has recognized the right to justice for those who have suffered loss during the conflict:

> The families of martyrs who sacrificed their lives in the people's movements, armed conflicts and revolutions for a democratic progressive change in Nepal, the families of those who were disappeared, persons who fought for democracy, victims of conflict and the displaced, persons who were physically maimed, the wounded and the victims, shall have the right with priority, as provided for by law, to education, health, employment, housing and social security, with justice and appropriate respect. (Constitution of Nepal, 2015, Article 42 Clause 50)

More specifically, Article 39 (Clause 9) specifies the right to special protection for vulnerable children:

> Children who are helpless, orphaned, physically impaired, victims of conflict and vulnerable, shall have the right to special protection and facilities from the State. (Constitution of Nepal, 2015)

Reconciliation through education also requires systemic change within the education system to redress the historical and contemporary economic, political and sociocultural injustices that underpin conflict. These may include provision of scholarships to children from poor and marginalized groups, ensuring adequate supply of textbooks in schools, especially in remote areas, and recruitment of new teachers from underrepresented communities. It is also crucial to examine education policies and practices that are linked with social integration and divisions, and to teach about the legacies of conflict and their relevance to peace and social cohesion at present and in the future (Novelli, Lopes Cardozo and Smith, 2017). Only through rebuilding trust with communities that have not been justly served in the past and mending the ruptured relationships between different identity groups can the education system support post-conflict reconciliation.

In conclusion, the 4Rs framework serves as a useful resource to analyse the interrelationship between education inequalities and conflict (UNICEF, 2016a) and pathways to redress these inequalities, as well as an advocacy tool through which development partners, national governments, civil society organizations as well as school communities can reshape education as a transformative process. It forewarns about the negative social and political outcomes of education unless the provision is deliberately and programmatically designed and delivered with the aim of paving the path to a peaceful future. More importantly, educational reforms in Nepal need to be informed by high-quality political economy analysis of how to implement the 4Rs principles in a situation where hill high castes continue to monopolize power and resources; hegemonic cultural groups dominate discourses about national identity; an elite political class resists representation of marginalized communities in educational decision-making and the terms of reconciliation are hijacked by those who control power. The potential of this analytical framework lies not optimistically at the macro structures of governance which still show resistance to relinquishing their powers, but at the grassroots where people's struggles for equity, inclusion and 'parity of participation' are building bottom-up pressures for peace with social justice. In this sense, local governments are the institutions of new hope for progressive reforms, but they need to be held accountable by local communities, especially by the groups that have been promised equity and justice by the new political system, to prevent them from inheriting the culture of patronage and rent-seeking that was deeply rooted in the centralized governments in the past.

8

Conclusion: Rethinking Education for Peace with Social Justice

Conflict is a major barrier to progress towards Sustainable Developmental Goals (SDGs). The debilitating impact of violence on educational access and quality of learning does not only delay conflict-affected countries in achieving the targets for SDG4 on education but also jeopardizes other goals that depend on educational success. Ensuring opportunities for children to remain at school and engage in learning without the fear of armed groups and security forces is fundamentally crucial. In this regard, the international humanitarian and development agencies, including the UN bodies and civil society organizations, have increasingly prioritized education as a key area of intervention in recent years even though unlike healthcare, food and shelter, education has, in the past, been ignored as a life-saving support during humanitarian crises. However, the increasingly protracted conflicts and humanitarian crises in several parts of the world have warranted a shift in the discourse on education aid, and there is a growing focus on education as a necessary emergency intervention (Nhan-O'Reilly, 2012). This led to the establishment of a global-funding initiative 'Education Cannot Wait' at the World Humanitarian Summit in 2016 aimed at protecting education in emergencies. The total Official Development Assistance (ODA) in the education sector accounted for just under 12 per cent in 2014, which increased to 14 per cent in 2019 (George, Johnson and Lüdemann, 2020). Due to the global refugee crisis posing 'threats' to donor countries, as well as the relentless advocacy of organizations supporting education in humanitarian settings, education aid in emergencies has also been rising. In emergency settings, education's share of humanitarian funding increased from 1 per cent in 2014 to almost 3 per cent in 2019 (George, Johnson and Lüdemann, 2020).

Nevertheless, there are still huge funding gaps in the education sector as well as in crucial support needed for children and young people in emergency situations. Where ODA in education is helpful, both in stable contexts and crisis-affected settings, it largely prioritizes school enrolments and development activities that concentrate on children's access to schooling. Less attention is given to the need for redressing systemic issues in educational systems, even though the growing evidence indicates that education can be complicit in hardening inequalities, social exclusion and cultural repression (King, 2014; Novelli and Higgins, 2017; Pherali, 2019; UNICEF, 2011). The central argument of this book is that increased educational access is vital but it does not alone guarantee education's contributions in redressing grievances of socially and politically marginalized groups, which serve as conflict drivers. The array of conflict-related experiences reported by teachers, education officers and students, and education's role in fuelling grievances of marginalized communities are not just part of mundane history portraying the uncomfortable effects on individuals; these are rather pertinent resources that offer insights and corrective measures to reshape the entire education system to one that is more just and conflict-sensitive.

Systemic Change in Education for Peace

Communities that have been excluded from fair representation in state institutions or abandoned in processes of educational development also suffer from marginalization in economic and social realms of the society. In such environments, people can easily relate to narratives of resistance and tend to organize, sometimes violently, to challenge these oppressive and exclusionary structures. Post-conflict peacebuilding hence requires reconfiguration of these unjust state structures to rebalance distribution of power across different identity groups. Education in this process is both a domain that requires fundamental change in its processes and a vehicle that consolidates, institutionalizes and strengthens the transformative policies aimed at building sustainable peace. In the former, the education system should be reshaped to serve everyone equitably, not only in the sense of its availability but also making it adaptable and acceptable to diverse communities (Tomaševski, 2001). The latter relates to laying foundations for and supporting transformative change – that the policies and practices are aimed at building an inclusive, fair and non-discriminatory society, which may involve curricular diversification to reflect and recognize civic identities, linking education to improving people's livelihoods, promoting peace and social justice through curriculum, pedagogies and school ethos, improving representation and diversity in the teaching workforce and redistributing educational resources to support the poorest.

However, progressive policy shifts in education require a serious commitment by political leaders. In societies where the foundations of power are elitist, serving the historically privileged groups, transformative policy changes in education are not without obstructions if not impossible. Ethnic minorities and oppressed social groups are also victims of epistemic oppression through the 'hegemonic hold', 'epistemic privilege' and 'successful positioning of the dominant groups' (Vaditya, 2018: 273) whose world view is deeply entrenched in production and legitimization of national identity. Social transformation is only possible when the hegemonic power structures are ruptured and new inclusive and participatory institutions are built to create space for the voices of historically marginalized groups. This is often a challenging task as it also requires the elite groups to relinquish some of their power and privileges and be willing to redefine conventional notions of nationhood. Inevitably, there is often resistance to or manipulation of demands for progressive shifts, so the post-conflict educational processes are often stressful and tend to return to more of the same old culture with some tokenistic gestures to pacify the dissent. Educational programming hence becomes part of liberal ideology and 'liberal peace' (Paris, 2004) rather than serving the needs of 'positive peace' (Galtung, 1969). As argued elsewhere:

> In the contexts where national education policies and the processes of development are governed by global capitalism and neoliberalism, social justice oriented redistributive policies which require affirmative actions to promote positive discrimination in favour of the poor and historically marginalized populations may find little currency. (Pherali, 2021: 14)

In order to promote peace and reconciliation, post-conflict societies should also reconcile the divisive narratives about the conflict and the nature of the peace that is being promoted. In the case of Nepal, there are strong disagreements about how to understand the People's War: a justifiable popular movement against the oppression of the poor and structurally excluded communities, versus an unnecessary, manipulative and pain-inflicting ultra-leftist violence orchestrated by a ruthless political group. Irrespective of the political positions, people endured losses and pain and the memories of the past continue to unsettle surviving families and victims of the conflict. These post-war tensions could be mitigated through truth and reconciliation programmes when they work at their best, and the education sector can support such programmes by producing learning materials and developing appropriate educational approaches to disseminate relevant information. However, the forward-looking pacification attempts of peace and human rights curricula on their own are likely to maintain 'negative peace over the commitments to positive peace through systemic transformation' (Paulson and Bellino, 2017: 373). Furthermore, education's capacity to contribute towards peace and reconciliation depends on the extent to which educational reconstruction pays attention to the particular ways that education has interacted with and generated conflict. In this sense, as Paulson and Bellino (2017: 373) argue, truth commissions need to engage in the 'backward gaze' at 'the difficult truths about education and its relationship to conflict and human rights violations' in order to address injustices through education.

Hence, reconstruction of education after conflict should not only be about rebuilding physical infrastructure of schools and improving school enrolments, but also must focus on conflict-sensitive educational policies including adopting learners' mother tongue for teaching and learning; creation of safe environments so that parents can send their children to schools without anxieties; recruitment of teachers and educational professionals from diverse ethnic, religious, caste and gender backgrounds and provision of peace-oriented professional development for teachers. This involves implementing a holistic post-war educational strategy that supports national goals of development and social transformation. In practical terms, such a strategy needs to 'focus reconstruction efforts on rebuilding a state's education system as well as devising short-term plans to help re-enroll students' (Lai and Thyne, 2007: 290).

Teachers and the People's War: A Complex Relationship

The discussion in this book has shown that the underlying causes and object of Nepal's Maoist rebellion were located within conditions of structural inequality. The rebellion was not only based on populist political campaigns but also on a rigorous process of political education drawn from Marxist ideology. This ideological doctrine was utilized to educate cadres and masses who could relate to the narratives of identity-based oppression and disparities along the lines of caste, ethnicity, region and gender, which helped the Communist Party of Nepal-Maoist (CPN-M) to mobilize them against the state. The Maoist educational approach was aimed at developing critical political consciousness among the masses to collectivize a sense of injustices in different forms that could resonate with the social realities of diverse marginalized social groups. The popular education campaigns penetrated formal, non-formal and informal learning spaces, and socialist narratives disseminated through cultural troupes, public assemblies involving leaders' speeches, cadre training programmes and military training produced new forms of militant knowledge. The narratives of class relations, monopoly of state power in the hands of a few, exploitative monarchy and feudalistic socio-economic conditions brought people together irrespective of their caste, ethnic and gender identities. This political strategy blurred the distinction between who should and should not be involved in the armed struggle, resulting in people even from high castes, educated groups and business communities either being involved directly or extending indirect or moral support to the rebellion. Schools, teachers and students were no different from those who were part of the armed resistance. More importantly, educational spaces became a tactical resource because of their collective nature, providing fertile ground for promoting the progressive agenda, mass mobilization and recruitment in the rebel ranks (van Wessel and van Hirtum, 2013).

Yet, there was also a strong opposition to the Maoist movement, including among people in the education sector. The Maoists used the tactics of ideological persuasion, fear and physical attacks to counter any opposition to their struggle. Those who were undeterred by threats often endured horrific consequences including physical assaults, injuries and loss of life. Some teachers were simply accused of being 'class enemies' and targeted violently because of their backgrounds, political affiliation or social status and were not even given a chance to comply with rebels' demands. They faced cruelty for the benefit of the rebels' strategy to create a culture of fear to weaken any dissent. The state and security forces that were supposed to protect schools and their stakeholders also waged war against education in a bid to defeat the insurgency. Hence, schools and their key actors – teachers, students and educational officials – were part of both assets and threats to the conflicting parties. This complex positioning of schools often revealed a multiplicity of ideologically contradictory responses to conflict by their stakeholders, who were simultaneously complying, enterprising, resisting and sometimes ambivalent. Ultimately, at a deep level, the impact of violent conflicts on educational stakeholders is explained by the very nature of their response.

Alternative Modes of Learning during Conflict

Given the risks of physical attacks on schools during conflict, it is important to rethink the notion of education in the current situation in which children and teachers travel to schools to learn and teach. When there are serious risks to life, the continued push for mass attendance at school may put teachers and students at risk of violent attack, including mass abduction, harassment by armed personnel and being caught in the crossfire, or schools may be targeted by arial bombing. Therefore, when the war is ongoing, temporary closure of schools may give more protection to children than continuation of schooling. The idea that schools are safe spaces for children may not hold true in all conflict situations. This is more pertinent especially in situations of conflict where conflicting parties do not respect the international laws on human rights and children's right to education. Instead, alternative security-sensitive modes of education may be more conducive. These may include homeschooling, change in the focus of learning (e.g. how to stay safe during war), use of remote teaching via digital technologies or small group community-based instruction and indigenous and home-based life skills/livelihood education. Schools can return to normal routines when political solutions to conflict are found or security situations improve and it becomes safer for teachers and students to resume schooling. Different communities can take different approaches, assessing the levels of risks in their own areas.

When schools cannot operate as normal during emergencies, children should be provided with learning opportunities at home and within their neighbourhoods. At the time of writing, the ongoing crisis of Covid-19 has exposed the limitations of mass education in the physically confined spaces of school classrooms. The pandemic has disrupted the education of the world's 1.6 billion children (UN, 2020), and learners in the most deprived and conflict-affected contexts have been hit the hardest (Education cannot Wait, 2021). It is 'the largest disruption of education systems in history' and 'with the combined effect of the pandemic's worldwide economic impact and the school closures, the learning crisis could turn into a generational catastrophe' (UN, 2020: 2–3). Nevertheless, the pandemic has also forced education providers, including governments, local communities, international organizations and private enterprises, to develop new methods, approaches and policies in education so that learning can continue even when students and teachers cannot gather in the physical spaces of educational institutions. The health emergency and conflict have similarities in terms of challenges posed to learners around disruption of education, loss of families' livelihood activities, lack of access to digital technologies and risks involved during travel to and from school. Amidst Covid-19, new possibilities of learning are emerging through innovations in digital learning, increased internet connectivity and access to wider knowledge and revival of community-based indigenous methods of education. For example, teachers in Nepal during August 2021 reported that the conventional practice of parents and older siblings teaching younger ones, teachers delivering lessons in local neighbourhoods or teaching smaller mixed groups of children alternately, and the traditional *tol shiksha* (township education) model were being adopted by local communities so that children's learning could continue while the schools remained closed. Despite the risks of international organizations and private technology firms dominating education to 'colonize' learning communities through digital monopoly (Morris, 2021), innovations around educational methodologies during the pandemic should be useful to educational communities in conflict and crisis.

Appreciating the Politics of Education

Schools should not be viewed as apolitical institutions merely providing students with literacy and numeracy skills. They are inherently political, aimed at inculcating particular sets of values and perspectives about life and society. The increasing corporatization of education and the economic logic of schooling in low-income conflict-affected contexts is underpinned by capitalism and neoliberal ideology, which essentially limits our understanding of the causes of attacks on schools. The micro-level analysis of lived experiences of Nepali teachers during conflict provides 'the reality of life on the front lines' (Robben and Nordstrom, 1995: 5), which encourages policymakers and educational practitioners to critically appreciate inherent social and political dimensions of schooling that interact with violent conflict.

The lived experiences of school leaders and the impact of decade-long conflict on schools discussed in this book have significant implications for re-envisioning school leadership in post-conflict Nepal and elsewhere. As a by-product of long-standing political tensions and involvement of teachers and school managers in party-based politics, educational processes such as teacher recruitment, school management processes and use of school development funding have become excessively corrupt, resulting in plummeting educational standards. Unless the traumatic impacts of conflict on teachers and school leaders, and the politicization of educational management, are appropriately addressed, the quality of education will continue to suffer even in the post-conflict period.

Nevertheless, there is an immense opportunity for transformatory reforms in the curricula and pedagogy, as the teaching workforce is politically conscious and has been immersed in critical debates about social inequalities and inclusive democracy. Yet, teachers' professionalism has declined due to incoherence between their political activism for educational transformation and dereliction of fundamental professional responsibilities. There is a misconception and, perhaps, lack of articulation of their roles as 'critical and transformative intellectuals' (Giroux, 1988) within their professional environments. So, there is also a real opportunity for progressive teacher development and systemic change in education that recognizes the potential of 'critical pedagogy' (Giroux, 2011) for Nepal's peace, democratization and social development.

Yet, the range of violent experiences endured by schools poses significant challenges to the task of educational reconstruction. The violent past and the kind of conflictual impasse which schools and head teachers were placed in belong to the forms of 'symbolic violence' (Bourdieu, 1977) that are essentially the same kind of dilemma. The protracted peace process combined with continued political instability and dominance of the pre-conflict hegemonic culture have obscured the contentious role of education before and during the conflict and undermined any meaningful debate on what 'more of the same' education might mean for reconstruction of a 'new Nepal'. The liberal form of education in post-conflict Nepal broadly concentrates on economic development while maintaining the status quo and limiting systemic change, unfortunately overlooking the connections between education and conflict, described throughout this book by those who experienced conflict.

Education, Conflict and Peace: A Framework of Analysis

Building upon the analysis of the historical process of educational development, effects of violence on schools and their actors and new debates about peace and prosperity in post-conflict Nepal, I consolidate the ideas into a new analytical framework that may be useful for educational practitioners, researchers and policymakers who work in conflict settings. I loosely call this a *Victim-Perpetrator-Liberator-Peacebuilder (VPLP) framework*, which could be used both as a pre-programme assessment tool and an ongoing evaluation mechanism of education systems for policy formulation and programme implementation in conflict-affected contexts, as shown Figure 8.1 and further elaborated in Table 8.1.

The above manifestations of the education and conflict nexus do not represent linear interactions, nor should these be understood as isolated parallel pathways. These interactions represent complex intersections often posing dilemmas

Figure 8.1 The VPLP Framework: Multi-directional interactions between education and conflict.

about policy response. Researchers should therefore historicize the process of analysis and closely draw upon contextual factors that are unique to the nature of the particular conflict and the society's sociocultural dynamics. For instance, cultural repression through education may be viewed as both education as a perpetrator of violence and victimization of indigenous practices of learning and knowledge production. Critical and humanizing pedagogies in education (Freire, 2014; Gill and Niens, 2014; Giroux, 2011) play emancipatory as well as peacebuilding roles. In conflict and protracted crisis, learning to cope with adversities and be safe from physical violence is vital. People who experience a sudden loss of home, forced displacement, loss of economic means and death in the family endure immense emotional and psychological stress. An adaptive and conflict-sensitive education in crisis contexts can enable learners to be resilient to hardships and identify new avenues of hope and change.

Resilient education systems have the capacity to bounce back after suffering destruction because of conflict or natural disasters such as earthquakes,

Table 8.1 The VPLP Framework to Analyse Multiple Roles of Education in Conflict

	Education: Analysis of the Interaction Using Diverse Methodological Tools
Victim (education as a target for violence)	• Disruptions in education (e.g. school closures, loss of school days and learning, teacher and student absenteeism due to fear of violence or other risks, occupation of schools by warring parties); • Types of attacks and effects on teachers, students and educational officials; • Different motivations for attacks/intrusions on schools (e.g. undermining state authority; serving rebel propaganda; disagreement with the system: liberal ideals, policies on enrolment, curriculum, language of instruction, and management of schools; ideological training; elimination of political opponents; denial of girls' education; abduction of girls and boys to be child soldiers; financial extortion; extraction of intelligence, arrests, detention and imprisonment by the state); • Destruction of school buildings and educational materials; • Neoliberal reforms in the education sector (e.g. curriculum and policies; reformed to serve the market undermining the local ecologies of knowledge); • Securitization of education (e.g. control of educational processes by armed groups and forces to achieve their military goals).
Perpetrator (creating or fuelling conditions of conflict)	• Exclusion of girls, refugees and cultural minority groups from the education system; • Divided and unjust provision of schooling, fuelling social, cultural and political divisions; • Promotion of biased history and 'othering' through curriculum, textbooks and teaching and learning; • Failing to promote equity, diversity and inclusion in educational policies and practices; • Repression of minority and indigenous languages through non-native language of instruction; • Education for violent extremism.
Liberator (enabling freedom and justice)	• Developing critical consciousness about social, political and economic conditions of society; • Empowerment of girls and historically oppressed social groups through development of individual capabilities, new knowledge and life skills; • Enabling learners' agency to participate in democratic processes and decision-making; • Skills to organize social movements to create bottom-up pressures for social justice; • Use of informal, non-formal and formal education spaces to build unity against structural violence and promote peace with social justice.

Table 8.1 The VPLP Framework to Analyse Multiple Roles of Education in Conflict (continued)

	Education: Analysis of the Interaction Using Diverse Methodological Tools
Peacebuilder (supporting sustainable peace and preventing violent conflict)	• Provision of peace-making training for conflict actors, political leaders and peace negotiators: dialogue, discussion, mediation, and human rights education; • Providing knowledge and skills for sustainable livelihood; • Redressing systemic inequalities within education to increase access and create a supportive environment for learners from historically excluded communities; • Equity and justice as core values in educational practices; • Promotion of peace and human rights through formal curriculum; • Transforming the pedagogical practices to help learners to transform conflicts peacefully and nurture their agency to enable social change; • Rewriting the history curriculum to promote inclusive and conflict-sensitive history teaching; • Support to post-war reconciliation by redressing systemic issues in education.

tsunamis and climate catastrophes (IIEP, 2014). Educating learners for disaster preparedness and risk reduction as well as to adapt to crisis can both protect educational provisions and build resilience to build back better after the crisis hits schools and communities (Kitagawa, 2020). Therefore, building institutional resilience by 'mainstreaming conflict and disaster risk reduction measures into education policies, plans and programmes helps countries strengthen their capacity to anticipate, prevent, and respond to conflict and disaster' (IIEP, 2021: n.p.). However, there is also a risk of the notion of 'resilience' being used to deflect the critical gaze from the underlying causes of conflict and emergencies only to reduce the intensity of impact. This alludes to possible manipulation or co-option of the liberatory ethos of education into hegemonic discourses. Reflecting on this trend, some scholars have argued as follows:

> The use of resilience has coincided with and facilitated a move away from conflict and natural or human-created disaster as the foci for EiE intervention towards risk mitigation. This reduces or even makes irrelevant the need to understand and seek to change the causes of the emergencies that EiE seeks to intervene in, and reduces or makes irrelevant the goal and possibility of a positive peace, which would require transformation of these root causes. (Shah, Paulson and Couch, 2020: 322)

Hence, I would stress that the above analytical framework enables researchers to ask critical questions about the education/conflict/peace nexus that delve into the systemic issues of education systems that relate to production of conflict drivers and the possibilities of education for transformative peacebuilding. Educational planners, practitioners and researchers who fail to fully appreciate the politics behind education and misrecognize its contentious role might be inadvertently perpetuating violence through education. Hence, the key message is that education should not only be seen as a responsive tool or a coping mechanism during conflict and crisis but also as an intervening force for redressing the causes of crises. The latter would challenge and seek to transform systemic inequalities and problematic power relationships into ones that are equitable and socially just. In conclusion, education should be protected from victimization and enhanced in its role as liberator and peacebuilder by redressing elements that are complicit in hardening conflict conditions. The capacity of education in building sustainable peace depends on the effectiveness and velocity of the process on these trajectories.

Conflict Analysis of the Education Sector: An Ongoing Process

In Nepal, Maoist ideologues promoted a narrative of injustices and oppressive structures as a justification for an armed rebellion. The use of violence in this situation was often argued as an acceptable action that defied elitist aggression against disenfranchised and indigenous populations, both in physical and symbolic terms. Gramsci's (1971) notion of hegemony elucidates the idea that violence, force and power are embedded in the social, cultural and political institutions that legitimize the ideology of the ruling class. The juxtaposition of social practices and hegemonic discourses normalizes and reproduces social injustices. To this end, education serves as a vehicle for social reproduction (Bourdieu, 1977). However, political movements and violent rebellions contribute to sensitization with regard to normalized conditions and destabilization of unequal power structures. In this process, structures of learning and their stakeholders are confronted by competitive dominance from conflicting powers. As discussed extensively in Chapters 3 and 4, this is manifested through attacks on education in conflict zones which include occupation or destruction of school buildings, abduction of children for forced recruitment or political indoctrination and killing of teachers and pupils, imposing alternative curricula and in some cases, denial of education entirely.

Armed rebellions that are inspired by 'revolutionary' ideologies often mobilize the tactics of political education, intimidation and persecution for any defiance of their movement. Rebels engage in mass mobilization through ideological indoctrination in which teachers and pupils either voluntarily participate or are forced into their campaign. Girls in particular face the additional risk of sexual exploitation and gender-based violence during conflict. Demonstration killings and brutal physical attacks serve as a war tactic in cultivation of fear and subjugation, which makes violent revolutions ironically disparate in their aims and approaches, in that the struggle is portrayed as necessary for liberation, but the tactics are inherently oppressive and unjustifiable. Schools not only represent the social, cultural and political disposition of a society but also serve as a contested political space. This complex positioning of schools often leads to a multitude of ideologically opposing responses to conflict that are supportive, compliant or disapproving of the rebellion. As reported elsewhere, teachers, school leaders, members of the school management committees and pupils are not mere passive victims of the conflict but also influential political agents in the struggle (Pherali, 2016a).

The provision of education in conflict-affected settings needs to account not only for the technical challenges such as the lack of school buildings, textbooks, trained teachers and institutional capacities, which are undoubtedly crucial, but also broader security and political economy factors involving 'the distribution of power and wealth between different groups and individuals, and the processes that create, sustain and transform these relationships over time' (Collinson, 2003: 3). A high-quality political economy analysis of education from a conflict perspective provides a critical understanding of the security, political, social and cultural dimensions of education at different levels and enables development partners, policymakers and educational practitioners to identify areas of priorities and intervention. Building upon the conflict assessment guidance suggested by Goodhand, Vaux and Walker (2002) and reflecting on arguments presented in this book, the following tool (Table 8.2) is proposed as a multilevel educational analysis from a conflict perspective. It is hoped the continuous assessment of education from a political economy perspective would help mitigate conflict drivers through contextually informed educational programmes.

Examining education in conflict-affected contexts by asking the above critical questions would allow policymakers and educational planners to unpack complex interactions between the provision of education and social, political and economic divisions at various levels of the society (Davies, 2005; Novelli et al., 2014; Pherali, Smith and Vaux, 2011). The issues around distribution of power and economic resources are central in social and political movements but these concerns are insufficiently embedded in post-conflict educational

Table 8.2 Conflict Analysis Framework in Education

	International	National	Local
Security	• How do the global and regional security discourses impact on education policies and practices? • Are there security-related conditions attached to education aid? • Are international armed forces present? How do they engage with education? • How are students and teachers affected by militarized educational support by international actors?	• Are schools targeted for violent attacks? By whom? • Are there risks and patterns of abduction, attacks and recruitment of teachers and pupils into armed groups? • Is there a national strategy to protect schools from violence? • What mechanisms are in place to protect schools from armed groups/forces?	• Are there ethnic, religious or political tensions that impact on the operation of schools in the communities? • Are there incidents of political and criminal violence affecting schools in the communities? • How do schools navigate security risks? • Are human rights promoted at schools and local communities? • Are pupils and teachers safe to travel to and from school?
Political	• How does the geopolitics of education aid affect education? Has international education aid increased due to increase in conflict intensity? • Which international organizations are actively involved in education in the country? • What are the donor interests in education? • What are the priority areas in education for international agencies?	• Who controls educational governance? State? Non-state actors? What are the tensions? • What is the nature of socio-political divisions in the country? Which groups control power? Is educational decision-making inclusive? • What are the political issues around curricula, language of instruction and teacher recruitment? • Is education featured in peacebuilding strategy?	• What are the effects of political instability on schools? • Are children involved in political activities such as demonstrations or mass resistance? • Who makes decisions on school matters? Are there mechanisms to prevent 'elite capture' of decision-making bodies?

Table 8.2 Conflict Analysis Framework in Education (continued)

	International	National	Local
Economic	• How does the global economic market affect education policies? • What is the role of large education corporations in education delivery? • What is the impact of international education policies on students living in poverty? • To what extent do neoliberal policies in education affect diverse social groups? • Is there evidence of corruption in managing donor funds?	• What is the link between education and the job market? Are refugees permitted to work? How is the education sector financed? How does conflict affect public school financing? • Are there economic motivations for young people to join armed groups? • Are there issues of child labour? • What is the proportion of private schools in the country? Where are they concentrated? Who has access to these schools? How are they different from public schools (financing, quality, certification etc.).	• Are there risks of extortion of school funds by armed groups? • Are there risks of corruption and misuse of school budget? What mechanisms are put in place to mitigate these? • How are teachers recruited and redeployed? • Do schools offer scholarships to children in poverty and those affected by conflict? • Are additional resources available to support refugee children?
Social	• How do the global education policies support equity and diversity? • What is the impact of globalization on family traditions? • Are there patterns of international migration? How do they impact on educational processes?	• What is the nature of ethnic and religious divisions in the country? • Are there issues of social status associated with private schools and English medium education? • How does the conflict affect enrolment of girls, minorities and children with disabilities? • What national policies and mechanisms exist to promote educational access of conflict-affected and marginalized groups?	• Do schools promote equity and diversity? • How are schools promoting girls' education? • Do civil society organizations support education? • How do schools provide psychosocial support to children affected by conflict? • How are controversial issues such as language of instruction, national identities, political interests, histories, gender, castes etc. addressed in teaching and learning?

reconstruction. Consequently, education is often limited to patchwork reforms rather than systemic change to redress deeply rooted structural problems. In Nepal, the School Sector Reform Plan 2009–2015 (SSRP) and the current School Sector Development Plan 2016–2023 (SSDP) do not respond adequately to systemic inequalities that obstruct progress towards equity, quality and efficiency in education and fail to address the impacts of both structural and physical violence endured by the education sector (MoE, 2009, 2016). In other words, the role of education in production of conflict has hardly been problematized at the policy level, and therefore the 'contentious role of education' (Davies, 2005) in fuelling the Maoist rebellion broadly remains unaddressed. Several years after the CPA was signed, school education in Nepal remains engulfed in the legacies of the 'People's War' and has failed to adopt a progressive approach to capitalize on the political gains of the socialist and ethnic movements.

Policy Recommendations for Peace and Inclusive Development

After the end of armed conflict and ethnic uprisings in Madhes, Nepal is now embarking upon a new phase of its political journey with the promulgation of 'a progressive federal constitution' that attempts to redefine the nation based on social and cultural diversity. There are, however, practical challenges in realizing the social justice aspirations of the constitution, as the structures of the state institutions are still dominated by the hegemonic discourses of the pre-conflict era which often resist attempts at radical change in policies. The people-centred discourses of the Nepali nation are still at large in new processes of nation-building, and the dominant Nepali psyche is paralysed by the national history constructed and enforced by the political class that denies the history of the ordinary peoples (Pathak, 2017). The education system also by and large reproduces the same old visions, goals and standards dictated by the ruling class. The devolution of powers in educational governance is positive but there are risks of 'elite capture' (Edwards, 2011) even at local levels, undermining the voices of the most marginalized. Drawing upon the foregoing chapters in the book, I now present some practical lessons for policymakers and agencies that support education in Nepal.

Political elites mobilize history to legitimize educational policies and define particular norms of behaviour demarcating social boundaries to shape the distribution of power and authority (Kern, 2009; Korostelina, 2017). In Nepal, national history has always been taught from the vantage point of the monarchy and the Khas-Arya ruling class, which has denied knowledge about the struggles of the grassroots and diverse ethnic groups. Peace with social justice demands recognition of previously obscured communities and celebration of their history and culture. Hence, there is an urgent need to rewrite the history curriculum so as to provide narratives about the past from the perspectives of the ordinary people who represent Nepal's geographical, cultural and religious diversity. For example, Yug Pathak's book *Mangena* lucidly tells an alternative history of Nepal from a critical standpoint (Pathak, 2017). Educating young people with a balanced history is crucial in order to return dignity and ownership of national identity to historically forgotten communities such as Madhesis, Janajatis and Dalits. Children should learn not only about the glorified past but also the pain and suffering of different social groups and misrecognition of their identities in the process of nation-building. It would serve as reparation for the long-standing cultural repression suffered by these communities.

Secondly, instruction in the mother tongue improves children's learning outcomes (Bühmann and Trudell, 2007; GPE, 2019; Pinnock, 2009), and when schools provide education in the child's first language, there are wider educational benefits: increase in classroom participation, decreased attrition and increase in the likelihood of family and community engagement in the child's learning (Trudell, 2016). Yet, Nepal has made little progress in this area, mainly because the state has historically taken an assimilationist approach with Nepali as the only unifying language, and now due to the lack of effective policy implementation. In a country where 123 different languages are spoken (CBS, 2014), formal education in the Nepali medium has disadvantaged non-Nepali-speaking learners. It has also functioned as a hegemonic power of the ruling class that destroys non-Nepali speaking parents' pride in their own language and culture. Consequently, parents view the policy on teaching and learning in the mother tongue as yet another barrier imposed upon them to limit their children's ability to participate in the national, political and economic realms (Pherali, Smith and Vaux, 2011). Even though proficiency in the dominant language combined with a higher level of education increases people's earnings (Casale and Posel, 2011), imposition of a non-native language as the medium of education adversely affects children's learning at an early age, reducing their chances of progressing to tertiary education. Hence, it is recommended that Nepal resourcefully adopt the policy of teaching and learning in the children's mother tongue while teaching foreign languages as additional subjects. More crucially, teaching English, Hindi and Chinese could open new economic opportunities in future.

Thirdly, it is vital that the federal government establish provincial education commissions to sketch out educational strategies that are aligned with the economic, geographical and cultural needs of each province. Nepal's geographical diversity and unique cultures and histories can be assets for economic and social development in which local communities can value and capitalize on their own economic and cultural resources to redefine the idea of development. Education and training can support skills development to harness the opportunities in tourism, production of unique agricultural products, herbal medicine and technological innovations locally. Provincial and municipal education policies could support youth to build local enterprises that tap into business and trade opportunities across the provinces as well as in the neighbouring countries – India and China.

Fourth, local governments should utilize technical and financial support from the federal institutions and Nepal's development partners to develop their education plans. From a peacebuilding perspective, these programmes should address inequities and social exclusion. Policies around language of instruction, local curriculum and teacher management could be geared towards redressing educational grievances endured by marginalized communities. Teachers should be provided with necessary skills to deliver conflict-sensitive education (INEE, 2013) – so that they reflect on their own political biases, deal with the history of conflict in a balanced manner and facilitate transformative learning. Initial teacher education and continuing professional development (CPD) programmes could be revised, incorporating new discourses and approaches that help teachers to teach controversial conflict-related topics. This could be a meaningful way of institutionalizing the outcomes of political and social movements and the aspirations of Nepal's new constitution. Local educational development must be seen beyond construction of school buildings, enrolment numbers and school upgrading (Schaffner, Sharma and Glewwe, 2020) to prioritize quality of learning and relevance of education for people's livelihood. In this process, school committees can benefit from capacity training for effective management and governance of schools.

Fifth, the state needs to regulate the private education sector and invest more to improve the quality of learning in community schools and public universities. The growth of private schools and constant underperformance of most community schools in the country has further expanded the educational gaps between the rural poor and urban better off populations. The public/private education divide in Nepal is likely to increase economic inequalities as higher levels of private education spending widen both wage dispersion and the education premium, whereas increases in public education spending have the opposite effects (Huber, Gunderson and Stephens, 2020: 184). Hence, from a social justice perspective, where the educational funding comes from does matter. Huber, Gunderson and Stephens (2020) further argue:

> Higher reliance on private spending creates greater room for social selectivity, both in access to educational opportunities and to careers. It has a particularly pernicious effect for those at the lower end of the academic and social scale. In contrast, higher levels of public education spending raise skills at all levels and reduce returns to education and ultimately earnings inequality. (Huber, Gunderson and Stephens, 2020:185)

Sixth, schools should mainstream teaching and learning about peace and social inclusion. The Truth and Reconciliation Commission needs to include education as a key domain of assessment so that the impact of conflict on teachers and students is accounted for and appropriate recommendations are made to build a forward thinking socially just education system. Schools could be provided with resources and toolkits to introduce programmatic interventions that promote an understanding of social justice, peace and reconciliation.

Finally, the provision of Global Citizenship Education can help learners develop skills for critical inquiry in 'order to dissect claims that do not stand up to rigorous scrutiny, logic and rational inquiry' and enhance their civic and political participation (UNESCO, 2018: 9). Critical peace education can equip learners with skills for civic and political engagement which can promote a culture of dialogue and discussion to deal with politically contested issues (Bajaj, 2019). Davies (2008: 181–2) argues that youth should learn to cast doubts on 'ideals' and to reject uncritical acceptance of single truths. Through a critical political education, learners can develop dialogic skills to engage with dominant cultural, political and religious ideologies and develop dynamic citizen subjectivities (Pherali, 2019).

Final Thoughts

Even though the Maoist rebellion formally ended some fifteen years ago, conflict survivors and their families continue to suffer from the trauma caused by horrific experiences during the conflict. The heartbreaking stories of the loss or disappearance of family members are still heard frequently and the current stark political divisions in Nepali society characterize the enduring impacts of the decade-long conflict. Suman Adhikari, the son of Muktinath Adhikari, a school head teacher in Lamjung whose murder was displayed by the Maoists as shot while kneeling on the ground with both hands tied behind to a tree, remembers his father on the auspicious Father's Day.

In an online interview with Indrasara Khadka titled 'That Shocking Picturing of My Father', Adhikari shares the following emotions:

> Today, Father's Day [Kushe Aushi]. The auspicious day to worship father. Everyone worshipped their father. Those whose fathers are not alive may have worshipped their fathers' pictures. But, that picture of my father still traumatizes me.
>
> Parents are considered gods. They really are gods. That's why, on the day of Kushe Aushi, father is visited and worshipped.
>
> I also remembered my father Muktinath Adhikari. I uploaded his picture on Facebook. While I was putting up his picture on Facebook, another picture of my father frightened me.
>
> It was on 16 Jan 2002. Maoists murdered my father brutally. I was 22 years old. I lived in Kathmandu and was studying and teaching.
>
> I had been home in Lamjung, Duradanda on 14th January and was planning to return to Kathmandu on 17th. We had added more grass on the thatched roof of our house. To mend the roof, we prepared bamboo strips. I walked ahead carrying them and father followed. We mended the roof together all day.
>
> In the evening, a message arrived for father from the district administration, asking him to collect the letter of appointment as the school headmaster.
>
> On the 2nd Jan, father got appointed as the school headmaster at the Education Office. He returned home in the evening. On the 3rd, he went to school. While he was teaching in the class, Maoists came to school and took him away. They hanged him on the tree alive and shot him.
>
> That scene still revolves around my eyes. No matter how much I try, I cannot forget. A teacher whose neck was tied on to the tree, hands tied on the back, spectacles on the ground, bullet on head and blood on his chest. How would a child feel to see such a scene of their father? Yes, I have seen that death of my father in front of my eyes. It hurts, badly hurts.
>
> Those sinners did not let me stay with my father. They took his life away in the name of politics. I still see him in my dreams sometimes. The dream also frightens me. I sometimes dream about that incident happening again. Sometimes, I dream about father staying with family.
>
> In the morning when I wake up, I get mortified. The same scene petrifies.

> ...
>
> I realize that many people like me lost their parents during the conflict. They were orphaned. They also have this pain. I was 22 when I lost my father. But many have been orphaned in their childhood. Such children have difficulties in their education and upbringing. The state should look after them.
>
> The rebels and state have orphaned many of us. I cannot get my father back no matter what I do. There is no measure for the sorrow we endured. Now, everyone must get justice.
>
> While uploading father's picture on Facebook, the same scene is reappearing so vividly. That tree is situated about 20 metres away from home on the slope. ... Since that incident, I have never been back to that spot. I still do not have the courage to visit that place. That scene continues to shock.
>
> ...
>
> Happy Father's Day!
>
> (Adhikari, 2021)

This was a school head teacher who was pulled out of the classroom in front of his students and killed near his own house twenty minutes after his abduction. The picture of his murder became a symbol of victimization of teachers during the conflict and still haunts the education community in Nepal. This book presented a comprehensive analysis of politics of education in which education became both a cause and victim of the armed conflict. Education's role in the sustainable peace and prosperity of Nepali society relies on both the way Nepal's political forces redress systemic problems in the education system and respond to the pain inflicted on teachers and students during the conflict.

References

Adhikari, S. (2021). 'That Shocking Picturing of My Father', in conversation with Indrasara Khadka, Kathmandu: Kathmandu Press, https://kathmandupress.com/news/20340, (accessed 7 September 2021).

Affolter, F. W., and Valente, A. A. (2020). 'Learning for Peace: Lessons Learned from UNICEF's Peacebuilding, Education, and Advocacy in Conflict-Affected Context Programme', in N. Balvin and D. J. Christie (eds), *Children and Peace: From Research to Action*, 219–38, Cham: Springer Open.

Ahlstram, C. (1991). *Casualties of Conflict: Report for the Protection of Victims of War*, Uppsala: Department of Peace and Conflict, Uppsala University.

Akanda, M. A. S. (2010). 'Returns to Education in Nepal: Evidence from Living Standard Survey', *Dhaka University Journal of Sciences*, 58(2): 257–64, https://papers.ssrn.com/sol3/papers.cfm?abstract_id=2146540 (accessed 20 August 2021).

Amnesty International. (2005). 'Nepal: Children Caught in the Middle', Kathmandu: Amnesty International.

Amusan, L., and Ejoke, U. P. (2017). 'The Psychological Trauma Inflicted by Boko Haram Insurgency in the North Eastern Nigeria', *Aggression and Violent Behavior*, 36: 52–9.

Andvig, J. C. (2006). 'Child Soldiers: Reasons for Variation in Their Rate of Recruitment and Standards of Welfare', working paper no. 704, Oslo: Norwegian Institute of International Affairs.

Annells, M. (1996). 'Hermeneutic Phenomenology: Philosophical Perspectives and Current Use in Nursing Research', *Journal of Advanced Nursing*, 23: 705–13.

Apple, M. (2004). *Ideology and Curriculum*, 3rd edn, London: Routledge.

Aronowitz, S., and Giroux, H. (1993). *Education Still under Siege*, Westport, CT: Bergin and Garvey.

Bajaj, M. (2019). 'Conceptualizing Critical Peace Education for Conflict Settings', *Education and Conflict Review*, 2: 65–9.

Bajaj, M., and Hantzopoulos, M. (2016). *Peace Education: International Perspectives*, New York: Bloomsbury.

Bajracharya, R., and Sijapati, B. (2012). 'The Kafala System and Its Implications for Nepali Domestic Workers', Policy Brief, Kathmandu: Centre for the Study of Labour and Mobility, Social Science Baha, https://www.ceslam.org/uploads/backup/Kafala_Nepali_Domestic_Workers_Female_Migration_Eng.pdf (accessed 25 August 2021).

Ball, S. (2007). *Education Plc*, London: Routledge.

Banda, F. (2000). 'The Dilemma of the Mother Tongue: Prospects for Bilingual Education in South Africa', *Language, Culture and Curriculum*, 13: 51–66.

Barakat, B., and Urdal, H. (2009). 'Breaking the Waves? Does Education Mediate the Relationship between Youth Bulges and Political Violence?' World Bank Policy Research working paper no. 5114, Washington, DC: The World Bank, Africa Region, Post Conflict & Social Development Unit, https://openknowledge.worldbank.org/bitstream/handle/10986/4304/WPS5114.pdf%3Bjsessionid%3D5097FB7EF7D2A297BEB3D571B7FF51A8?sequence%3D1.

Barro, R. J. (2013). 'Education and Economic Growth', *Annals of Economics and Finance*, 14(2): 301–28.

Bar-Tal, D. (1998). 'The Rocky Road toward Peace: Beliefs on Conflict in Israeli Textbooks', *Journal of Peace Research*, 35(6): 723–42.

Basabose, J. D., and Habyarimana, H. (2019). 'Peace Education in Rwandan Secondary Schools: Coping with Contradictory Messages', *Journal of Peacebuilding & Development*, 14(2): 138–49.

Becker, G. S. (1975). *Human Capital: A Theoretical and Empirical Analysis, with Special Reference to Education*, Chicago: University of Chicago Press.

Bengtsson, S. (2011). 'Fragile States, Fragile Concepts: A Critical Reflection on the Terminology of Fragility in the Field of Education in Emergencies', in J. Paulson (ed.), *Education, Conflict and Development*, 33–58, Oxford: Symposium Books.

Bennett, L. (2005). 'Gender, Caste and Ethnic Exclusion in Nepal: Following the Policy Process from Analysis to Action', World Bank Conference Paper, http://siteresources.worldbank.org/INTRANETSOCIALDEVELOPMENT/Resources/Bennett.rev.pdf.

Bennett, L., Tamang, S., Onta, P., and Thapa, M. (2006). 'Unequal Citizens: Gender, Caste and Ethnic Exclusion in Nepal', report on Gender and Social Exclusion Assessment (GSEA), The World Bank, available at: http://documents.worldbank.org/curated/en/745031468324021366/pdf/ 379660v20WP0Un00Box0361508B0PUBLIC0.pdf (accessed 2 July 2021).

Bhatta, P. (2009). 'Introduction: 60 years of Educational Development in Nepal', in P. Bhatta (ed.), *Education in Nepal: Problems, Reforms, and Social Change*, 1–16, Kathmandu: Martin Chautari.

Bhatta, P. (2011). 'Aid Agency Influence in National Education Policy-Making: A Case from Nepal's "Education for All" Movement', *Globalisation, Societies and Education*, 9(1): 11–26.

Bhatta, P., and Budathoki, S. B. (2013). 'Understanding Private Educationscape(s) in Nepal, ESP', working paper 57, Private Education Research Initiative, http://peri-global.org/role-state/document/understanding-private-educationscapes-nepal (accessed 4 April 2022).

Bhatta, P., and Pherali, T. (2017). *Nepal – Patterns of Privatization in Education: A Case Study of Low-Fee Private Schools and Private Chain Schools*, Brussels: Education International.

Bhatta, P., Adhikari, L., Thada, M., and Rai, R. (2008). 'Structures of Denial: Student Representation in Nepal's Higher Education', *Studies in Nepali History and Society*, 13(2): 235–63.

Bhattarai, B. R. (2003). 'The Political Economy of the People's War', in A. Karki and D. Seddon (eds), *The People's War in Nepal: Left Perspectives*, 117–164, New Delhi: Adroit Publishers.

Bishwakarma, M. (2019). *Political Transformations in Nepal: Dalit Inequality and Social Justice*, Oxon: Routledge.

Bista, D. B. (1991). *Fatalism and Development: Nepal's Struggle for Modernization*, New Delhi: Orient Longman.

Biton, Y., and Salomon, G. (2006). 'Peace in the Eyes of Israeli and Palestinian Youths: Effects of Collective Narratives and Peace Education Program', *Journal of Peace Research*, 43(2): 167–80.

Borchgrevink, K. (2008). 'Book Note: The Madrassah Challenge: Militancy and Religious Education in Pakistan', *Journal of Peace Research*, 45(6):853.

Bourdieu, P. (1977). *Outline of a Theory of Practice*, R. Nice, trans., Cambridge: Cambridge University Press.

Bourdieu, P. (1984). *Distinction: A Social Critique of the Judgement of Taste*, Cambridge, MA: Harvard University Press.

Bourdieu, P. (1986). 'The Forms of Capital', in J. E. Richardson (ed.), *Handbook of Theory of Research for the Sociology of Education*, 241–58, Westport, CT: Greenwood Press.

Bourdieu, P. (1990). *In Other Words*, Cambridge: Cambridge University Press.

Bourdieu, P., and Wacquant, L. J .D. (1992). *An Invitation to Reflexive Sociology*, Cambridge: Polity Press.

Brock-Utne, B. (2012). 'Language and Inequality: Global Challenges to Education', *Compare: A Journal of Comparative and International Education*, 42, 773–93.

Brun, C., and Shuayb, M. (2020). 'Education in Emergencies: Five Critical Points for Shifting the Power', Beirut: Center for Lebanese Studies, https://lebanesestudies.com/education-in-emergencies-at-20-five-critical-points-for-shifting-the-power/ (accessed 27 August 2021).

Buckland, P. (2005). *Reshaping the Future: Education and Post-Conflict Reconstruction*, Washington, DC: World Bank.

Bühmann, D., and Trudell, B. (2007). *Mother Tongue Matters: Local Language as a Key to Effective Learning*, Paris: UNESCO.

Burde, D. (2014). *Schools for Conflict or for Peace in Afghanistan*, New York: Columbia University Press.

Burghart, R. (1984). 'The Formation of the Concept of Nation-State in Nepal', *Journal of Asian Studies*, 44(1): 1–25.

Bush, K. D., and Saltarelli, D. (2000). *The Two Faces of Education in Ethnic Conflict: Towards a Peacebuilding Education for Children*, Florence: UNICEF Innocenti Research Centre.

Caddell, M. (2006). 'Private Schools as Battlefields: Contested Visions of Learning and Livelihood in Nepal', *Compare: A Journal of Comparative Education*, 36: 463–79.

Carney, C., and Rappleye, J. (2011). 'Education Reform in Nepal: From Modernity to Conflict', *Globalization, Societies and Education*, 9(1): 1–9.

Carney, S., and Bista, M. B. (2009). 'Community Schooling in Nepal: A Genealogy of Education Reform Since 1990', *Comparative Education Review*, 53(2): 189–211.

Carney, S., and Madsen, U. A. (2009). 'Schooling and the Formation of Identities in Modern Nepal: A place of One's Own', in J. Zajda, H. Daun and L. Saha (eds), *Nation-Building, Identity and Citizenship Education: Cross-Cultural Perspective*, 171–87, New York: Springer.

Carney, S., Bista, M., and Agergaard, J. (2007). 'Empowering the "Local" through Education? Exploring Community-Managed Schooling in Nepal', *Oxford Review of Education*, 33: 611–28.

Carnoy, M. (1999). *Globalization and Educational Reform: What Planners Need to Know*, Paris: United Nations Educational, Scientific, and Cultural Organization (UNESCO).

Casale, D., and Posel, D. (2011). 'English Language Proficiency and Earnings in a Developing Country: The Case of South Africa', *Journal of Socio-Economics*, 40(4), 385–93.

CDC (2005). Primary Education Curriculum 1–3, 2062 BS, Sanothimi, Bhaktapur: Curriculum Development Centre.

CDC (2010). The Local Curriculum: Resource and Training Manual (In Nepali), Sanothimi, Bhaktapur: Curriculum Development Centre.

Cederman, L-K., Weidmann, N. B., and Gleditsch, K. S. (2010). 'Horizontal Inequalities and Ethnonationalist Civil War: A Global Comparison', *American Political Science Review*, 105(3): 478–95.

Central Bureau of Statistics (2003). Population Monograph of Nepal, vol. 1, Kathmandu: National Planning Commission Secretariat.

Central Bureau of Statistics (2004). Nepal Living Standard Survey 2003/2004, Kathmandu: Central Bureau of Statistics.

Central Bureau of Statistics (CBS) (2014). Population Monograph of Nepal, Kathmandu: CBS.

Chauvet, L., and Collier, P. (2008). 'What Are the Preconditions for Turnarounds in Failing States?' *Conflict Management and Peace Science*, 25: 332–48.

Child Workers in Nepal Concerned Centre (2004). 'The State of the Rights of the Child in Nepal', Kathmandu: Child Workers in Nepal Concerned Centre, https://resourcecentre.savethechildren.net/document/state-rights-child-nepal-2004/ (accessed August 20, 2021).

Chinwokwu, E. C., and Arop, S. K. (2014). 'Socio-Psychological Effects of Political Violence and War on Gender in Nigeria', *Mediterranean Journal of Social Sciences*, 5(26): 44–50.

Clandinin, D. J., and Connelly, F. M. (2000). *Narrative Inquiry: Experience and Story in Qualitative Research*, San Francisco: Jossey Bass.

Cohen, R. (1978). 'Ethnicity: Problem and Focus in Anthropology', *Annual Review of Anthropology*, 7: 379–403.

Collier, P., and Hoeffler, A. (2004). 'Greed and Grievance in Civil War', *Oxford Economic Papers*, 56(4): 563–95.

Collier, P., and Sambanis, N. (2002). 'Understanding Civil War: A New Agenda', *Journal of Conflict Resolution*, 46(1): 3–12.

Collier, P., Hoeffler, A., and Soderbom, M. (2008). 'Post-Conflict Risks', *Journal of Peace Research*, 45(1): 461–78.

Collinson, S. (ed.) (2003). *Power, Livelihoods and Conflict: Case Studies in Political Economy Analysis for Humanitarian Action*, London: Overseas Development Institute.

Connolly, K. (2007). 'Introduction to Part 2: Exploring Narrative Inquiry Practices', *Qualitative Inquiry*, 13: 450–3.

Constitution of Nepal (2015). The Constitution of Nepal, https://www.mohp.gov.np/downloads/Constitution%20of%20Nepal%202072_full_english.pdf (accessed 1 September 2021).

Cornwall, A., and Brock, K. (2005). 'What Do Buzzwords Do for Development Policy? A Critical Look at "Participation", "Empowerment" and "Poverty Reduction"', *Third World Quarterly*, 26: 1043–60.

CPA (2006). 'Comprehensive Peace Accord': Signed between Nepal Government and the Communist Party of Nepal (Maoist), https://peacemaker.un.org/nepal-comprehensiveagreement2006, (accessed 22 November 2006).

Credit Suisse (2020). Global Wealth Report 2020, Zürich: Credit Suisse Research Institute, https://www.credit-suisse.com/about-us/en/reports-research/global-wealth-report.html (accessed 6 September 2021).

Crotty, M. (1998). *The Foundations of Social Research*, London: Sage.

Cuellar-Marchelli, H. (2003). 'Decentralization and Privatization of Education in El Salvador: Assessing the Experience', *International Journal of Educational Development*, 23: 145–66.

Dahal, M., and Nguyen, Q. (2014). 'Private Non-state Sector Engagement in the Provision of Educational Services at the Primary and Secondary Levels in South Asia: An Analytical Review of its Role in School Enrollment and Student Achievement', Policy Research working paper 6899, Washington, DC: World Bank.Davies, L. (2004). *Education and Conflict: Complexity and Chaos*, London: Routledge.

Davies, L. (2005). 'Schools and War: Urgent Agendas for Comparative and International Education', *Compare: A Journal of Comparative Education*, 35: 357–71.

Davies, L. (2008). *Educating against Extremism*, Stoke-on-Trent: Trentham Books.

Deraniyagala, S. (2005). 'The Political Economy of Civil Conflict in Nepal', *Oxford Development Economics*, 33: 47–62.

DFID (2010) 'Working Effectively in Conflict-Affected and Fragile Situations', A DFID practice paper, March 2010, London: Department for International Development, https://assets.publishing.service.gov.uk/government/uploads/system/uploads/attachment_data/file/67701/building-peaceful-states-D.pdf (accessed 18 August 2021).

Dhital, T. (2006). Sashastra dwandako chapetama balbalika: Sashastra dwandaka kramma mritu, ghaite, pakrau tatha apaharanma pareka balbalikako biwaran 1996–2006, (Children Caught in the Armed Conflict: Details of the Children Dead, Wounded, Arrested and Abducted during the Armed Conflict 1996–2006), Kathmandu: CWIN, Nepal.

Dhungana, R. K. (2021). 'Peace Education Initiative in Nepal: Redressing the Value of "Celebrating Diversity"', *Journal of Contemporary Issues in Education*, 16(1): 3–22.

Dhungana, S. (2019). 'Exploitation of Teachers Goes Unchecked at Private Schools', *My Republica*, 30 January 2019, https://myrepublica.nagariknetwork.com/news/overworked-and-underpaid/ (accessed 1 September 2021).

Díaz-Ríos, C. M. (2021). 'The Politics of Education Reforms in Post-Conflict Societies: A Cautionary Tale for the Colombian Case', in J. L. Fabra-Zamora, A. Molina-Ochoa and N. C. Doubleday (eds), *The Colombian Peace Agreement: A Multidisciplinary Assessment*, 246–60, London: Routledge.

Do, Q-T., and Iyer, L. (2007). 'Poverty, Social Divisions and Conflict in Nepal', World Bank Policy Research working paper 4228, May, Washington, DC: World Bank.

DOE (2073BS-2016). 'A Study on Identification of Scientific Basis of Fee Structure in the Institutional Schools', Sanothimi, Bhaktapur: Ministry of Education, Department of Education, http://www.doe.gov.np/assets/uploads/files/3c44e3902f19affc4f9e8d00e7d91a66.pdf.

Dong, T. B. (2016). 'Social Inequality in the Civil Service and a Review of Affirmative Action in Nepal', *South Asianist*, 4(2): 119–42.

Education Cannot Wait (2021). 'COVID-19 and Education in Emergencies', https://www.educationcannotwait.org/covid-19/ (accessed 12 September 2021).

Education Cannot Wait (2018). 'Strategic Plan 2018–2021', https://www.educationcannotwait.org/wp-content/uploads/2018/05/Strategic_plan_2018_2021_web_PAGES.pdf (accessed 5 September 2021).

Edwards, R. (2011). 'Disconnect and Capture of Education Decentralisation Reforms in Nepal: Implications for Community Involvement in Schooling', *Globalisation, Societies and Education*, 9: 67–84.

Escobar, A. (1995). *Encountering Development: Making and Unmaking of the Third World*, New Jersey: Princeton University Press.

Ezati, B. A., Ssempala, C., and Ssenkusu, P. (2011). '"Teachers" Perceptions of the Effects of Young People's War Experiences on Teaching and Learning in Northern Uganda', in J. Paulson (ed.), *Education, Conflict and Development*, Oxford Studies in Comparative Education, 167–85, Oxford: Symposium.

Feinstein, C., Giertsen, A., and O'Kane, C. (2010). 'Children's Participation in Armed Conflict and Post-Conflict Peace Building', in B. Percy-Smith and N. Thomas (eds),

A Handbook of Children and Young People's Participation Perspectives from Theory and Practice, 53–62, Oxon: Routledge.

Feldman, S., and Stenner, K. (1997). 'Perceived Threat and Authoritarianism', *Political Psychology*, 18: 741–70, http://dx.doi.org/0162-895X.00077.

Ferguson, J. (2006). *Global Shadows: Africa in the Neoliberal World Order*, London: Duke University Press.

Fraser, N. (2005). 'Reframing Justice in a Globalized World', *New Left Review*, 36: 79–88.

Freeman, M. (2006). *International Child Abduction Effects*, Reunite International Child Abduction Centre, http://takeroot.org/ee/pdf_files/library/freeman_2006.pdf (accessed on 26 August 2021).

Freire, P. (1974). *Education for Critical Consciousness*, London: Continuum.

Freire, P. (2014). *Pedagogy of the Oppressed*, 30th edition, London: Bloomsbury.

Fukuyama, F. (1992). *The End of History and the Last Man*, London: Penguin.

Gallagher, T., Robinson, G., Hughes, J., and Connolly, D. (2019). Education in Conflict-Affected Areas: Final Report, London: British Council, https://www.britishcouncil.org/sites/default/files/global_education_security_and_stability_report_0319.pdf.

Galtung, J. (1964). 'An Editorial', *Journal of Peace Research*, 1:1–4.

Galtung, J. (1969). 'Violence, Peace and Peace Research', *Journal of Peace Research*, 6: 167–91.

Galtung, J. (1971). 'Structural and Direct Violence: A Note on Operationalization', *Journal of Peace Research*, 8: 73–6.

GCPEA (2014). *Education under Attack 2014*, New York: Global Coalition to Protect Education from Attack, https://protectingeducation.org/publication/education-under-attack-2014/ (accessed date 2 April 2022).

GCPEA (2020). *Education under Attack 2020: A Global Study of Attacks on Schools, Universities, Their Students and Staff, 2017–2019*, New York: Global Coalition to Protect Education from Attack, https://protectingeducation.org/publication/education-under-attack-2020/ (accessed 1 September 2021).

Gellner, D. N. (2007). 'Caste, Ethnicity and Inequality in Nepal', *Economic and Political Weekly* (May), 1823–8.

Gellner, D. N. (2016) 'The Idea of Nepal', The Mahesh Chandra Regmi Lecture 2016, Social Science Baha, Kathmandu.

Geo-Jaja, M. A. (2004). 'Decentralisation and Privatisation of Education in Africa: Which Option for Nigeria?' *International Review of Education*, 50: 307–23.

George, S., Johnson, Z., and Lüdemann, C. (2020). 'Decades of Neglect: Donor Financing for Education in Emergencies', *Development Tracker Insights*, https://donortracker.org/insights/decades-neglect-donor-financing-education-emergencies, (accessed 9 November 2020).

George, T. (2020). *Hermeneutics*, Stanford Encyclopedia of Philosophy, https://plato.stanford.edu/entries/hermeneutics/ (accessed 15 August 2021).

Gettleman, J., Kushkush, I., and Callimachi, R. (2015). 'Somali Militants Kill 147 at Kenyan University', *New York Times*, 2 April 2015, https://www.nytimes.

com/2015/04/03/world/africa/garissauniversity-college-shooting-in-kenya.html (accessed 25 August 2021).

Ghobarah, H. A., Huth, P., and Russett, B. (2003). 'Civil Wars Kill and Maim People-Long after the Shooting Stops', *American Political Science Review*, 97: 189–202.

Gill, S., and Niens, U. (2014). 'Education as Humanization: A Theoretical Review on the Role of Dialogic Pedagogy in Peacebuilding Education', *Compare: A Journal of Comparative and International Education*, 44(1): 10–31.

Giroux, H. (1988). *Teachers as Transformative Intellectuals: Towards a Critical Pedagogy of Learning*, Westport, CT: Bergin and Garvey Publishers.

Giroux, H. (2011). *On Critical Pedagogy*, London: Bloomsbury.

Goldwyn, R., and Chigas, D. (2013). 'Monitoring and Evaluating Conflict Sensitivity Methodological Challenges and Practical Solutions', London: DFID, https://www.cdacollaborative.org/wp-content/uploads/2016/02/Monitoring-and-Evaluating-Conflict-Sensitivity.pdf (accessed 20 August 2021).

GoN, (1971). 'The National Education System Plan for 1971–76', Kathmandu: Ministry of Education, Government of Nepal, https://www.moe.gov.np/assets/uploads/files/2028_English.pdf (accessed 20 August 2021).

GoN (2006). 'Comprehensive Peace Agreement between the Government of Nepal and the Communist Party of Nepal (Maoist)', Kathmandu: Government of Nepal, https://peacemaker.un.org/nepal-comprehensiveagreement2006 (accessed 20 August 2021).

GoN (2015). 'School Level Educational Statistics of NEPAL', https://www.doe.gov.np/assets/uploads/files/b9f2323936f096fd40a4a34cce9198d7.pdf (accessed 11 September 2019).

GoN (2016). 'Flash II report 2072 (2015–016)', Bhaktapur: Ministry of Education, Department of Education, https://www.doe.gov.np/assets/uploads/files/9c1b2b977abc775a7b132863f6f4cd31.pdf (accessed 20 August 2021).

GoN. (2016). 'School Sector Development Plan (SSDP) 2016–2023', Kathmandu: Ministry of Education, Government of Nepal, http://www.moe.gov.np/assets/uploads/files/SSDP_Book_English_Final_July_5,_20171.pdf.

GoN (2018). 'Flash I Report 2075 (2018/19)', Bhaktapur: Ministry of Education, Science and Technology Centre for Education and Human Resource Development, Government of Nepal, https://www.doe.gov.np/assets/uploads/files/cbe2b2b1ae68bb5bdaa93299343e5c28.pdf (accessed 29 August 2021).

GoN (2020). 'Nepal Labour Migration Report 2020', Kathmandu: Government of Nepal, https://nepalindata.com/resource/nepal-labour-migration-report-2020/.

Goodhand, J., and Walton, O. (2009). 'The Limits of Liberal Peacebuilding? International Engagement in the Sri Lankan Peace Process', *Journal of Intervention and Statebuilding*, 3(3) 303–23, doi: 10.1080/17502970903086693.

Goodhand, J., Vaux, T., and Walker, R. (2002). *Conducting Conflict Assessments: Guidance Notes*, London: Department for International Development, https://gsdrc.org/document-library/conducting-conflict-assessments-guidance-notes/ (accessed 4 April 2022).

Goyal, S. (2009). 'Inside the House of Cleaning: The Relative Performance of Public and Private Schools in Orissa', *Education Economics*, 17(3): 315–27.

GPE (2020). 'Supporting Countries Affected by Fragility and Conflict', Washington, DC: Global Partnership for Education, August 2020, https://www.globalpartnership.org/sites/default/files/document/file/2020-08-GPE-factsheets-Fragility.pdf (accessed 5 September 2021).

Gramsci, A. (1971). *Selections from the Prison Notebooks*, Q. Hoare and G. Nowell-Smith, trans, London: Lawrence and Wishart.

Grewal, B. S. (2003). 'Johan Galtung: Positive and Negative Peace', available from: http://www.activeforpeace.org/no/fred/Positive_Negative_peace.pdf.

Green, L. (1995). 'Living in a State of Fear', in C. Nordstrom and A. Robben (eds), *Fieldwork under Fire: Contemporary Studies of Violence and Survival*, 105–28, Berkeley: University of California Press.

Gounari, P. (2010). 'Manufacturing Fear: The Violence of Anti-politics', in J. Schostak and J. F. Schostak (eds), *Researching Violence, Democracy and the Rights of People*, 180–95, Oxon: Routledge.

Guichon, A. (2014). Into the Unknown Exploitation of Nepalese Migrant Domestic Workers in Lebanon, London: Anti-Slavery International, https://ecommons.cornell.edu/bitstream/handle/1813/102238/ASI_2014_DWS_Lebanon_Into_the_Unknown.pdf?sequence=1 (accessed 20 August 2021).

Gurr, T. R. (1970). *Why Men Rebel*, Princeton: Princeton University Press.

Gurung, Y., Pradhan, M. S., and Shakya, D. (2018). *State of Social Inclusion in Nepal: Caste Ethnicity and Gender, Evidence from Nepal Social Inclusion Survey 2018*, Kathmandu: Central Department of Anthropology, Tribhuvan University.

Hachhethu, K., Kumar, S., and Subedi, J. (2008). *Nepal in Transition: A Study on the State of Democracy*, Kathmandu: DSA/Nepal Chapter and International IDEA.

Haider, H. (2014). *Conflict: Topic Guide,* revised edition with B. Rohwerder, Birmingham: GSDRC, University of Birmingham.

Hanson, M. E. (1998). 'Strategies of Educational Decentralization: Key Questions and Core Issues', *Journal of Educational Administration*, 36(2): 111–28.

Harbom, L., and Wallensteen, P. (2007). 'Armed Conflict, 1989–2006', *Journal of Peace Research*, 44: 623–34.

Harbom, L., Högbladh, S., and Wallensteen, P. (2006). 'Armed Conflict and Peace Agreements', *Journal of Peace Research*, 43(5): 617–31.

Harriss, J. (2011). 'How Far Have India's Economic Reforms Been "Guided by Compassion and Justice"?: Social Policy in the Neoliberal Era', in Sanjay Ruparelia, Sanjay Reddy, John Harriss and Stuart Corbridge (eds), *Understanding India's New Political Economy: A Great Transformation?*, 66–80, New York: Routledge .

Hart, J. (2001). 'Conflict in Nepal and Its Impact on Children', Discussion paper, Oxford: Refugee Studies Centre, University of Oxford, https://www.rsc.ox.ac.uk/publications/conflict-in-nepal-and-its-impact-on-children.

Harvey, D. (2007). *A Brief History of Neoliberalism*, Oxford: Oxford University Press.
Haviland, C. (2007). 'End of Nepal Monarchy – or Trouble?' BBC, http://news.bbc.co.uk/2/hi/south_asia/7159258.stm (accessed 29 Aug 2021).
Hendry, P. M. (2007). 'The Future of Narrative Inquiry', *Qualitative Inquiry*, 13(4): 487–98.
Hoelscher, K., Miklian, J., and Nygård, H. M. (2015). 'Understanding Attacks on Humanitarian Aid Workers', *Conflict Trends* – June 2015, https://www.prio.org/utility/DownloadFile.ashx?id=101&type=publicationfile (accessed 15 September 2021).
Hornberger, N., and Vaish, V. (2009). 'Multilingual Language Policy and School Linguistic Practice: Globalisation and English-Language Teaching in India, Singapore and South Africa', *Compare*, 39: 305–20.
Hoxby, C., and C. Avery. (2013). *The Missing 'One-Offs': The Hidden Supply of High-Achieving, Low-Income Students*, https://theconversation.com/the-psychology-of-riots-and-why-its-never-just-mindless-violence-125676 (accessed 25 September 2021).
HMG (1971). *National Education System Plan for 1971–76*, Kathmandu: His Majesty's Government of Nepal.
HMG (1998). *The Ninth Plan (1997–2002)*, Kathmandu: National Planning Commission (NPC)
Huber, E., Gunderson, J., and Stephens, J. D. (2020). 'Private Education and Inequality in the Knowledge Economy', *Policy and Society*, 39(2): 171–88.
Human Rights Watch (2016). *World Report 2016: Events of 2015*, New York: Human Rights Watch, https://www.hrw.org/world-report/2016/country-chapters/nigeria (accessed 15 September 2021).
Human Rights Watch (2021) *World Report 2021: Events of 2020*, New York: Human Rights Watch, https://www.hrw.org/sites/default/files/media_2021/01/2021_hrw_world_report.pdf (accessed 14 September 2021).
Humphreys, M., and Weinstein, J. (2008). '"Who Fights?" The Determinants of Participation in Civil War', *American Journal of Political Science*, 52(2): 436–55.
Hung, C. (2005). 'The Dance of Revolution: Yangge in Beijing in the Early 1950s', *China Quarterly*, 181: 82–99, https://www.jstor.org/stable/20192445 (accessed 14 September 2021).
Hutt, M. (2004). 'Introduction: Monarchy, Democracy, and Maoism in Nepal', in M. Hutt (ed.), *Himalayan 'People's War': Nepal's Maoist Rebellion*, 1–20, London: C. Hurst & Co.
Hutt, M. (2012). 'Singing the New Nepal', *Nations and Nationalism*, 18(2): 306–25.
Ibrahim, B., and Mukhtar, J. I. (2017). 'An Analysis of the Causes and Consequences of Kidnapping in Nigeria', *African Research Review*, 11(4): 134–43.
IIEP (2014). 'Safety, Resilience, and Social Cohesion: A Guide for Education Sector Planners', Paris: UNESCO, International Institute for Educational Planning, http://education4resilience.iiep.unesco.org/sites/default/files/booklets/1_planning_en.pdf (accessed 14 September 2021).

IIEP (2021). 'Education System Resilience', Paris: UNESCO, International Institute for Educational Planning, http://www.iiep.unesco.org/en/our-mission/education-system-resilience (accessed 14 September 2021).

INEE (2010). *Minimum Standards for Education: Preparedness, Response, Recovery*, New York: Inter-Agency Network for Education in Emergencies.

INEE (2013). *INEE Conflict Sensitive Education Guiding Principles*, New York: Inter-Agency Network for Education in Emergencies.

INEE (2018). *Strategic Framework 2018–2023*, New York: Inter-Agency Network for Education in Emergencies, https://inee.org/system/files/resources/INEE_Strategic_Framework_2018-2023_ENG.pdf (accessed 20 August 2021).

Informal Sector Service Centre (INSEC) (2007). *Human Rights Year Book*, Kathmandu: Informal Sector Service Centre.

International Alert (2006). Education for All Nepal, Kathmandu: International Alert/Embassy of Finland.

Internal Displacement Monitoring Centre (2011). Nepal, http://www.internal-displacement.org/idmc/website/countries.nsf/(httpEnvelopes)/1949E98C81942B55C12571FE004D8821?OpenDocument (accessed 1 August 2021).

International Commission of Jurists (2009). 'Disappearances in Nepal: Addressing the Past, Securing the Future. International Commission for Jurists', Briefing paper, http://reliefweb.int/node/300176 (accessed 21 January 2011).

International Labour Office (2003). 'Wounded Childhood. The Use of Children in Armed Conflict in Central Africa', Geneva: ILO Publication Bureau.

Jamil, I., and Baniamin, H. M. (2020). 'Representative and Responsive Bureaucracy in Nepal: A Mismatch or a Realistic Assumption?' *Public Administration and Policy*, 23(2): 141–56.

Jeffery, R. (2021). 'Truth Commissions and Democratic Transitions: Neither Truth and Reconciliation nor Democratization in Nepal', *Journal of Human Rights*, 20(3): 318–38.

Jha, H. B. (2019). *The Janajati of Nepal*, New Delhi: Vivekananda International Foundation.

Jones, S. (2010). 'Lessons from Political Economy Analysis in Nepal', Oxford Policy Management.

Joshi, P. (2019). 'The Growth, Roles and Needs of the Private Education System: Private Stakeholder Perspectives from Nepal', *International Journal of Educational Development*, 65: 57–67.

Joshi, P. (2020). 'The Consequences – and Causes – of Private School Growth: A Look at Nepal', World Education Blog, https://gemreportunesco.wordpress.com/2020/02/04/the-consequences-and-causes-of-private-school-growth-a-look-at-nepal/ (accessed 22 August 2021).

Karki, A., and Seddon, D. (eds) (2003). *The People's War in Nepal: Left Perspectives*. New Delhi: Adroit Publishers.

Kang, S., and Meernik, J. (2005). 'Civil War Destruction and the Prospects for Economic Growth', *Journal of Politics*, 67, 88–109.

Kaufman, S. (2006). 'Escaping the Symbolic Politics Trap: Reconciliation Initiatives and Conflict Resolution in Ethnic Wars', *Journal of Peace Research*, 43(2): 201–18.

Kern, T. (2009).'Cultural Performance and Political Regime Change', *Sociological Theory*, 27(3): 291–316.

King, E. (2014). *From Classrooms to Conflict in Rwanda*, Cambridge: Cambridge University Press.

Kingdon, G. (1996). 'The Quality and Efficiency of Public and Private Education: A Case Study of Urban India', *Oxford Bulletin of Economics and Statistics*, 58(1): 57–82.

Kitagawa, K. (2020). 'Disaster Risk Reduction Activities as Learning', *Natural Hazards*, doi:10.1007/s11069-020-04443-5.

Korostelina, K. (2017). 'The Normative Function of National Historical Narratives: South Korean Perceptions of Relations with Japan', *National Identities*, 21(2): 171–89.

Kothari, R. (1997). 'The Agony of the Modern State', in M. Rahnema and V. Bawtree (eds), *The Post-Development Reader*, 143–51, London: Zed Books.

Kreutz, J. (2010). 'How and When Armed Conflicts End: Introducing the UCDP Conflict Termination Dataset', *Journal of Peace Research*, 47(2): 243–50.

Kumar, D. (2003). 'Consequences of the Militarized Conflict and the Cost of Violence in Nepal', *Contributions to Nepalese Studies*, 30(2): 167–216.

Kumar, D. (2005). 'Proximate Causes of Conflict in Nepal', *Contributions to Nepalese Studies*, 32: 51–92.

Lai, B., and Thyne, C. (2007). 'The Effect of Civil War on Education, 1980–97', *Journal of Peace Research*, 44: 277–92.

Lal, C. K. (2012). *To Be a Nepalese*, Kathmandu: Martin Chautari.

Lall, M. (2020). *Myanmar's Education Reforms: A Pathway to Social Justice?* London: UCL Press.

Landau, S. F., Gvirsman, D. S., Huesmann, R., Dubow, E. F., Boxer, P., Ginges, J. and Sikaki, K. (2015). 'The Effects of Exposure to Violence on Aggressive Behaviour: The Case of Arab and Jewish Children in Israel', Hebrew University of Jerusalem Legal Research Paper, 16–19, 1–39, https://papers.ssrn.com/sol3/papers.cfm?abstract_id=2708492 (accessed 8 August 2021).

Langer, A., and Kuppens, L. (2019). 'Horizontal Inequalities and Conflict: Education as a Separate Dimension of Horizontal Inequalities', *Education and Conflict Review*, 2: 38–43.

Lawoti, M. (2005). *Towards a Democratic Nepal: Inclusive Political Institutions for a Multicultural Society*, London: Sage.

Lawoti, M. (2007). 'Contentious Politics in Democratizing Nepal', in M. Lawoti (ed.), *Contentious Politics in Democratization in Nepal*, 17–47, London: Sage.

Lawoti, M. (2010). Evolution and Growth of the Maoist insurgency in Nepal, in M. Lawoti and A. Pahari (eds), *Evolution and Growth of the Maoist Insurgency in Nepal*, 3–29, London, Routledge.

Lawoti, M., and Hangen, S. (2013). *Nationalism and Ethnic Conflict in Nepal*, Oxford: Routledge.

Lawoti, M., and Pahari, A. K. (eds) (2010). *Evolution and Growth of the Maoist Insurgency in Nepal*, London: Routledge.

Lederach, J. P. (1995). *Preparing for Peace: Conflict Transformation Across Cultures*, New York: Syracuse University Press.

Leve, L. (2007). '"Failed Development" and Rural Revolution in Nepal: Rethinking Subaltern Consciousness and Women's Empowerment', *Anthropological Quarterly*, 80(1): 127–72.

Lieblich, A., Tuval-Mashiach, R., and Zilber, T. (1998). *Narrative Research: Readings, Analysis, and Interpretation*, London: Sage.

Liechty, M. (2003). *Suitably Modern: Making Middle Class Culture in a New Consumer Society*, Princeton: Princeton University Press.

Liow, J. C., and D. Pathan (2010). *Confronting Ghosts: Thailand's Shapeless Southern Insurgency*, Sydney: Lowy Institute for International Policy.

Machel, G. (1996) 'The Impact of Armed Conflict on Children', an expert report by the Special Representative of the Secretary-General, New York: United Nations, https://digitallibrary.un.org/record/223213?ln=en (accessed 12 August 2021).

Machel, G. (2001). *The Impact of War on Children: A Review of Progress Since the 1996 United Nations Report on the Impact of Armed Conflict on Children*, London: C. Hurst & Co. Publishers.

Magee, A., and Pherali, T. (2019). 'Paulo Freire and Critical Consciousness in Conflict-Affected Contexts', *Education and Conflict Review*, 2: 44–8.

Makkawi, I. (2002). 'Role Conflict and the Dilemma of Palestinian Teachers in Israel', *Comparative Education*, 38(1): 39–52.

Malagodi, M. (2013). *Constitutional Nationalism and Legal Exclusion: Equality, Identity Politics, and Democracy in Nepal (1990–2007)*, Oxford: Oxford University Press.

Maoist Statements and Documents (2003). In A. Karki and D. Seddon (eds), *The People's War in Nepal: Left Perspectives*. New Delhi: Adroit Publishers.

Marginson, S. (2019). 'Limitations of Human Capital Theory', *Studies in Higher Education*, 4(2): 287–301.

Mason, D. (2006). 'Ethnicity', in G. Payne (ed.), *Social Divisions*, 2nd edition, 102–30, Basingstoke: Palgrave.

Matsumoto (2011). 'Expectations and Realities of Education in Post-Conflict Sierra Leone: A Reflection of Society or a Driver for Peacebuilding?' in J. Paulson (ed.), *Education, Conflict and Development, Oxford Studies in Comparative Education* (D. Phillips (Series ed.)), 119–44, Oxford: Symposium.

McCaffrey, G., Raffin-Bouchal, S., and Moules, N. J. (2012). 'Hermeneutics as Research Approach: A Reappraisal', *International Journal of Qualitative Methods*, 11(3): 214–229.

McCowan, T. (2012). 'Human Rights within Education: Assessing the Justifications', *Cambridge Journal of Education*, 42(1): 67–81.

McEvoy-Levy, S. (ed.) (2006). *Troublemakers or Peacemakers? Youth and Post-Accord Peacebuilding*, Notre Dame: University of Notre Dame.

McGinn, N., and Welsh, T. (1999). *Decentralisation of Education: Why, When, What and How?* Paris: United Nations Educational, Scientific, and Cultural Organization (UNESCO).

Miklian, J. (2008). 'Nepal's Terai: Constructing an Ethnic Conflict', South Asia Briefing Paper No.1, Oslo: International Peace Research Institute, www.prio.no (accessed 10 September 2021).

Miles, R. (1993). *Racism After Race Relations*, London: Routledge.

Milton, S., and Barakat, S. (2016). 'Higher Education as the Catalyst of Recovery in Conflict-Affected Societies', *Globalisation, Societies and Education*, 14(3): 403–21.

Ministry of General Administration (2010). 'Department of Civil Personnel Records', Lalitpur: Government of Nepal, Ministry of General Administration.

Ministry of General Administration (2014). 'Department of Civil Personnel Records', unpublished government records, Ministry of General Administration, Government of Nepal, Nepal.

MoE (2007). National Curriculum Framework, Bhaktapur: Curriculum Development Centre, http://www.moe.gov.np/assets/uploads/files/National-Curriculum-Framework-2007-English.pdf (accessed 28 July 2021).

MOE (2009). School Sector Reform Plan 2009–2016, Kathmandu: Ministry of Education, Government of Nepal, https://www.moe.gov.np/assets/uploads/files/SSRP_English.pdf (accessed 30 July 2021).

MOE (2016). School Sector Development Plan 2016/17-2022/23, Kathmandu: Ministry of Education, https://www.globalpartnership.org/sites/default/files/2019-05-nepal-education-sector-plan.pdf (accessed 30 July 2021).

Morris, P. (2021). 'Covid and the Future of Education: Global Agencies "Building Back Better"', a presidential address delivered at the UKFIET Conference 15/09/2021, (online).

Mundy, K., and Dryden-Peterson, S. (2011). 'Educating Children in Zones of Conflict: An Overview and Introduction', in K. Mundy and S. Dryden-Peterson (eds), *Educating Children in Conflict Zones: Research, Policy, and Practice for Systemic Change – A Tribute to Jackie Kirk*, 1–12, New York: Teachers College Press.

Murshed, S. M., and Gates, S. (2005). 'Spatial-Horizontal Inequality and the Maoist Insurgency in Nepal', *Review of Development Economics*, 9: 121–34.

Neupane, G. (2000). 'Nepālko jātiya prasna: Sāmājik banot ra sājhedāriko sambhāvanā' (Nepal's Nationality Question: Social Structure and the Possibilities of Compromise), Kathmandu: Centre for Development Studies.

Neupane, P. (2017). 'Barriers to Education and School Attainment – Evidence from Secondary Schools in Rural Nepal', *International Education Studies*, 10(2): 68–83.

Newman, E., and Richmond, O., (eds) (2006). *The Challenges of Peacebuilding: Managing Spoilers during Conflict Resolution*, Tokyo: United Nations University Press.

Nhan-O'Reilly, J. (2012). 'New Funding for Education in Emergencies', Global Partnership for Education, 19 December 2012, https://www.globalpartnership.org/blog/new-funding-education-emergencies (accessed 21 August 2021).

Nicolai, S., and Triplehorn, C. (2003). 'The Role of Education in Protecting Children in Conflict, Humanitarian Practice Network', HPN Paper 42, London: Overseas Development Institute.

NIRT (2016). Nepal Education Sector Analysis, Kathmandu, Nepal, https://www.globalpartnership.org/sites/default/files/2019-05-nepal-education-sector-analysis.pdf (accessed 13 August 2021).

Novelli, M. (2010). 'The New Geopolitics of Educational Aid: From Cold Wars to Holy Wars?' *International Journal of Educational Development*, 30(5): 453–9.

Novelli, M. (2011). 'Are We All Soldiers Now? The Dangers of the Securitization of Education and Conflict', in K. Mundy and S. Dryden-Peterson, *Educating Children in Conflict Zones: Research, Policy, and Practice for Systemic Change: A Tribute to Jackie Kirk*, 49-66, New York: Teachers College Press.

Novelli, M. (2017). 'Education & Countering Violent Extremism: Western Logics from South to North', *Compare: A Journal of Comparative and International Education*, 47(6): 835–51.

Novelli, M. (2019). *Knowledge Production on Education in Conflict Contexts: Towards an Ecology of Knowledge*, Norrag, https://www.norrag.org/knowledge-production-on-education-in-conflict-contexts-towards-an-ecology-of-knowledge-by-mario-novelli/ (accessed 2 April 2022).

Novelli, M., and Higgins, S. (2017). 'The Violence of Peace and the Role of Education: Insights from Sierra Leone', *Compare: A Journal of Comparative and International Education*, 47(1): 32–45.

Novelli, M., and Lopes Cardozo, M. T. A. (2008). 'Conflict, Education and the Global South: New Critical Directions', *International Journal of Educational Development*, 28(4): 473–88.

Novelli, M., and Smith, A. (2011). 'The Role of Education in Peacebuilding: A Synthesis Report of Findings from Lebanon, Nepal and Sierra Leone', New York: UNICEF, https://reliefweb.int/sites/reliefweb.int/files/resources/EEPCT_PeacebuildingSynthesisReport%20%281%29.pdf (accessed 20 October 2020).

Novelli, M., Lopes Cardozo, M. T. A., and Smith, A. (2017). 'The 4Rs Framework: Analyzing Education's Contribution to Sustainable Peacebuilding with Social Justice in Conflict-Affected Contexts', *Journal on Education in Emergencies*, 3(1): 14–43.

Novelli, M., Lopes Cardozo, M. T. A., and Smith, A. (2019). 'The "4 Rs" as a Tool for Critical Policy Analysis of the Education Sector in Conflict-Affected States', *Education and Conflict Review*, 2: 70–5.

Novelli, M., Higgins, S., Ugur, M., and Valiente, V. (2014). 'The Political Economy of Education Systems in Conflict-Affected Contexts: A Rigorous Literature Review', Department for International Development.

Novelli, M., Benjamin, S., Çelik, A., Kane, P., Kutan, B., and Pherali, T. (2021). '"Laboratories of Learning" Education, Learning and Knowledge-Making in Social Movements: Insights from Colombia, Nepal, South Africa and Turkey', Brighton: University of Sussex.

Nowak, A. Z., and Dahal, G. (2016). 'The Contribution of Education to Economic Growth: Evidence from Nepal', *International Journal of Economic Sciences*, V(2): 22–41.

OCE (2016). 'School-Leaving Certificate Records, 2014–15', Sano Thimi, Bhaktapur: Office of the Controller of Examinations.

OHCHR (2008). 'Investigation by the Office of the High Commissioner for Human Rights in Nepal into the Violent Incidents in Kapilvastu, Rupandehi and Dang Districts of 16–21 September 2007', Kathmandu: UN Human Rights Office (OHCHR), https://nepal.ohchr.org/en/index.html.

O'Malley, B. (2007). 'Education under Attack: A Global Study on Targeted Political and Military Violence against Education Staff, Students, Teachers, Union and Governmental Officials, and Institutions', Paris: United Nations Educational, Scientific and Cultural Organization.

O'Malley, B. (2010) 'Education Under Attack, 2010: A Global Study on Targeted Political and Military Violence against Education Staff, Students, Teachers, Union and Government Officials, Aid Workers and Institutions', Paris: United Nations Educational, Scientific and Cultural Organization.

Onta, P. (1996). 'Ambivalence Denied: The Making of Rastriya Itihas in Panchayat Era Textbooks', *Contributions to Nepalese Studies*, 23: 213–54.

Osler, A., and Starkey, H. (2005). *Changing Citizenship: Democracy and Inclusion in Education*, Maidenhead: Open University Press.

Østby, G., Nordås, R. and Rød, J. K. (2009). 'Regional Inequalities and Civil Conflict in Sub-Saharan Africa', *International Studies Quarterly*, 53(2): 301–24.

Oyefusi, A. (2008). 'Oil and the Probability of Rebel Participation among Youths in the Niger Delta of Nigeria', *Journal of Peace Research*, 45(4): 539–55.

Pandey, R. R., K. C., K. B., and Wood, B. H. (eds) (1956). 'Education in Nepal: Report of the Nepal National Education Planning Commission', Kathmandu: College of Education.

Pandey, N. N. (2010). *New Nepal: Fault Lines*, London: Sage.

Parajuli, L. (2019). 'Schools as an Arena of Struggle: Reexamining the Panchayat Era Politics of Education', *Studies in Nepali History and Society*, 24(2): 381–414.

Paris, R. (2004). *At War's End: Building Peace after Civil Conflict*, Cambridge, UK: Cambridge University Press.

Pathak, Y. (2017). *Mangena: Nepal Manthan [Mangena: Nepal Churning]*, Kathmandu: Fine Prints.

Paudel, N. R. (2018). 'Limits of Inclusion: Women's Participation in Nepalese Civil Service', in N. Ahmed (ed.), *Women in Governing Institutions in South Asia*, 193–208, London: Palgrave Macmillan.

Paulson, J. (2006). 'The Educational Recommendations of Truth and Reconciliation Commissions: Potential and Practice in Sierra Leone', *Research in Comparative and International Education*, 1, 335–50.

Paulson, J. (2011). *Education, Conflict and Development, Oxford Studies in Comparative Education*, Oxford: Symposium.

Paulson, J., and Bellino, M. (2017). 'Truth Commissions, Education and Positive Peace: An Analysis of Truth Commission Final Reports (1980–2015)', *Comparative Education*, 53(3): 351–78.

Peters, M. (2014). '"Western Education Is Sinful": Boko Haram and the Abduction of Chibok Schoolgirls', *Policy Futures in Education*, 12(2): 186–90, http://dx.doi.org/10.2304/pfie.2014.12.2.186

Pettigrew, J. (2003). 'Living Between the Maoists and the Army in Rural Nepal', *Himalaya*, XXIII(1): 9–20.

Pherali, T. (2007). *The Role of Youth in Peacebuilding and Community Decision-Making in Nepal. A Baseline Research Report*. Kathmandu: Search for Common Ground Nepal.

Pherali, T. J. (2011). 'Education and Conflict in Nepal: Possibilities for Reconstruction', *Globalisation, Societies and Education*, 9: 135–54.

Pherali, T. (2012). 'The World Bank, Community Schooling, and School-Based Management: A Political Economy of Educational Decentralization in Nepal', in D. Kapoor, B. Barua and A. Datoo (eds), *Globalization, Culture and Education in South Asia: Critical Excursions*, 71–86, New York: Palgrave Macmillan.

Pherali, T. (2016a). 'School Leadership during Violent Conflict: Rethinking Education for Peace in Nepal and Beyond', *Comparative Education*, 52(4): 473–91.

Pherali, T. (2016b). 'Education: Cultural Reproduction, Revolution and Peacebuilding in Conflict-Affected Societies', in O. P. Richmond, S. Pogodda and J. Ramovic (eds), *Dimensions of Peace: Disciplinary and Regional Approaches*, 296–313, London: Palgrave Macmillan.

Pherali, T. (2017). 'Educational Accountability in Post-Conflict Settings: A Case Study of Nepal', a Background Paper for the Global Education Monitoring Report 2017/8, https://unesdoc.unesco.org/ark:/48223/pf0000259544 (accessed 21 August 2021).

Pherali, T. (2019). 'Education and Conflict: Emergence, Growth and Diversification of the Field', *Education and Conflict Review*, 2: 7–14.

Pherali, T. (2021). 'Social Justice, Education and Peacebuilding: Conflict Transformation in Southern Thailand', *Compare: A Journal of Comparative and International Education*, doi:10.1080/03057925.2021.1951666.

Pherali, T., and Garratt, D. (2014). 'Post-Conflict Identity Crisis in Nepal: Implications for Educational Reforms', *International Journal of Educational Development*, 34, 42–50, doi:10.1016/j.ijedudev.2012.12.004.

Pherali, T., and Lewis, A. (2019). 'Developing Global Partnerships in Higher Education for Peacebuilding: A Strategy for Pathways to Impact', *Higher Education*, 78: 729–44, 10.1007/s10734-019-00367-7.

Pherali, T., and Millican, J. (eds) (2020). 'Rebuilding Syrian Higher Education for a Stable Future', *Education and Conflict Review*, 3(whole issue), https://discovery.ucl.ac.uk/id/eprint/10108657/ (accessed 4 April 2021).

Pherali, T., and NEMAF (2021). 'Knowledge Production and Learning in Nepal's Madhes Movement: Struggle, Achievements and Disappointments', ESRC Grant No: ES/R00403X/1, Nepal Case Study: The Nepal Madhesh Foundation (NEMAF), Brighton: University of Sussex, https://knowledge4struggle.org/ (accessed 20 August 2021).

Pherali, T. J., Smith, A., and Vaux, T. (2011). *A Political Economy Analysis of Education in Nepal*, Brussels: European Union.

Phyak, P., and Ojha, L. P. (2019). 'Language Education Policy and Inequalities of Multilingualisms in Nepal: Ideologies, Histories and Updates', in A. Kirkpatrick and A. J. Liddicoat (eds), *The Routledge International Handbook of Language Education Policy in Asia*, 341–54, London: Routledge.

Pigg, S. (1992). 'Inventing Social Categories through Place: Social Representations and Development in Nepal', *Comparative Studies in Society and History*, 34(3): 491–513.

Piketty, T. (2013). *Capital in the 21st Century*, Massachusetts: Harvard University Press.

Pinnock, H. (2009). 'Language and Education: The Missing Link. How the Language Used in Schools Threatens the Achievement of Education for All', London: Save the Children.

Polkinghorne, D. E. (2007). 'Validity Issues in Narrative Research', *Qualitative Inquiry*, 13: 471–86.

Poppema, M. (2009). 'Guatemala, the Peace Accords and Education: A Post-Conflict Struggle for Equal Opportunities, Cultural Recognition and Participation in Education', *Globalisation, Societies and Education*, 7: 383–408.

Poudel, L. (2007). 'Power, Knowledge and Pedagogy: An Analysis of the Educational Exclusion of Dalits in Nepal', unpublished Doctoral Thesis, Canterbury: University of Kent.

Poudyal, C. S. (2017). 'Nepali Private Schools and Tolerated Illegality: A Foucauldian Analysis of Privatization of Education in Nepal', *Policy Futures in Education*, 15(4) 537–49.

Pradhan, U. (2020). *Simultaneous Identities: Language, Education and the Nepali Nation*, Cambridge: Cambridge University Press.

Psacharopoulos, G., and Patrinos, H. A. (2018). 'Returns to Investment in Education: A Decennial Review of the Global Literature', New York: World Bank, https://openknowledge.worldbank.org/bitstream/handle/10986/29672/WPS8402.pdf.

Pyakurel, S. 2006. 'Kranti' ra'Shanti' ko chyapoma manabadhikar (Human Rights in between the Rebellion and Peace), *Himal Khabarpatrika*, 13–27 February, 55.

Pyakurel, U. (2021). *Reproduction of Inequality and Social Exclusion: A Study of Dalits in Caste Society, Nepal*, Singapore: Springer.

Radburn, M. and Scott, C. (2019). 'The Psychology of Riots – And Why It's Never Just Mindless Violence', *The Conversation*, 15 November.

Ragsdale, T. A. (1989). *Once a Hermit Kingdom: Ethnicity, Education and National Integration in Nepal*, New Delhi: Manohar.

Rahnema, M., and Bawtree, V. (eds) (1997). *The Post-Development Order Reader*, London: Zed Books.

Rai, S. (2018). *Conflict, Education and People's War in Nepal*, New Delhi: Routledge India.

Rappleye, J. (2011). 'Different Presumptions about Progress, Divergent Prescriptions for Peace: Connections between Conflict, "Development" and Education in Nepal', in J. Paulson (ed.), *Education, Conflict and Development*, Oxford Studies in Comparative Education, 59–98, Oxford: Symposium.

Reardon, B. (2000). 'Peace Education: Review and Projection', in B. Moon, M. Ben-Peretz and S. Brown (eds) *International Companion to Education*, 397–425, New York: Routledge.

Regmi, K. (2021). 'Educational Governance in Nepal: Weak Government, Donor Partnership and Standardised Assessment', *Compare: A Journal of Comparative and International Education*, 51(1): 24–42.

Regmi, K. D. (2017). 'World Bank in Nepal's Education: Three Decades of Neoliberal Reform', *Globalization, Societies and Education*, 15(2): 188–201.

Reicher, S. D., and Stott, C. (2011). *Mad Mobs and Englishmen? Myths and Realities of the 2011 Riots*, London: Constable and Robinson.

Robben, A. C. G. M., and Nordstrom, C. (1995). 'The Anthropology and Ethnography of Violence and Sociopolitical Conflict', in A. C. G. M. Robben and C. Nordstrom (eds), *Fieldwork under Fire: Contemporary Studies of Violence and Survival*, 1–23, Berkeley: University of California Press.

Rose, P., and Greeley, M. (2006). 'Education in Fragile States: Capturing Lessons and Identifying Good Practice', Centre for International Education, Prepared for the DAC Fragile States Group Service Delivery Workstream Sub-Team for Education Services.

Rummel, R. J. (1994). *Death by Government*, New Burnswick, NJ: Transaction Books.

Save the Children (2013). 'Education for All Global Monitoring Report Policy Paper, 10 July 2013 Children still Battling to Go to School', https://unesdoc.unesco.org/ark:/48223/pf0000221668 (accessed 24 September 2021).

Save the Children (2019). 'Stop the War on Children: A Report from Save the Children', London: Save the Children, https://www.stopwaronchildren.org/report.pdf (accessed 24 September 2021).

Schaffner, J., Sharma, U., and Glewwe, P. (2020). 'Federalism in Nepal: Early Implications for Service Delivery in Education', Kathmandu, doi: 10.13140/RG.2.2.16574.61763.

Schultz, T. W. (1961). 'Investment in Human Capital', *American Economic Review*, 51(1): 1–17.

Scott, C., and Drury, J. (2017). 'Contemporary Understanding of Riots: Classical Crowd Psychology, Ideology and the Social Identity Approach', *Public Understanding of Science*, 26(1): 2–14.

SDGs (2015). 'The 17 Goals', New York: United Nations, Department of Economic and Social Affairs Sustainable Development, https://sdgs.un.org/goals (accessed 20 August 2021).

Selenica, E., and Novelli, M. (2021). 'The Political Economy of Education Systems in Conflict-Affected Contexts in a Changed World Order 2021: A Narrative Literature Review', Political Economy of Education Research Network, PEER Working Paper 3, https://peernetworkgcrf.org/wp-content/uploads/2021/08/Selenica-Novelli-Report-PE-EDU-CAFS-2021.pdf (accessed 20 August 2021).

Sen, A. (1999). *Development as Freedom*, Oxford: Oxford University Press.

Sengupta, S. (2016). 'United Nations Chief Exposes Limits to His Authority by Citing Saudi Threat', *New York Times*, http://www.nytimes.com/2016/06/10/world/middleeast/saudi-arabia-yemenchildrenban-ki-moon.html?_r=0, (accessed 25 August 2021).

SFCG (2020). 'Mission Statement', Washington, DC: Search for Common Ground, https://www.sfcg.org/our-mission/ (accessed 20 August 2021).

Shah, R., Paulson, J., and Couch, D. (2020). 'The Rise of Resilience in Education in Emergencies', *Journal of Intervention and Statebuilding*, 14(3): 303–26.

Shah, S. (1993). 'Throes of a Fledgling Nation', *Himal*, 6: 7–10.

Shah, S. (2004). 'A Himalayan Red Herring? Maoist Revolution in the Shadow of the Legacy Raj', in M. Hutt (ed.), *Himalayan 'People's War': Nepal's Maoist Rebellion*, 192–224, London: Hurst Publications.

Shakya, A. (2011). 'Experiences of Children in Armed Conflict in Nepal', *Children and Youth Services Review*, 33: 557–63.

Shangraw, J. (2019). 'Local Democracy and Education Policy in Newly Federal Nepal', Independent Study Project (ISP) Collection, 3183, https://digitalcollections.sit.edu/isp_collection/3183 (accessed 5 August 2021).

Sharma, K. (2006). 'The Political Economy of Civil War in Nepal', *World Development*, 34: 1237–53.

Sharma, S. (2007). 'Maoist Use of Ethnic Groups Complicates Peace', http://www.gulf-times.com/site/topics/article.asp?cu_no=2&item_no=184787&version=1&template_id=44&parent_id=24, (accessed 20 August 2010).

Sharma, J. R., and Donini, A. (2010). *Towards a Great Transformation: The Maoist Insurgency and Local Perceptions of Social Transformation in Nepal*, Medford: Tufts University.

Sharma, R., and Khadka, B. (2006). 'Impact of Armed Conflict in Education', Kathmandu: Education Journalists Group, Nepal.

Sharma, M., Dangal, M. R., and Pande, R. N. (2015), 'School Education Financing in Nepal: Bracket vs. Blanket Approach', Kathmandu: National Campaign for Education-Nepal.

Shields, R., and Rappleye, J. (2008a). 'Differentiation, Development, (Dis) Integration: Education in Nepal's "People's War"', *Research in Comparative International Education*, 3(1): 91–102.

Shields, R., and Rappleye, J. (2008b). 'Uneven Terrain: Educational Policy and Equity in Nepal', *Asia Pacific Journal of Education*, 28(3): 265–76.

Shiva, B. (1997). 'Western Science and Its Destruction of Local Knowledge', in M. Rahnema and V. Bawtree (eds), *The Post-Development Reader*, 161–7, London: Zed Books.

Shrestha, B. G. (2007). 'Ethnic Nationalism in Nepal and the Newars', in M. Lawoti (ed.), *Contentious Politics and Democratization in Nepal*, 199–224, London: Sage.

Shrestha, N. (1997). *In the Name of Development: A Reflection on Nepal*, Kathmandu: Educational Publishing House.

Shrestha, S. K., and Paudel, N. R. (2019). 'Civil Service Management in Nepal', in I. Jamil, T. N. Dhakal and N. R. Paudel (eds), *Civil Service Management and Administrative Systems in South Asia*, 99–119, London: Palgrave Macmillan.

Simkhada, D. 2006. 'Kshikshaka Lagi Shanti [Peace for Education]', *Himal Khabarpatrika*, 13–27 February, 63–78.

Singer, P. W. (2006). *Children at War*, Berkeley: University of California Press.

SIPRI (2005). *Year Book 2005: Armaments, Disarmament and International Security, Summary*, Stockholm International Peace Research Institute, https://www.sipri.org/yearbook/2005.

SIPRI (2016). *Year Book 2016: Armaments, Disarmament and International Security, Summary*, Stockholm International Peace Research Institute, https://www.sipri.org/yearbook/2016.

SIPRI (2021). *SIPRI Year Book 2021: Armaments, Disarmament and International Security, Summary*, Stockholm International Peace Research Institute, https://www.sipri.org/sites/default/files/2021-06/sipri_yb21_summary_en_v2_0.pdf (accessed 12 September 2021).

Skinner, D., and Holland, D. (1996). 'Schools and the Cultural Production of the Educated Person in a Nepalese Hill Community', in B. Levinson, D. E. Foley and D. C. Holland (eds), *The Cultural Production of the Educated Person: Critical Ethnographies of Schooling and Local Practice*, 273–300, New York: State University of New York Press.

Sluka, J. A. (2000). 'Introduction: State Terror and Anthropology', in J. A. Sluka (ed.), *Death Squad: The Anthropology of State Fear*, 1–45, Philadelphia: University of Pennsylvania.

Smith, A. (2010). 'Children, Education and Reconciliation', Innocenti Working Paper, Florence: UNICEF Innocenti Research Centre, http://www.peacewomen.org/assets/file/childreneducationandreconciliation_unicef.pdf (accessed 3 September 2010).

Smith, D. (2004). *Trends and Causes of Armed Conflict*, Berlin: Bergh of Foundation, https://berghof-foundation.org/library/trends-and-causes-of-armed-conflict (accessed 8 September 2021).

Smith, M. (2015). *Nepal: Lessons from Integrating Peace, Human Rights, and Civic Education into Social Studies Curricula and Textbooks*, Paris, France: UNESCO, International Institute for Educational Planning.

Smith, A., and Ellison, C. (2015). 'The Integration of Education and Peacebuilding: A Review of the Literature', https://www.eccnetwork.net/resources/integration-education-and-peacebuilding (accessed 2 August 2018).

Smith, A., and T. Vaux (2003). 'Education, Conflict and International Development', DFID Issues Paper, London: Department for International Development.

Smith, A., Datzberger, S., and McCully, A. (2016). *The Integration of Education in Peacebuilding. Synthesis Report on Findings from Myanmar, Pakistan, South Africa and Uganda*, UK: UNICEF New York & Ulster University.

Standing, K., and Parker, S. (2011). 'The Effect of the "People's War" on Schooling in Nepal, 1996–2006', *Education, Citizenship and Social Justice*, 6(2): 181–195.

Stash, S., and Hannum, E. (2001). 'Who Goes to School? Educational Stratification by Gender, Caste, and Ethnicity in Nepal', *Comparative Education Review*, 45: 354–78.

Stewart, F. (2000). 'Horizontal Inequalities: A Neglected Dimension of Development', Working Paper, Centre for Research on Inequality, Human Security and Ethnicity: University of Oxford.

Stewart, F. (2003). 'Conflict and Millennium Development Goals', *Journal of Human Development*, 4: 325–51.

Stewart, F. (2008). *Horizontal Inequalities and Conflict: Understanding Group Violence in Multiethnic Societies*, Basingstoke: Palgrave Macmillan.

Stewart, F. (2010). 'Horizontal Inequalities as a Cause of Conflict: A review of CRISE Findings, World Development Report 2011', background paper, https://openknowledge.worldbank.org/bitstream/handle/10986/9126/WDR2011_0029.pdf?sequence=1&isAllowed=y (accessed 2 July 2021).

Stott, C., and Drury, J. (2017). 'Contemporary Understanding of Riots: Classical Crowd Psychology, Ideology and the Social Identity Approach', *Public Understanding of Science*, 26(1): 2–14.

Strand, H., Rustad, S. A., Nygård, H. M., and Hegre, H. (2020). 'Trends in Armed Conflict, 1946–2019', PRIO Policy Brief, https://www.prio.org/utility/DownloadFile.ashx?id=2193&type=publicationfile (accessed 21 August 2021).

Suárez-Orozco, J. (1987). 'The Treatment of Children in the "Dirty War": Ideology, State Terrorism and Abuse of Children in Argentina', in N. Scheper-Hughes (ed.), *Child Survival: Anthropological Perspectives on the Treatment and Maltreatment of Children*, 227–46, Amsterdam: Reidel.

Subba, C., Pyakuryal, B., Bastola, T. S., Subba, M. K., Raut, N. K., and Karki, B. (2014). *A Study on the Socio-economic Status of Indigenous Peoples in Nepal*, Kathmandu: Lawyers' Association for Human Rights of Nepalese Indigenous Peoples (LAHURNIP).

Subedi, K. R. (2018). 'Local Curriculum in Schools in Nepal: A Gap Between Policies and Practices', *Crossing the Border: International Journal of Interdisciplinary Studies*, 6(1): 57–67.

Subedi, M. (2016). 'Caste in South Asia: From Ritual Hierarchy to Politics of Difference', *Politeja*, 40: 319–40, https://www.jstor.org/stable/10.2307/24920210 (accessed 17 August 2021).

Sullivan, D. (2007). 'Tinder, Spark, Oxygen and Fuel: The Mysterious Rise of the Taliban', *Journal of Peace Research*, 44(1): 93–108.

Sunam, R., and Shrestha, K. (2019). 'Failing the Most Excluded: A Critical Analysis of Nepal's Affirmative Action Policy', *Contributions to Nepalese Studies*, 46(2): 283–305.

Taka, M. (2020). 'The Role of Education in Peacebuilding: Learner Narratives from Rwanda', *Journal of Peace Education*, 17(1): 107–122.

Thapa, A. (2015). 'Public and Private School Performance in Nepal: An Analysis Using the SLC Examination', *Education Economics*, 23(1): 47–62, doi: 10.1080/09645292.2012.738809.

Thapa, D., and Sijapati, B. (2004). *A Kingdom under Siege: Nepal's Maoist Insurgency, 1996 to 2004*, London: Zed Books.

The Worker (1996). 'The Historic Initiation and After', *The Worker*, The Communist Party of Nepal (Maoist).

Themnér, L., and Wallensteen, P. (2011). 'Armed Conflict, 1946–2010', *Journal of Peace Research*, 48: 525–36.

Tiwari, B. N. (2007). 'An Assessment of the Causes of Conflict in Nepal', Second Annual Himalayan Policy Research Conference, Madison: Nepal Study Centre, http://tribhuvan.academia.edu/BishwaTiwari/Papers/947761/An_Assessment_of_the_Causes_of_Conflict_in_Nepal (accessed 20 October 2019).

Tiwari, B. N. (2010). 'Horizontal Inequalities and Violent Conflict in Nepal', in M. Lawoti and A. Guneratne (eds), *Ethnicity, Inequality and Politics in Nepal*, 55–92, Kathmandu: Himal Books.

Tomaševski, K. (2001). *Human Rights Obligations: Making Education Available, Accessible, Acceptable and Adaptable*, Stockholm: Swedish International Development Cooperation Agency, https://www.right-to-education.org/sites/right-to-education.org/files/resource-attachments/Tomasevski_Primer%203.pdf (accessed 21 August 2021).

Toots, A., Worley, N., and Skosireva, A. (2014). 'Children as Political Actors', in G. B. Melton, A. Ben-Arieh, J. Cashmore, G. S. Goodman and N. K. Worley (eds), *The SAGE Handbook of Child Research*, 54–80, London: Sage, https://dx.doi.org/10.4135/9781446294758 (accessed 25 August 2021).

Trudell, B. (2016). *The Impact of Language Policy and Practice on Children's Learning: Evidence from Eastern and Southern Africa*, Nairobi: UNICEF ESARO.

UN (1989). *The United Nations Convention on the Rights of the Child*, New York: United Nations, http://www.ohchr.org/EN/ProfessionalInterest/Pages/CRC.aspx (accessed 27 September 2021).

UN (1992). *An Agenda for Peace Preventive Diplomacy, Peacemaking and Peace-Keeping, Report of the Secretary-General*, New York: United Nations, https://www.un.org/ruleoflaw/files/A_47_277.pdf.

UN (2010a). *UN Peacebuilding: An Orientation*, Peacebuilding Support Office, United Nations http://www.un.org/en/peacebuilding/pbso/pdf/peacebuilding_orientation.pdf.

UN (2010b). 'Nepal: UN Hails Release of All Child Soldiers by Maoists', http://www.un.org/apps/news/story.asp?NewsID=33696&Cr=Nepal&Cr1 (accessed 10 August 2021).

UN (2020). *Policy Brief: Education during COVID-19 and Beyond*, New York: United Nations, https://www.un.org/development/desa/dspd/wp-content/uploads/sites/22/2020/08/sg_policy_brief_covid-19_and_education_august_2020.pdf. (accessed 15 September 2021).

UN (2021). 'Children and Armed Conflict: Report of the Secretary-General', https://reliefweb.int/sites/reliefweb.int/files/resources/N2111309.pdf (accessed 20 September 2021).

UNESCO (2000). 'The Dakar Framework for Action: Education for All: Meeting Our Collective Commitments', Dakar: United Nations Educational, Scientific and Cultural Organization.

UNESCO (2007). *Education under Attack: A Global Study on Targeted Political and Military Violence against Education Staff, Students, Teachers, Union and Government Officials, and Institutions*, Paris: United Nations Educational, Scientific and Cultural Organization.

UNESCO (2010). *Education under Attack, 2010: A Global Study on Targeted Political and Military Violence against Education Staff, Students, Teachers, Union and Government Officials, Aid Workers and Institutions*, Paris: United Nations Educational, Scientific and Cultural Organization.

UNESCO (2011). *EFA Global Monitoring Report 2011 – The Hidden Crisis: Armed Conflict and Education*, Paris: United Nations Educational, Scientific and Cultural Organization.

UNESCO (2015). 'Education for All 2000–2015: Achievements and Challenges', EFA Global Monitoring Report', Paris: United Nations Educational, Scientific and Cultural Organization.

UNESCO (2018). 'Global Citizenship Education and the Rise of Nationalist Perspectives', Paris: United Nations Educational Scientific and Cultural Organization, http://unesdoc.unesco.org/images/0026/002654/265414e.pdf (accessed 10 September 2021).

UNESCO (2019). 'New Methodology Shows that 258 Million Children, Adolescents and Youth Are Out of School', Toronto: UNESCO Institute for Statistics, http://uis.unesco.org/sites/default/files/documents/new-methodology-shows-258-million-children-adolescents-and-youth-are-out-school.pdf (accessed 10 September 2021).

UNESCO Institute for Statistics (2018). 'Nepal: Education and Literacy', http://uis.unesco.org/en/country/np?theme=education-and-literacy (accessed 11 September 2019).

UNHCR (2020). *Figures at a Glance, The UK Refugee Agency*, https://www.unhcr.org/uk/figures-at-a-glance.html (accessed November 2020).

UNHCR (2021). 'Refugee Data Finder: Key Indicators', Geneva: United Nations High Commissioner for Refugees, https://www.unhcr.org/refugee-statistics/ (accessed 27 September 2021).

UNICEF (2002). 'Adult Wars, Child Soldiers: Voices of Children Involved in Armed Conflict in the East Asia and Pacific region', Bangkok: UNICEF Eastern and Southern Africa Regional Office.

UNICEF (2010a). 'Child Protection from Violence, Exploitation and Abuse: Children in Conflict and Emergencies', New York: UNICEF, www.unicef.org/protection/index_armed conflict.html. (accessed 10 August 2021).

UNICEF (2010b). 'Schools as Zones of Peace (SZOP): Education for Stabilization and Peace Building in Post-Conflict Nepal', https://protectingeducation.org/wp-cont ent/uploads/documents/documents_schools_as_zones_of_peace_szop_education_for_stabilization_and_peace_building_in_post-conflict_nepal.pdf, (accessed 2 September 2021).

UNICEF (2011). 'The Role of Education in Peacebuilding: A Synthesis Report of Findings from Lebanon, Nepal and Sierra Leone', New York: UNICEF.

UNICEF (2014). 'Thailand Case Study in Education, Conflict and Social Cohesion', Bangkok: UNICEF East Asia and Pacific Regional Office, https://deepsouthwatch. org/sites/default/files/archives/docs/unicef_thailand_education_conflcit_socialcohes ion2014.pdf (accessed 21 August 2021).

UNICEF (2015). 'Nepal's Study within the Global Initiative on Out-of-School Children, Final Report', (28 October 2015), Kathmandu: UNICEF Nepal Country Office, https://www.unicef.org/nepal/sites/unicef.org.nepal/files/2018-07/All%20child ren%20in%20school-report%202016.pdf (accessed 11 August 2021).

UNICEF (2015a). 'Evaluation of UNICEF's Peacebuilding, Education and Advocacy Programme (PBEA)', New York: United Nations Children's Fund, https://gdc.unicef. org/resource/2015-global-evaluation-unicefs-peacebuilding-education-and-advoc acy-programme-pbea (accessed 18 May 2019).

UNICEF (2015b). 'Investment in Equity and Peacebuilding Uganda Case Study', Washington, DC: FHI 360 Education Policy and Data Center, https://www.epdc.org/ node/5988.html (accessed 9 September 2020).

UNICEF (2015c). 'Investment in Equity and Peacebuilding: South Africa Case Study', Washington, DC: FHI 360 Education Policy and Data Center, https://www.epdc.org/ node/5989.html (accessed 23 August 2021).

UNICEF (2016a). 'Does Horizontal Education Inequality Lead to Violent Conflict? A Global Analysis', New York: UNICEF and FHI 360 Education Policy and Data Center, https://www.fhi360.org/projects/horizontal-inequality-education-and-violent-conflict-research (accessed 4 April 2022).

UNICEF (2016b). 'Four Schools or Hospitals Attacked or Occupied Every Day', UNICEF Press Release, 19 May 2016, https://www.unicef.org/turkey/en/press-releases/four-schools-or-hospitals-attacked-or-occupied-every-day-unicef.

UNICEF (2017). 'Education Uprooted: For Every Migrant, Refugee and Displaced Child, Education', https://www.unicef.org/media/48911/file/UNICEF_Education_Uprooted-ENG.pdf (accessed 25 September 2021).
UNICEF (2022). 'Six Grave Violations against Children in Times of War: How Children Have Become Frontline Targets in Armed Conflicts', https://www.unicef.org/stories/children-under-attack-six-grave-violations-against-children-times-war.
Vaditya, V. (2018). 'Social Domination and Epistemic Marginalization: Towards Methodology of the Oppressed', *Social Epistemology*, 32(4): 272–85, doi:10.1080/02691728.2018.1444111.
Valente, C. (2014). 'Education and Civil Conflict in Nepal', *World Bank Economic Review*, 28(2):354–83.
van Wessel, M., and van Hirtum, R. (2013). 'Schools as Tactical Targets in Conflict: What the Case of Nepal Can Teach Us', *Comparative Education Review*, 57(1): 1–21.
Vaux, T. (2011). 'The Role of Education in Peacebuilding: Case Study – Nepal', New York: UNICEF, https://www.eccnetwork.net/resources/role-education-peacebuilding-4 (accessed 20 October 2019).
Vaux, T., Smith, A., and Subba, S. (2006). 'Education for All – Nepal: Review from a Conflict Perspective', Kathmandu: International Alert.
Verger, A., Novelli, M., and Altinyelken, K. (2012). 'Global Education Policy and International Development: An Introductory Framework', in A. Verger, M. Novelli and K. Altinyelken (eds), *Global Education Policy and International Development: New Agendas, Issues and Policies*, 3–32, London: Bloomsbury.
Waever O., Buzan B., and Kelstrup, M. (1993). *Identity, Migration and the New Security Agenda in Europe*, London: Palgrave Macmillan.
Walker, K. L. M. (2008). 'Neoliberalism on the Ground in Rural India: Predatory Growth, Agrarian Crisis, Internal Colonization, and the Intensification of Class Struggle', *Journal of Peasant Studies*, 35(4): 557–620, doi: 10.1080/03066150802681963.
Walter, B. F. (2010). 'Conflict Relapse and the Sustainability of Post-Conflict Peace', World Development Report 2011, background paper, https://openknowledge.worldbank.org/bitstream/handle/10986/9069/WDR2011_0008.pdf?sequence=1&isAllowed=y (accessed 10 August 2021).
Wankhede, G. G., and Sengupta, A. (2005). 'Village Education Committees in West Bengal, India: Planned Vision and Beyond', *International Journal of Educational Development*, 25: 569–79.
Watchlist (2005). 'Caught in the Middle: Mounting Violations against Children in Nepal's Armed Conflict', New York: Watchlist on Children and Armed Conflict.
Watchlist (2007). 'Children in the Ranks: The Maoists' Use of Child Soldiers in Nepal', vol 19(2C), New York: Watchlist on Children and Armed Conflict.
Wessells, M. (2006). *Child Soldiers. From Violence to Protection*, Cambridge: Harvard University Press.

Whittall, J. (2015). 'Is Humanitarian Action Independent from Political Interests?' *Sur Journal*, 2(21): 1–5, sur.conectas.org (accessed 30 August 2021).

Wille, Belkis (2020). 'Why Are Russians Paying for Bombing Schools in Syria?' New York: Human Rights Watch, https://www.hrw.org/news/2020/12/17/why-are-russians-paying-bombing-schools-syria (accessed 20 August 2021).

Wimmer, A., Cederman, L-E., and Min, B. (2009). 'Ethnic Politics and Armed Conflict: A Configurational Analysis of a New Global Data Set', *American Sociological Review*, 74: 316–37.

Winthrop, R., and Matsui, E. (2013). 'A New Agenda for Education in Fragile States', Washington, DC: Brookings Institution, https://www.brookings.edu/wp-content/uploads/2016/06/08-education-agenda-fragile-states-winthrop.pdf (accessed 16 August 2021).

World Bank (2001). 'Nepal: Priorities and Strategies for Education Reform', Kathmandu: World Bank.

World Bank (2010). 'Project Performance Assessment Report, Nepal, Community School Support Project (CR. 3808)', retrieved from http://www.worldbank.org.

World Bank (2011). 'World Development Report 2011: Conflict, Security, and Development', http://siteresources.worldbank.org/INTWDRS/Re- sources/WDR2011_Full_Text.pdf (accessed 23 April 2018).

Wyness, M. (2006). *Childhood and Society: An Introduction to the Sociology of Childhood*, New York: Palgrave Macmillan.

Yadava, Y. P. (2007). 'Linguistic diversity in Nepal: Perspectives on Language Policy', paper presented at the Seminar on Constitutionalism and Diversity (22–24 August), Kathmandu, Nepal, http://www.uni-bielefeld.de/midea/pdf/Yogendra.pdf (accessed 20 June 2016).

Zur, J. (1994). 'The Psychological Impact of Impunity', *Anthropology Today*, 10(3): 12–17.

Index

4Rs framework 41-2, 158-9, 164, 166, 171

abduction 24, 33, 82, 85-106, 178-93
abduction and disappearance 102-4
adhar ilaka (base territory) 70
afno manchhe (favour towards one's own people) 132
All Nepal National Free Students' Union Revolutionary (ANNFSU-R) 111
All Nepal Teachers Organization (ANTO) 88
alternative Modes of Learning 177
attacks on education 20-4, 49, 68-79, 85, 98, 154, 179, 182-6

bhautik karbahi (physical action) 71
bikas 2, 46,134
bourgeois system 103

capitalist system 30
chanda atanka (terror of donations) 71, 90
civil service examinations 131
collusion 86, 90
Communist Party of Nepal - Maoist (CPN-M) 14, 45-6, 102
Comprehensive Peace Accord (CPA) 15, 48, 124, 138, 156
conflict analysis 184, 186-7
conflict sensitive education 14, 37, 39-43, 138, 144, 156, 174, 176, 178, 183, 190
conscientization 12, 146
constituent Assembly (CA) 46-7, 58, 135
Constitution of Nepal 1990 57, 125
Constitution of Nepal 2015 48, 57, 58, 125, 127, 132, 137, 159, 163, 167, 170,
counter-hegemonic narratives 76
Covid-19 139, 178,
critical peace education 158, 191
Crown Prince Dipendra 47
cultural violence 12
culture of terror 71, 85

curriculum Development Centre (CDC) 57-8

Dakar Framework for Action 56
Dalit children 4, 8, 62
Dalits 1, 4, 8, 15-17, 20, 33, 45, 47, 49, 56, 75, 124, 132, 140, 159, 163-5, 189
decentralization 160, 162-3, 166
demonstration killing 80, 82, 185
direct violence on Schools 44, 79, 147
District Education Offices 50, 60, 86-7, 104
Dr Babu Ram Bhattarai 78
Durbar High School 7

ecologies of knowledge 31, 63, 182
economic catastrophe 30
economic Relevance of Education 55, 71
educated person 3
education and social disparities 52
Education for All 28-9, 38, 56
education for peace 145-6, 173-4
education for peacebuilding 23, 37, 41, 158
education for revolution 75, 148, 185
education in emergencies 37-8, 64, 94, 155, 173
education under attack 20, 24, 31, 49, 68-70, 79, 85, 86-7, 93, 98, 108, 164, 182, 186
educational Divide 72, 190
educational inequalities 14, 36
educationism 27, 159
Ek Madhes Ek Pradesh (the entire southern plains as one federal Madhes state) 136
epistemic oppression 175
equity in Education 36, 43, 55, 74
ethnic and Indigenous Agency 57
ethnic Discrimination 125, 130, 133, 141
ethnic diversity 123
ethnic minorities 8, 16, 41, 45, 56, 116, 130-2, 175
ethnic Violence 19, 25, 113-14, 136

Father's Day 192–3
five Year Plan for Education in Nepal (1956–61) 51
forced displacement 16, 23, 32, 37, 114, 181
fragility 10, 13, 24–5, 64, 136, 150

general Strikes 81
genocidal ideology 25
Global Coalition to Protect Education from Attack (GCPEA) 31, 68
greed and grievance theory 33
grievances 14, 16–17, 30, 32–6, 41–4, 49, 115, 120, 132, 137, 151, 174, 190

hearts and minds 26
Hill high-caste groups 124, 147, 163
homeschooling 178
homogenization 9, 25, 128
horizontal inequalities 12, 35–6, 125, 142, 146, 161
human capital theory 145
humanitarian response 155
humanizing pedagogies 181

identity crisis 135
ideological indoctrination 12, 185
inclusive development 21, 188
indigenous communities 5, 7, 45, 49, 62, 131
indigenous knowledge 146
indigenous nationalities 47, 49, 58, 62, 65, 114, 123–4, 131, 134, 139–40, 159, 164, 166
indoctrination 11–12, 75, 134, 146, 184–5
institutional schools 52
intrastate civil wars 12, 23

King Gyanendra 47–8

liberal democracy 14, 15, 26, 46, 149
liberal peacebuilding 149–50
Limbuwan Mukti Morcha 133
linguistic repression 42

Madhes movement 136–8
Madhesi 49, 62, 113–15, 124, 126, 131–3, 135–7, 139
Madhesi Mukti Morcha 133

madrasas 52
mandatory donations 50, 60, 79, 86, 90, 119
Mangena 189
Maoist movement 15–16, 33, 58, 60, 62, 73, 100, 102, 115–17, 120, 164, 177
mass demonstrations 117
middle school 1–3
migrant workers 55
Ministry of Education 8, 51, 57, 130, 138, 154, 160, 166
modern education 1, 3, 50–1, 65, 93, 128
modernity 2, 8, 65, 73, 134
monarchy 8–9, 14–15, 45–6, 48, 51, 90, 102, 113, 129, 134, 152, 177, 189
monopoly in education 127
Muktinath Adhikari 82, 192
Muluki Ain (National Code) 123–4

narrative research 19, 96–7
narrative writing 18, 95, 96
National Civil Service (NCS) 140
National Education Planning Commission (NEPC) 51
National Education System Plan (NESP) 8, 51, 129
national homogenization 9, 25
national identity 9, 11, 21, 36, 46, 62, 114, 123, 126–8, 136–8, 141–3, 166, 168, 171, 175, 189
national reconciliation 21, 149, 168
negative face of 'development' 64
negative peace 147, 176
neoliberal reforms 15, 89, 182
neoliberalism 29–30, 167, 175
Nepali nationalism 8, 72, 132
Newa Mukti Morcha 133
northern hegemonies 38

Official Development Assistance (ODA) 173
orotracted violent conflicts 99

pacification 149, 175
Panchayat system 8–9, 46, 51, 76, 129, 135, 164
peace pathways 31
Peace, Human Rights and Civic Education (PHRCE) 156–7
People's Liberation Army (PLA) 48, 108

People's War 14–18, 58, 64, 71, 75–9, 89, 100, 120, 127, 175, 188
policy recommendations 188
political activism 9, 100, 117, 147, 180
political allegories 126
political consciousness 7, 176
political economy analysis 19, 39, 163, 171, 185
political socialization 21, 24, 75, 101, 116, 120
politics of language 61, 125
positive peace 147, 148, 175–6, 183
post-conflict peacebuilding 19
power equilibrium 48
Pratikar Samuha 113
private education 9, 53, 59, 60–1, 73–4, 79, 91, 161, 190
privatization of education 9, 24, 89
professional motivation 83, 84, 93
psychological distress 90
Pushpa Kamal Dahal (Prachanda) 78

radicalization 11, 38
rajanitik prakshiksan (political training) 71
Rajbhakti 51
Rana oligarchy 7–8, 45, 50
rastrabhasha 125
rebel recruitment 27, 32, 34
recognition 10, 13, 41–2, 63, 125, 138, 142, 152, 158–9, 160, 163–5, 189
reconciliation 21, 25, 41–2, 44, 82, 138, 149–50, 159, 167–71, 175–6, 183, 191
redistribution 41, 44, 124, 128, 158, 160
refugee population 28, 32
regional politics 133, 143
relational disequilibrium 91
representation 17, 24, 41, 43, 63, 97, 126–7, 132, 134–6, 140, 158, 165–6, 174
revolutionary songs 108
Royal family 47
Royal Nepalese Army 89

Sanskrit 5, 7, 50, 80, 87
School Leaving Certificate (SLC) 57, 59, 74, 78
School Management Committee (SMC) 151, 162, 166, 185
School Sector Development Plan 2016–2023 (SSDP) 188

School Sector Reforms Plan 2009–2016 (SSRP) 52, 138, 188
Schools as Zones of Peace (SZOP) 102, 151–4
Schools in the Crossfire 2004 82
Secondary Education Examinations (SEE) 57
securitization of education aid 26, 182
Seventh Amendment of Nepal's Education Act 1971 52
social capital 49, 76, 140
social Inclusion Survey 49
social inequalities 3, 9, 35, 179
social justice 21, 37, 42, 48, 49, 89, 100, 108, 116, 123, 141, 143, 145–6, 158–9, 171, 173–5, 182, 188–91
social reproduction 5, 53, 123, 127, 158, 184
spying 82, 86–7
state 'terror' 50, 81
state of emergency 48, 81, 89–90
state of fear 154
state oppression 21, 88
structural inequalities 5, 15–16, 27, 42, 102, 133, 147, 148, 176
suicide bombers 99
Sustainable Development Goals (SGDs) 12, 29, 32, 73
symbolic violence 20, 49, 124, 126, 128–30, 180
sympathizers 50, 71, 77, 111, 119

teachers in the revolution 77
Tharuwan Mukti Morcha 133
tol shiksha (township education) 179
Truth and Reconciliation Commission 82, 138, 168, 169, 175, 191

undemarcation of the battlefields 29, 98
United Nations Convention on the Rights of the Child (UNCRC) 99
untouchable 1, 4, 124, 147

victim-Perpetrator-Liberator-Peacebuilder (VPLP) framework 180
VPLP framework 180, 182–3

youth bulge theory 34

www.ingramcontent.com/pod-product-compliance
Lightning Source LLC
Chambersburg PA
CBHW062216300426
44115CB00012BA/2093